Margaret (Muggie) Dembowski

A Single Woman's Journey

FINDING JOY AFTER DIVORCE

A Single Woman's Journey

FINDING JOY AFTER DIVORCE

MARGARET (MAGGIE) DEMBOWSKI

XULON PRESS

Xulon Press
2301 Lucien Way #415
Maitland, FL 32751
407.339.4217
www.xulonpress.com

Paperback ISBN-13: 978-1-6628-0314-7

Hard Cover ISBN-13: 978-1-6628-0315-4

Ebook ISBN-13: 978-1-6628-0316-1

Dedication

This book is lovingly dedicated to the following people:
Julie Epperson
Terri Trickel
Bobbi Nelson
Susan Betancourt
Heidi Pletsch
"You are my sunshine"

My precious five daughters,
who have supported and encouraged me.
God so graciously and abundantly blessed and honored me
when he brought you into my life.

You are loved beyond words by our heavenly Father and your mother.

To my mother Florence Roemer Volz
(December 19, 1912–September 5, 2008)
for her impartation of prayer and godly upbringing.

To my many family members and friends who walked alongside me
during my forty-years as a single woman.
I am humbled by your love and kindness.

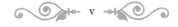

Table of Contents

My Timeline: Retracting My Steps

"For I know the thoughts that I think toward you, says the Lord, thoughts of peace and not of evil, to give you a future and a hope" (Jeremiah 29:11).

My story sheds light on how God made a way. The following timeline provides an overview of how God guided me.

1940–1958: Birth to childhood through elementary and high school

1958: High school graduate followed by marriage—Sebewaing, Michigan

1958–1978: Military wife—Military travel (multiply trips to Newport News, Virginia; Fort Eustis, Virginia; Williamsburg, Virginia; Fort Rucker, Alabama; Savannah, Georgia; Fort Knox, Kentucky; Fort Huachuca, Arizona; and Germany. Multiply spouse unaccompanied temporary duty trips (TDY) and two Viet Nam tours.

1960–1990: Family—five daughters

1979–Present: Singleness

1980–1995: City of Sierra Vista, Arizona—employment and retirement

1983: Community college to graduation with a BA in 1990—Sierra Vista/Tucson, University of Phoenix (UOPX)

1993: Mission tour with Barnabas Ensemble to Ghana and Ivory Coast, Africa

1995–2000: State employment with the Governor's Advisory Council on Aging (GACA), Phoenix

1997: Internship with Christian Family Care Agency (CFCA), Phoenix

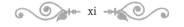

1995–1998: Graduate Student University of Phoenix-MC (UOPX), Phoenix

1997–2000: Employment with Christian Family Care Agency (CFCA), Phoenix

2000–2013: Mission's counselor with Wycliffe Bible Translators (WBT)—Travels to Dallas and multiple international trips to Papua New Guinea, Pakistan, Canada, Africa, Germany, Australia, Israel, and the Philippines

2003: Licensures—National Certified Counselor, Arizona State License Counselor, Registered Play Therapist

2013: Retirement from Wycliffe Bible Translators

2014–2021: Volunteer time: Cochise County Juvenile Detention Facility-Bible Study, Chaplain Assistant Canyon Vista Medical Center

2021: Book - A SINGLE WOMAN'S JOURNEY: FINDING JOY AFTER DIVORCE

God, my navigator, carried me through the valuable journey of various life lessons, experiences, seasons, and exposures of life. I celebrate the gift of singleness. God taught me along the way through his Word, my mother, and the mentors he placed into my path during my eighty years of life and along the forty-year stretch as a single woman and single parent.

Introduction

*M*y story takes you from childhood to a young woman's devastating divorce to an extraordinary relational journey with the God of the universe. The God of creation loves divorcees, widows, and singles. First, I was a young single woman, and then I found the love of my life. This story is written to encourage and give hope to singles and follows me, Margaret Volz Dembowski, when I again became a single woman at age thirty-nine and my journey through the following forty-one years. My narrative is to honor the Father, Son, and Holy Spirit.

A life of opportunities awaits a single woman, if she finds herself alone or left behind in the middle of life. God has a plan and purpose for her whether she is single, divorced, or widowed.

When I became a single woman and a single parent, my five daughters ranged in age from seven to eighteen. My daughters have since graduated from high school and a few from college. During the many years

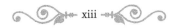

that followed, my daughters, their future spouses, and their children have filled my quiver with many grandchildren and great-grandchildren.

My marriage of twenty years abruptly ended, resulting in a life of singleness before I even realized what had happened. Throughout the following forty years, I lived in close relationship with our heavenly Father. He carried me through the storms and sunshine of life into an adventure and an extraordinary life journey.

We struggled during the earlier years, yet God brought victory into our lives. Each obstacle strengthened our walk with him. God, in his limitless, infinite wisdom and ways, uses life's disruptions, hindrances, and detours, if we allow him to do so, for our good and his glory. My family focused on living a purpose-filled life through the teachings of Jesus imparted to them on the path with him. God has included all of us for a productive life in and through him in every season.

At one point, I no longer wanted to live. I consider what I would have missed had I followed through with my wish to die. Only God saved me from the speed of my car and the brokenness of my heart. He knew my life was worth saving. He brought healing and restoration to others through the life of this daughter. His plan saves lives and brings a desire to live like never before to the hurting and beaten down.

This story is to offer hope and encouragement. Our God will carefully and confidently raise up a single's life for his purpose. We are in his plan for good, expectation, and a future. He customizes our hardships to further his kingdom if we allow him to do so.

Transitioning from marriage to singleness was initially painful but eventually immeasurably productive. It took perseverance and intentional living for him. Likewise, transitioning into a new normal takes time and effort. The outcome is an abundant and bountiful life. He miraculously opens doors that help us and closes those that will be to our detriment. For me, the process offered unique personal, parental, and professional skills along with the opportunity for further growth. God continually refined my character in new ways and gave me unexpected opportunities.

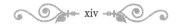

Doors opened for employment from a city job to a state job. He allowed me to travel domestically and internationally and to become a mission's family counselor with Wycliffe Bible Translators two days before turning sixty.

God is my strength and source. At age sixty-four, I entered and completed the Mission's Pacific Orientation Course (boot camp) in Papua New Guinea. He was my endurance and courage. His strength brought healing, health, and courage. Some observers reflected that my strength and stamina were healthier than others half my age.

I moved to Papua New Guinea and then to the Philippines. While stateside and living in these countries, counseling opportunities took me to various other nations. As he walked with me through my struggles, he also gave me the privilege and honor of providing counseling and crisis management to others.

My life also consists of twenty years as a military wife, twenty-plus years of employment between city and state positions, and a dozen-plus years as a counselor after that. Eventually, I retired after my time in the working world, and since retirement, I volunteer for enjoyment and to pay the blessings forward.

This story honors the healer of broken hearts—a husband to the widow and father to the fatherless. As a single woman, God sustained me with every biblical promise. God's plan and purpose for life is a relationship process, a daily walk with the Creator of heaven and earth. He transforms his children from the inside out and from ordinary to extraordinary.

I trust you will enjoy the stories interspersed within my book and see God's hand in each. Some stories have pleasing outcomes, and then some could have better results.

I pray that my story offers hope and encouragement to divorced, widowed, and never-married sisters and brothers. *A Single Woman's Journey* demonstrates that there really is life and joy after divorce, widowhood, and for the never-married. The new normal of singleness can lead to contentment, fulfillment, and a celebration of life.

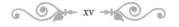

1

God's Purpose—
Overview from Child to Adult

My real name is Margaret, but everyone calls me Maggie. My life began eighty years ago, an adventure planned explicitly by God before I entered my mother's womb. My childhood was spent wandering the rural community sidewalks, the beginning of a lifetime of adventure.

When I was seventeen, my high school graduating class went to Washington, DC. With a suitcase in hand, a Greyhound bus took me, at age eighteen, through many states to join my husband. A decade plus later, a Lufthansa flight carried my five daughters and me to Germany to join my military husband. Nearly a decade after that, three daughters and I traveled unescorted in a diesel Chevrolet from the far west to middle America. By then, I was a single mother.

Those first baby steps—on treks, scooters, and skates traveling up and down our street block—taught me to venture out on short trips away from home. In my teen years, I took more risks as I rode that Greyhound across the country. I eventually advanced to travels on 747 flights across the ocean into many continents.

Unbeknownst to me, through each baby step to the end of the block and back, like a fearless warrior, I was safely in the protective arms of our Lord and Savior. His plan for my life led me forward slowly but surely. Eventually, he unfolded all that he had ahead for me. He was ever-present in each step that I took. "I am with you always, even to the

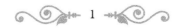

end of the age" (Matthew 28:20). I would, in time, realize that my total dependence was on the one who planned my life even before my conception in my mother's womb. Little steps later developed into more significant, bolder, broader steps.

Life's process happens little by little. Visualize, for a moment, a bunch of neighborhood kids lined up in a row. They are riding bikes, wagons, roller skates, and other modes of transportation. They all neatly follow the leader, traveling from one end of the block to the other. These kids then learned to test their boundaries, becoming braver. They venture out a little further, perhaps to surrounding neighborhood blocks. Ultimately, some of these kids spread their wings by moving away from their home state and venturing into states, some near, some across the country. Eventually they are led on a journey around the world, stopping in many countries and cultures. I was one of those kids who continued the adventure into faraway lands. Life happens when God calls.

The riverbank was perfect for sledding onto the frozen river. Ice skaters occupied this patch in the winter, and children fished in the running water in the summer. Lanterns and the huge Michigan moon set the scene for nighttime ice skating and summertime fishing.

A child's delight was riding snow horses and throwing snowballs at the pretend enemy during those young years. All of us kept busy for long hours, playing cowboys and Indians on the hilly, bushy riverbank. Back then, all kids owned a Roy Rogers, Gene Autry, or Lone Ranger and Tonto gun and holster fastened from the waist. Cap guns echoed throughout the riverbank when we could afford caps. Otherwise, we just pointed and said, "*Bang*! *Bang*! You're dead."

This winter ice rink became a thrilling water flow during the spring and summer months. My brother built a log dock, which became an ideal spot to drop a fishing pole line into the river while hanging over the bottom edge of the riverbank water. From there, young feet dangled over the shallow, murky river. Fun, imaginary kid play included soaking up the summer sunshine, munching on a favorite snack, and acting like a pioneer or, perhaps, Tom Sawyer. The log raft tied to the dock carried us throughout the shallow river and was perfect for catching perch and other unusual fish.

Those Michigan winters called for bundling up. A hat, mitts, and a scarf over the face prevented chapped skin and frostbite. The basement coal furnace was a nice spot for thawing out while devouring mom's warm homemade cookies. Mom was intentional about creating a homey atmosphere. When I became a single mom, our kitchen was a favorite meeting place as well. I, like my mother, focused on establishing a pleasant atmosphere. Shoveling coal was a permanent job to help keep the house somewhat warm. I, too, did what I had to in order to take care of my girls, including cutting wood for the fireplace. These chores are usually a man's job, but a man's job can become a woman's job when a man is not present. Mom did an incredible job of keeping the fire aglow and often baked just to warm the kitchen, which took hard work and money.

Outdoor play became a great outlet for releasing anxiety and the pressures of young life. Mom used the river fish as fertilizer in her garden. Since the river was polluted, we imitated the Mayflower pilgrims. Mom dug corn hills roomy enough for a few kernels of corn and a fish or two, depending on the size of our catch. We kids added to the bountiful crop of sweet corn from our fish catch.

I grew up in a small township in Huron County, an ideal location for kids to be raised. The village population was about twenty-five hundred people and consisted primarily of German settlers. My parents grew up on farms within five miles of our childhood home that were located in the heart of this small community. Our modest two-story house with a basement was set on a fifty-foot by one-hundred-and-fifty-foot plot, perfect for a flower and vegetable garden and a play area for active children and their friends.

Our church and the Christian school were located a short walk from our home. Our high school was a short block away, heading the other direction. The heart of the township was about two blocks past the high school—all entities set within the perfect distance for a family that either walked or biked. Traveling with relatives twenty-five miles down the road to the big city to shop was huge and an adventurous road trip for our family.

Our community was safe, and parents let their kids venture out from early morning to supper time during the summer months with brief break for a lunch of a peanut-butter-and-jelly sandwich. We trekked the town, each with our own mode of transportation. We learned to become future leaders and followers as we took turns in our travels up and down the sidewalk. The grass between the sidewalk's cracks barely had time to grow as we repeatedly trampled it down. If the paths could talk, they surely would tell a story.

Life was a young child's delight. Although hungry, no one wanted to give up the fun playtime when parents called us in for supper. Often, I fell asleep at the family supper table after an active day. To wake up, wash up, put on pajamas, and go to bed was an imposition. And I had to climb up the many stairs to my bedroom. My little legs were worn to a frazzle, so climbing from the bottom to the top step was a real chore. Even more difficult was when it was my turn to do the dishes as my legs screamed with growing pains.

Most of the neighbors were permanent residents, yet the corner rental house on the block saw several families come and go. The neighborhood families welcomed newcomers, yet the more permanent families probably were a bit territorial, especially with the families that moved in and out.

The neighborhood kids, for the most part, happily played together and got along—perhaps even better at times than our parents did. Occasionally, we had a dispute over someone else's child. Moms went to bat for their children whenever a situation with the kids got out of hand. Later, in my child-rearing days, I, too, went to bat for my daughters, and on occasion, I was proven wrong. As parents, we want to believe our children, even when they tell stories.

The kitchen door stayed closed to the rest of our house during the winter months. Our kitchen and bathroom were the two warmest

rooms. Getting up in the mornings in our freezing upstairs bedrooms called for action. A dense layer of ice covered our inside windows and stayed there until spring. Once out of bed, we quickly dressed and got a move on. The furnace kept the house from freezing over, yet the temps were so low that it stayed chilly. Mom later inherited enough money to replace the coal furnace with an oil furnace. This gift was a huge blessing. Mom, especially in her older years, liked a nice cozy warm home.

Mom's days started early during the summer months. After lunch, she was ready for a much-needed sofa rest. I often looked closely to see if she was still breathing. As I watched her chest rise and fall, I was so relieved.

I was sometimes ashamed of my attitude, knowing how my words and sassiness hurt her. My pride kept me from saying, "I'm sorry," even though the Holy Spirit convicted me. As a middle child, I sometimes felt that the older and younger children were favorites. Birth order can sometimes causes issues with middle siblings. As a counselor, I helped these middle children work through some of these issues in play therapy. Thankfully, we have a God of forgiveness. He wants to clean us up from the inside out.

Mom came from a family that knew how to work. Sometimes this strong work ethic in every area of life nearly drove me crazy. Later in life, I learned to appreciate doing a job to the best of my ability. We cleaned the house each Saturday, and the sheets were washed each Monday. The heels of the socks faced the same direction, working from the largest to the smallest. And yes, much to my surprise, this habit accompanied me throughout life. Consequently, Mom is still often in my actions.

Mom maybe reached five feet, five inches at her tallest. She was of a medium build, energetic with noticeable and appealing freckles that matched her beautiful chestnut hair. Her sparkling eyes complemented the rest of her coloring and expressed her warmth and humor.

Most of the women I knew let their hair turn gray as they grew older. However, my mother bucked the trend and dared to color her hair—the only one of her siblings who was so brave. About every six months, she visited the local beautician who carefully permed her hair too.

Her weekly walks to the grocery store, church, school, or wherever she went were most likely the reason for her firm calves. Her pace was swift, as lollygagging did not fit her lifestyle, and she covered much ground every day.

We filled many daily hours by pretending in our beach sand in the sandbox located under the grapevine. We dug deep into the mounds of sand, just knowing we would eventually reach China or Russia on the other side of the world.

Years later, as a play therapist, I learned that play in a child's world is considered work. Adults verbally communicate while children cannot always express themselves verbally. Play then helps them work through their emotions, replay situations, and learn to resolve problems. As children play, they are sorting through their feelings with toys, art, and other types of therapy. Meaningful play rehearsal benefits them. Girls nurture their baby dolls, and boys build and work with their cars and trucks.

I spent hours playing with my dollhouse and baby dolls, dressing and undressing them, and pretending to wash and iron their clothes on my home-made ironing board. My baby doll received much nurturing. This activity, no doubt, prepared me to recognize the ins and outs of motherhood, which come about a few years later. I imitated the older adults as a young girl.

My mom and dad both grew up on nearby farms. Their siblings moved out of their parent's farms and into their own farms, all except us township folk. Mom and Dad ended up in the middle of a near-by township. Mom relished her childhood with her parents. God used her to become a rock for her children. Her example aided me in the years when I became a single woman.

I spent summer vacations on these farms. I often babysat my younger cousins since I was the second oldest cousin. I also learned to help with the various farm chores. The farm always offered some excitement. The birth of baby pigs and other animals; gathering eggs; and feeding and milking the cows certainly fast-forwarded my knowledge about the birds and the bees.

Our kinsfolk celebrated the birthdays of all family members. The kids played hide-and-go-seek in the large yards or the barn while our parents played cards. The evening came to a close shortly after ice cream and cake and a birthday song or two. We fell asleep in the back seat of my grandfather's car, a place of comfort, on our drive home after a time of much play. We hated waking up and getting out of the warm car to go into our house, especially during those cold Michigan nights—no fun. The evening play with our cousins kept us going so once we slowed down, sleep came quickly.

My mom's dad emigrated from Germany at age seventeen, and soon after, he married my grandmother. Grandpa was ambitious, dependable, wise, and the father of four children. My mom and her siblings regularly spoke of their parents and their farm days with great fondness. Grandpa purchased a farm and later sold it for a bigger farm. He and his family were self-sufficient and grew fruits and vegetables and raised cattle, chickens, and pigs. He tended to his grape vineyard, corn in the field, wheat, and sugar beets. They baled hay and straw sufficient to feed their dairy cattle. Grandpa and Grandma were committed Christians, yet they worshiped in different churches. I never understood why they attended different churches as they did everything else together. Eventually, age caught up with them, and they left the farm and moved kitty-corner from our home in the heart of town.

As I share each childhood experience, I want to honor all parties involved in the story. Hindsight showed me that God had a plan for my life. Likewise, he has a purpose for your life. He knew the ups and the downs that we would encounter, and ultimately, these happenings draw us closer to him for his glory and the answers to our lives. To think he has a plan for our lives before we were yet in existence is mind-boggling. Scripture says that "before I formed you in the womb I knew you" (Jeremiah 1:5).

I have always felt that God carefully selects the parents that will benefit our growth and preparation for what is in store for us. Our parents, siblings, family, environments, exposures, and experiences are all planned and figured out to glorify the God of the universe. The task of our parents is to groom their children for the future. God makes no mistakes even through the hard times, and we are fashioned to his liking.

God knew my father's life would be short and that my mother would remain a widow from age thirty-two until she reached ninety-five years and seven months of age. I add the seven months as the days and months count when you reach the age she reached. He knows our all. God knew each detail of my mom's life, from becoming a widow, raising her children, and teaching the generations that followed. "I am the Alpha and the Omega, the Beginning and the End, the First and the Last" (Revelation 22:13).

I scarcely remember my dad's short twenty-nine years. I was six days into my fifth birthday when he passed away from heart and lung conditions. My newly widowed mom was now assigned to raise her three children solo. It's hard to believe, but this was in God's plan. Mom was our rock and kept our family together. Her faith in her heavenly husband kept her going throughout nearly a century of life.

"Sing to God, sing praises to His name; extol Him who rides on the clouds, by His name Yah, and rejoice before Him. Father of the fatherless and protector of widows is God in his holy habitation" (Psalm 68:4–5).

Before conception, God had my purpose all planned out, a purpose more significant than I could imagine. He knew the ups and the downs that I would encounter and, ultimately, these up and downs drew me closer to him for his glory. Our lives and future are in his hands—yours, mine, each of ours. He gives us gifts and talents to be used for his glory. I was not aware of this, yet life goes on, and we mature emotionally and spiritually. The Bible is our roadmap. His Word and godly people teach us, and it somehow comes together. "Train up a child in the way he should go, and when he is old, he will not depart from it" (Proverbs 22:6).

What are our gifts and talents? We, in time, begin to recognize our strengths and what brings us joy, and we become good at our individual gifts and skills. Everyone has a gift. Even a tree and a chicken have a gift. The tree drops a seed, which eventually gives us an apple or an orange or whatever. A chicken gives us eggs. "There are diversities of gifts, but the same Spirit." (1 Corinthians 12:4).

He plans to prosper me and to prosper you. It may take a few years to understand this, yet as we grow mentally, emotionally, and spiritually through the years of our trials and the testing of our faith, we discover his unique method for us. That twenty-twenty hindsight has shown me this truth: God does know best.

Previous years, perhaps unbeknownst to us, prepared us for the later years of life. Little did I know that one day, I would be a single mom raising her children, similar to how my mom raised me and my siblings. The difference was that mom was widowed early in her marriage, and I was single through a divorce. But we both raised our children as single parents. In my case, my oldest daughter had just turned eighteen, and the rest followed on down in age, with the youngest daughter seven. Mom's children were six, five, and one year of age. Thankfully, Mom let us children play hard after Dad died. I think those hours of "work" helped in the grieving and healing process.

My memories of my dad are few. One memory is being in a gravel stone pit with dad. He was filling up his trailer with gravel, and I was splashing through ankle-deep puddles of water nearby. A second memory is in our backyard amid dad's scrap metal, which he collected during the war to sell and manufacture for weapons. Dad did not qualify for the United States Army due to his condition of his weak heart and lung, but he wanted to help the World War II efforts and did so through contributing scrap metal.

My mom's camera was always within arm's reach. She was a photographer at heart, so she blessed her children with a few thousand photos from birth to our early birthdays to our graduation gowns and onward. Sometimes I wonder if my recall is not an actual memory but might come from a picture or two instead. My last memory of him is in his casket, laid at rest in our home. My siblings and I stayed with a neighbor lady until our father's burial.

I have one more vague memory as a youngster: waking up to the noise of airplanes flying over our home. My brother and I had bedrooms upstairs, a long way from mom's bedroom downstairs if we woke up afraid and wanted to be next to her. My young ears tuned in to the war stories and bomb conversations. Between the radio news of war and family talk, this was an ongoing topic in our family.

Our townships catered to small airplanes that regularly flew in and out. This activity was different while World War II was going on. My mom took turns watching at the community lookout tower for activity directly overhead. Grandpa, a German immigrant, stayed current on his home country happenings.

My mom left an impressive spiritual legacy. Even ten years after her death, she continues to be missed. We know she is exuberant about being with her heavenly Maker, her husband, her parents, siblings, and friends. Mom and I were weekend phone buddies and faithful letter writers throughout the years. She saved my letters, which I eventually inherited, and I saved her correspondence, all of which are now neatly placed in sequential order.

She fed her children fresh vegetables and fruits. Just as she fertilized and cared for her plants, she nurtured her family spiritually with her focus on the Lord. She had to know that her children knew and loved the Lord. We were all baptized, attended a Christian elementary school, were confirmed, and, in my case, even married in this particular church. We were permitted to leave the table only after we completed our family devotions.

Mom was a supporter of our small township activities. She mostly went by herself if there was no one to join her. Later, I, too, learned that there are times of doing things alone. My mother's built-in energy and determination carried her through many difficult situations, and God accompanied her every day. Volunteering and receiving compensation in the form of food, along with her welfare check, helped to provide for our family needs. Mom was dedicated, enthusiastic, and committed in whatever she did. She knew how to make life happen. Her will power, strength of character, and work ethic was in her favor as a single parent.

My brother became a polio victim at thirteen in the 1954 Michigan epidemic. From that time until he met mom in heaven at age seventy-seven, he could not use his left arm. Mom did a physical therapy regime on his left arm each day, diligently laboring over her son for the first few years. He and I ended up together in the same high school class and graduated together. He later earned his BA and became a teacher. He eventually opened a business and became a forty-year bike repair specialist and a Michigan fur harvester. He created a variety of gadgets to compensate for the use of one arm. He demonstrated much determination and tenacity and led a successful life.

From grade school through college and until he went to be with Jesus, my brother sang in the church choir and the college choir. He even worked an apparatus to help him hold his choir song books. Scripture verses written on poster board, cardboard pieces, small index cards, and scraps of paper were scattered throughout his home. Verses even filled the pages of his journals. He was focused on living a life for Jesus.

My sister became a nurse, a wife, and a mother to three children who grew up to be very accomplished adults.

My high school extracurricular activities consisted of band and varsity cheerleading. These activities boosted my self-esteem. My freshmen classmates chose me as their freshman queen. Later, the principal choose me as one of two girls to attend Girls State during our junior year. Girls State took place at a state university where many girls from throughout Michigan learned how the government functions.

As I think about it years later, our small family had much going for us: plenty to eat, relatives that cared for us, and mom's energy making life happen. Even so, I sometimes suffered from shame and humiliation. I had no dad and a family member with a disability, and we were on welfare. All that was hard, yet it prepared me for life and made me who I am today. Although my young life was a struggle, I learned much about not only my life but the lives of others and living conditions in general. We can decide to be happy and love or feel inadequate or inferior. The decisions we make determine our future. We choose, and the result follows.

Thankfully, God has forgiven my sinful thoughts. As we mature in the Lord, we increase in both wisdom and knowledge. I walked in those shoes, so familiarity and firsthand information gave me insight. God did give me the right parents to mentor me and fulfill his personal purpose for me as I was growing up. As difficult as life sometimes is, I would not change anything about how I was raised, other than those times when I was sassy and gave my mother a hard time.

My friends' dads accompanied them to the high school father-and-daughter banquets. Fathers occupied the school bleachers, cheering for their offspring. Since my dad was not around, Mom filled that spot. She seldom missed a school event and was likely more supportive than many moms. From day one, through my high school years, she was there. Having her by our side was significant. Unfortunately, some activities catered only to dads and daughters. The teachers, however, made sure I was at ease, even without a dad as an escort. The presence of a father would have been a blessing. Some teachers took care of me in that respect.

The unexpected disruptions and detours in life result in zigzags all over the place. Life does not consist of a scenic linear route. We get to z by tackling all the letters from a to z in order or sometimes out of order. We reach our goal one step at a time and sometimes a half step at a time. Detours can be valuable. God wants to work within us. He knows what he is doing even when his ways are not clear to us. I'm convinced life's detours strengthen our spiritual muscles and work for our good and ultimately his glory.

Life's interferences cause us to stretch in ways we had not previously thought of. We see the hand of God guiding us all the way. Determination and consideration carry us forward. When the road gets bumpy, we can give up or carry on. The choice is ours. As we reflect on how God previously made a way, it helps us to pick ourselves up again and move forward. In other words, venture out. We should not get too comfortable as these comfort zones may be harmful. We sometimes just settle there instead of pursuing God with all our hearts.

We had near-perfect Sunday school attendance, and mom found a way for us to attend summer church and 4-H camps. She undoubtedly made sacrifices to make these camps possible. She possibly hoped to compensate for our unavailable deceased dad. Maybe that's why she made sure her children had the little extras in life. Welfare did not take into consideration the importance and the expense of children experiencing time at summer camp.

Welfare limited our earnings. When we exceeded that amount, that surplus was reported and deducted from our next monthly check. We worked the fields, and mom's siblings provided beef, pork, and chickens during butchering times. Between our garden and the aunts' and uncles' gardens, we had plenty of fresh fruit and vegetables. These supplements provided for healthy meals. We possibly had a better diet than wealthier people.

God had it going for us. His footsteps in the sand were never washed away by the incoming waves. He had us under his wing. Dad's life insurance paid off our home. When we returned from the day's activities, Mom was usually home to meet us. We had a heavenly Daddy who cared for this widow and was a father to her children. We had much to be thankful for. And I complained!

Mom supported me in all my efforts. I learned to cook, bake, grow a garden, preserve fruits and vegetables, and sew. Mom's effort to keep life going after dad died was extraordinary. I modeled her example and attempted to keep life going in my home after the divorce. A homey atmosphere and the aroma of baked goods and Christian music helps maintain peace and tranquility when raising children in a single-parent home. My specialty was baking and donating these baked goods at the church bazaars.

Mom always had enough money to purchase fabric for my 4-H garments. My largest project was my prom dress. Some twenty years later, my youngest daughter insisted on wearing this same formal to her high school prom. With the help of a senior seamstress who had excellent alteration skills, the dress added beauty to my already beautiful daughter.

Insecurity can invade a child's mind. But as a young child, I did not lack a male figure in our home. Grandpa had an unmistakable twinkle in his eye and a big and tender heart. I loved the smell of his pipe or his cigar. He helped my mother fix whatever was broken. He brought us all fresh berries and other fruits and vegetables from his garden. He made himself at home while drinking a cup of coffee and telling us stories of his childhood and sharing life lessons.

Grandpa and Grandma moved into town when they became too old to manage the farm. I felt more secure with our grandparents across the street, a mere minute away. Mom often sent me to Grandpa's when my attitude needed adjustment or when I needed help with my math. Grandpa never really scolded me. We talked about doing better, being kind, and showing respect to my mom. Because of his attentiveness, I became a good checkers player and learned how to whistle with the use of two fingers in my mouth. And my math improved as well.

Once I completed my driver's education classes, he and I went out for a few practice drives. Eventually, he trusted me to take his car to town to pick up groceries. His Chevrolet smelled like cigar and pipe tobacco. When I was young, we did not have a car or a TV. The neighbor lady who cared for us during the showing of my deceased dad occasionally invited us over to watch TV with her kids.

Yes, our younger years caravanning around the block were good years. When I reached school age, times changed somewhat. We kept busy with school, homework, and church activities, and by nine or ten, we began working in the fields, picking strawberries, raspberries, and cucumbers with the Mexican workers that came into our community each year.

In addition, I became a babysitter and worked in my uncle's field in the summer, hoeing various crops. I learned to drive a tractor and an old truck at an early age. Of course, we only operated vehicles in the fields. Driver's training and Grandpa's training came a little later when I turned fifteen and had a driver's course behind me.

The farm days and babysitting contributed to a solid work ethic. This ethic aided me through life when my daughters and I kept the home fires burning while their dad served two separate Viet Nam tours and, later in life, when I became a single woman. My childhood years taught me to work, to be dependable, to be responsible, and, most importantly, to never give up.

Energetic and eager kids of German upbringing filled our four-room school, which was just what I needed. I didn't like being on welfare and having no daddy. I think the teachers of German descent saw the potential within me. To top it off, I wore brown stockings to keep from freezing in the winter months while walking to school. I hated those stockings, which came complete with a harness-type garter belt. Mom and I struggled each school day about those stockings. Those were the days of my more extreme high spirits.

Our teachers were skilled musicians and played all the instruments, including a violin. They taught band, choir, musical instruments, sports, and Bible. I did well in most subjects yet could have done better in Bible. Those days are still quite vivid in my memory. Once a month, these teachers showed a Shirley Temple movie on the big reel-to-reel projector. That day, we could bring snacks. Together, the teachers and kids watched little Miss Shirley and consumed snacks.

As a young middle-schooler, I helped Grandpa keep the cemetery lawn clipped and mowed during the summer. I followed behind Grandpa, clipping the grass around the grave markers while he mowed. I was continually interested in making a few dollars. The older widows on our street were always in need of someone to help clean their homes and rake the fallen leaves. If you were willing to work, you could always find plenty to do around a farming community.

At a young age, I spent the night at a newly widowed woman's home down the street from our house. She was afraid to be home alone each night, so I stayed with her for a few weeks while she adjusted. I went into her dark home many nights and lay in her bed, waiting for her to return. This boisterous little round German lady liked spending time with her friends more than she liked being in her own home. Her home was always toasty warm, yet her basement furnace and cooking equipment filled the air with scary noises through the night, especially to a preteen and early teen. My incentive to stay with her was my weekly payday. She was a good friend of the family, and Mom thought it right that I should help out until she was ready to face the nights alone again.

I also stayed with my grandmother, my father's mother, when Grandpa died. I rode the bus out to the farm after school and back to school in the mornings. I guess God knew that one day, I would be working with older adults as a recreation coordinator for a city where my daughters and I grew up together.

I learned to appreciate doing a job to the best of my ability. Eventually, after about twenty years of being single, I retired from my employment with the city and state. I then became a licensed professional counselor and a registered play therapist. My younger years as a single woman and parent taught me much about life and, most importantly, that God is faithful and true. This is my story.

We can count on him. He uses every area of our lives for his purpose and glory. His unconditional love for you and me is the best. He satisfies the desires of our hearts. He wants to build our spiritual muscles in preparation for a life adventure of serving him.

God purposely filled the empty spot in my heart and gave me much joy and purpose. I appreciate the detours and disruptions of life and what these ups and downs have done for me. God uses every circumstance to bring us into spiritual maturity, buff in the Lord. With the trials and tribulations in our lives, we have that opportunity. From now on, let's count it all joy while he prepares us for the greatest adventure of his kingdom work.

In his book, James tells us to "count it all joy when you fall into various trials, knowing that the testing of your faith produces patience" (James 1:2–3).

2

The Anointing Flows— Holy Spirit Nudges

*A*n airport security guard once seized one of my valuable therapy items while traveling overseas. At the stateside airport, my baggage weight exceeded the maximum amount, so I just reached into the overweight bag and pulled out a readily available object and tucked it into my carry on. Of course, this added weight made for a heavier carry-on, but this was better than leaving the item behind.

We stopped in several places, and my carry-on bag was not questioned. But at the Paris International Airport, a security guard searched, questioned, confiscated, and eventually tossed this item into a nearby trash can.

My appeal was to no avail, and neither was my second attempt to retrieve the item at the security station. I was so let down. I had traveled a great distance and had a full day's layover. After sitting, contemplating, and much prayer, I received a nudge, a Holy Spirit nudge. I recognized this familiar nudge as I have often experienced it. I returned to the security checkpoint for a third time as the relentless Spirit within me was working.

Initially, I only checked in one cargo bag when this trip allowed for two cargo bag check-ins at no cost. While traveling, I usually carry an extra, small lightweight duffle bag in my carry-on bag—just in case.

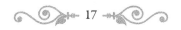

Maybe this bag could be checked in as a second bag with my three-pound item inside, I thought. Tears of excitement now rolled down my flushed cheeks. Eagerly returning to the security checkpoint, I had high expectations of retrieving my therapy item.

Meanwhile, the security station had a change of guards. A very kind guard, fresh on the job, was just beginning his shift. He listened carefully with a kind heart and heard my plea.

Together, we rummaged through several large blue trash cans filled to near capacity, and finally, we found my tropical play dough item. The security guard was as elated as I was. He mentioned before we began the search that yes, I could check in this lightweight duffle bag. Still, it was a very long walk to that check-in point.

I had plenty of remaining hours before take-off in my long day at this terminal. A jog and a stretch were probably a healthy idea, so I started to walk—or maybe skip—the entire way. It was a perfect day. I watched as that little duffle bag moved down the conveyor amid large bags. What a sight! It was so tiny in comparison with the others.

Once that conveyer belt started tossing out baggage in that big airport in Africa, I waited with great anticipation, high expectations, and excitement at the baggage conveyer for my small bag to show up. I could only imagine what it might have felt like for this little item to be in the cargo belly of the 747 aircraft among the enormous bags. The conveyer belt then began to roll, and finally, there amid the grown-up and giant bags and boxes came my miniature duffle bag.

My heart can be very childlike at times, full of play and laughter. I visualized the smile on that small duffle bag when it saw me. I imagined that this little bag, weighing perhaps three pounds, had plenty of bumps and bruises along the way among the bigger bags. In my childlike imagination, I could hear it calling out. "Here I am, here I am. I made it, I made it! Hurry—pick me up. I'm so glad to see you."

For a moment or two, much praise and worship filled my inner being and echoed within the walls of that African airport. God was there. His plan was to restore his children in the middle of their stormy crises by using this item.

Nearly twenty-four hours later, this small duffle bag and I were reunited. Yes, God wanted the healing of his sons and daughters in the continent of Africa. And yes, He was also about taking care of my item among the rest of the suitcases!

The Holy Spirit nudge assured me he was in this place! "Surely the Lord is in this place, and I did not know it" (Genesis 28:16). The Holy Spirit nudges are my blessed assurance and peace.

While I lived in Papua New Guinea, I attended church in a building called the meeting house. I lived quite close to this building, just a short walk away. Each Sunday morning, I heard the PNG worship team practicing, an extraordinary choir, a heavenly moment. My spirit groaned, and my soul sobbed, a cry from deep within my heart. God was doing significant weekly work in this intense sob.

This is not a prideful statement. I often felt God working in a mighty way during these profound encounters, these times of assurance and encouragement. A single person living in a faraway country and culture needs the Lord to sustain them from loneliness. In reality, all missionaries need this reassurance that God is always with us.

"The Spirit also helps in our weaknesses. For we do not know what we should pray for as we ought, but the Spirit Himself makes intercession for us with groanings which cannot be uttered" (Romans 8:26).

Years ago, I realized that God wants to be involved in every area of our lives, in every breath we breathe. He carefully regulates our blood pressure, our heartbeats, and our every bodily function while we sleep and throughout every day. I love this. Each morning, when I wake up, I realize God restored me through the night and prepared me for what he had for me to do in my new day.

As a full-time wife and mother, I was somewhat mindful of this, yet my life was busy, keeping up with the doings of being a wife and mom. However, since becoming single, I realize that God is in every breath breathed. He even cares for a small therapy tool among the huge, intimidating suitcases. Possibly Gabriel or Michael, God's special angels, hand-carried this little bag in that loaded down cargo space.

"I am the Alpha and the Omega, the Beginning and the End, the First and the Last" (Revelation 22:13). He is all-knowing and ever-present and, yes, in every single breath you and I breathe. Yes, and everything in between. He is our breath of life.

"Let everything that has breath praise the Lord" (Psalm 150:6). "The Spirit of God has made me, and the breath of the Almighty gives me life." (Job 33:4). "And the Lord God formed man of the dust of the ground, and breathed into his nostrils the breath of life; and man became a living being." (Genesis 2:7). We depend on God for every breath we take. The air he provides is essential to our every breath, to life itself.

On a crisis management trip overseas, I planned to work with families and children, so I brought along my tools of the trade, including puppets. Years prior, at the Dallas Counseling Office, I had lost a unique ring but never found it. On this particular trip overseas, God showed up and endorsed our work with his presence. The children, a colleague, and I were working with puppets when one of the children said, "Ms. Maggie, look what I found." My long-lost ring was snuggled in the arm of the puppet he was playing with.

Much time had passed since this ring was lost and then found. God perhaps knew this was the perfect time for a solid dose of encouragement and reinforcement. That ring was just like me; I once was lost and now am found, as we sing in "Amazing Grace." God cares about a lost ring and, more importantly, his children. This memory of God's gentle concern to me brings tears to my eyes even many years later.

I reflected on God's goodness while in Israel as a counselor. We had just completed an extensive workshop for field singles from many areas around the world. The workshop coordinators and leaders blessed us with a thoughtful message on God's covenant with his people. As I reflected on the week, I heard in my Spirit that "the best is yet to come." Already I had experienced many bests as a single woman, yet there was more to come.

One client in crisis in Ethiopia gave me a note before our good-byes. The note read, "We were like Peter in the midst of the stormy sea. We were all over the place. Your presence calmed that storm." God so graciously steps in and calms our storms with his mobile vessels on planet Earth.

A different time, another client in the Philippines handed me her special note. She wrote, "I am sure you are an angel disguised as a counselor. You probably noticed that through all the teaching and mentoring, I fell in love with my husband." God was busy using the hands and feet of his children to care for people just like others cared for us when we hurt.

This woman's story shows God working through and within his children. The confidence I have come to know as God walks alongside, guiding and protecting, has kept me going. With God, all things are possible. I better understand this through my experiences. Every day is an insightful day.

Sometimes, I was overwhelmed when I walked into a situation that was out of hand and I had to calm the waters. Yet God's direction and the nudges of the Holy Spirit make the impossible, possible. Without God, I would never accept the assignment to bring health, healing, and normalcy to others while calming the storms within a crisis. This healing is all about God's anointing oil. These assignments are not to be taken lightly.

My faith story takes you from my years as a youngster to the later phases and places of my life. God's goodness has me standing in awe. Who would have thought? He knew my life and yours before that seed entered our mother's womb. His breath of life includes glory for him and you and me.

"We are the clay, and You our Potter" (Isaiah 64:8). In each valuable stage of life, from childhood to adulthood, from blindness to seeing the light, the Potter's hand continues the molding process to his liking and according to the future he has for our lives. "Every good gift and every perfect gift is from above" (James 1:17). God breathes in us the breath of life, which excites me. (See Genesis 2:7.) To think, the moment life is breathed into you and me, our lives, each stage and season, now have a purpose.

My appreciation for life and his goodness increased once my spiritual eyes opened. When I invited Jesus into my heart, the spiritual awaking began. A transitioning, a transformation took place. This makeover is unexplainable; it just happens, and suddenly, life is worth living. "But we have this treasure in earthen vessels, that the excellence of the power may be of God and not of us" (2 Corinthians 4:7).

God became my navigator, which was especially prominent for me after becoming single. He carried me through many valuable life lessons, experiences, periods, and seasons. I deeply value these forty years of single life, a development beyond my comprehension. This describes my joyful reason for celebrating the gift of my singleness.

Had I known earlier even half of what I learned from mid-life forward, life just might have been easier and more straightforward. Mountain peaks, valley lows, and desert wilderness have accompanied the experience. Hindsight is remarkable. We come to recognize and realize how the seasons of life offered growth, wisdom, knowledge, discernment, insight, and direction. I want all of this in my life, don't you?

This journey of life resembles a road map. We sometimes face a fork in the road, a detour, or a roundabout way, or we even become lost if we don't pay attention to the signs. Perhaps we have taken a similar path as Moses and the children of Israel with their forty-year wilderness trek that they should have completed in eleven short days.

My prayer is that my story demonstrates that there is life and joy after divorce. With God, what appears to be an impossible event becomes possible. We move out of the victim status to a victorious state, from barely living to reaching our full potential. Unusual happenings come into play when we invite and allow God to be the anchor of our lives. The disciples called out to Jesus who was asleep in the boat when the stormy sea roared, and with just a word, Jesus calmed the sea. The winds and water even obey him (Luke 8:23). Just like Jesus calmed the sea and the disciples, my storm ceased when I invited Jesus into my life in a friend's living room. I experienced calmness and an unexplainable hope.

God is in control. Life happens, and although we sometimes feel as if we are drowning, God can calm the storm and take us to the other side. He desires to make the most of our spiritual purpose, bringing us to our complete potential.

Yes, he does give us free will. His will, however, is the best to follow, and when we oppose his will as shown in Scripture, we exercise our own free will. When we follow Scripture, we apply God's will. His will is the most excellent way.

I love it when God takes our disappointments and uses them for his good (Romans 8:28). We can truly benefit from the losses, successes, and recoveries of life's happenings.

If you or someone you know is going through a hard time, please share my story. God is available to help each one of us. He wants us to hang in there and never give up on living, to stay in the race of life and finish victoriously.

He waits for us to call on him. We have the opportunity to overcome difficulties, to accomplish much, to appreciate life, and to pass on a legacy. When challenges come, we pick ourselves up and wipe the dust off our knees and the sweat off our brows. With our eyes on Jesus, he calms our storms. He is all about forgiveness, promises, and provisions.

God says he will never leave or forsake us. Promises made at the altar of marriage were forgotten. The journey of our lives offers challenges, hardships, and times of facing failure. Sometimes, we feel like giving up. Through it all, we can gain a wealth of strength and spiritual growth that we might have missed if it were not for the struggles. These broken seasons can bring us into an intimate relationship with God. God restores and makes us strong. He wants to be an intimate part of our lives. Come, Lord Jesus. Here I am, Lord, send me and use me.

"Therefore God, Your God, has anointed You with the oil of gladness" (Psalm 45:7). My oil of thankfulness and joyfulness increased as time went by while learning more about what God offers his children. I wanted it all. God anointed me with much joy, and I experienced God's amazing faithfulness beyond my every expectation after becoming single. Since then, I now see him in a bright light, almost like an LED.

Marriage does not define me; God defines me. James 1:2–4 tells us, "Count it all joy when you fall into various trials, knowing that the testing of your faith produces patience. But let patience have its perfect work, that you may be perfect and complete, lacking nothing." It's not about counting the pain as joyful but about knowing he will carry us through the painful times.

God just shows up in reassuring ways. He knows how to take care of us and what will delight our hearts. His anointing falls and flows, and here we go—no time to think twice about the immediate situation. I have many stories about how God made a way for me as a single woman.

My daughter was on her way home for Christmas break. Her college exams and time of burning the midnight oil were now behind her until the next time around. The trip home involved some twelve hundred miles and twenty hours of travel, much through conditions with winter snow. She was about three hundred miles from home when she called. "Mom, I'm so tired, so exhausted. I don't think I can drive another mile without sleep. I only have enough money for gas and maybe a snack for breakfast." She was in Flagstaff, Arizona, and it was too cold to just pull over and take a nap.

I had escorted a bus trip that stopped overnight in Flagstaff months prior while working for the city. I thought that this hotel management just might remember me. I called this hotel and asked if they remembered me as I needed a favor. They remembered me and kindly gave my daughter a room. They trusted me to drop a check in the mail the next day. They not only put up my daughter for the night but left snacks in the room. God is in our every breath and our every step.

While living overseas, a family flew in for a lengthy time of counseling. Every effort to help this family through the sufferings had been of no avail. Within a session or two, nudges from the Holy Spirit led us to the family's God-given gifts. "This also comes from the Lord of hosts, who is wonderful in counsel and excellent in guidance" (Isaiah 28:29). For nearly two weeks, this family carefully, through the guidance of these God-given gifts, worked on each crisis encountered through the previous year. The family drawings, detailed discussions, and discourses guided this family into the path of peace and healing. "You will guide me with Your counsel, and afterwards receive me to glory" (Psalm 73:24).

The traumas should never have happened, yet we live in a dangerous world. And yes, God, in his miraculous way, restored. The drawings, the discussions, prayers, and God's healing touch restored. God showed up, and months later, it was confirmed. God healed. My life is filled with similar stories and divine godly appointments.

Our lives consist of stormy times. I, at one time, thought hard times came about because of sin, and yes, sin does cause struggles. I thought our life's voyage meant sweetness, smooth sailing, and sunshine—every day. I didn't realize what hard times do for a person. Simply put, tough times have the potential to draw us closer to Jesus. The challenges he went through and his sacrifice expressed his unconditional love for his children. The good news is how much he loves you and me.

The bumps and bruises in life can draw us into a closer, more intimate walk with Jesus. Hard times have the potential to pull us to the source that heals and brings hope and joy into our lives. We look for answers, and he is ultimately the only answer. He brings people into our experience to help us. This mercifulness tells me he is ever present (Psalm 46:1).

People become God's hands and feet. The time even comes when we are comfortable in the solitude of our homes because of the peace he gives that surpasses all understanding (Philippians 4:7). When we are the weakest, he is active (2 Corinthians 12:10). "I am the way, the truth, and the life" (John 14:6).

I tell you this as my story is accurate, and I am still very much alive. Jesus became the lifter of my head (Psalm 3:3) and the healer of my broken heart (Psalm 147:3). His love replaced my marriage partner, who was once my dear friend. He can keep us on track and give us a fulfilled life. When we aren't sure what to do, he guides us. Any diffi-culty—a divorce, death, loss of a job or limb—whatever the situation, Jesus can exchange our sorrow for joy (2 Timothy 1:7).

Jesus is the only one who can calm a raging storm within us. The storms in life are many. And each storm builds strength and persever-ance and has the potential to diminish the winds with little effort. This assurance is good news.

My tough time—a true test—involved a failed marriage. Eventually, I realized that even though this marriage had ended, much good and gain came through our time together. I learned what it is like to have a strong marriage, and I learned the issues that bring about a divorce. I learned that one cannot do much if a spouse is determined to leave a relationship.

Looking at the remarkable happier side, I gained children and grandchildren through this matrimony. Likewise, I experienced God's work in my life through what I learned while single. My children and I have gained immeasurable insight and matured greatly through the recovery process. God's message of renewal and salvation expands and continues into the generations that follow.

Working through my spousal calamity prepared my children and me to aid others. My reliance on the Lord grew stronger as a single person. I had much to do and learn through the years. This learning required strength from the Spirit of the living God. "'Not by might nor by power, but by My Spirit,' says the Lord of hosts" (Zechariah 4:6). As a single of many years, I can attest that God has a track record of excellence in taking care of his children of all ages, married or single. His grace "is sufficient for you and me" (2 Corinthians 12:9).

The Word assures us that God is the husband to the husbandless widow and the father to the fatherless children (Psalm 68:5). I whole-heartedly agree as I have seen him in action. We learned that God is the healer, and through it all, we learned to walk in both the steps of defeat and restoration.

Since retirement, I took several creative writing classes and workshops to find out how to write a book. The highlight of one workshop was hearing an author tell his story of how it took seven years of hard work to publish his first book. I am nearing this magical number for this book as well.

The number seven is often listed in Scripture. This number represents completion. God rested on the seventh day after creating the heavens and the earth. No doubt I will take full advantage of the seventh year of rest as I have labored hundreds of hours in writing my story.

The passage about forgiving seventy times seven (Matthew 18:21–22) is also significant. Forgiving those who hurt us is not always easy, yet necessary, for healing within the depths of our souls. God can then freely work in our lives, freeing us from burdens.

God's plans for you and me offer hope, a future, peace (Jeremiah 29:11, 14), and freedom from captivity. His anointing is for you and me. His anointing oil removes the burdens from our shoulders (Isaiah 10:27).

3

I Once Was Blind—
Spiritual Awakening

*Y*es, I once was blind, and now I see. How did this happen? My hero, the God of the Bible, did this.

In the book of John, Jesus healed a blind man. He had lived in darkness since birth; perhaps his arms were stretched out for alms while his olive wood walking stick lay beside him. One day, Jesus came along and anointed the blind man's eyes with spit and clay and told the blind man to wash his eyes in the pool of Siloam. The blind man's eyes were opened, and he could see light. The blind man had no explanation other than, "I can see." People who knew him and knew he was born blind asked, "'This man, is he the same—?' And the man said, 'I am he.'" (See John 9.)

I can only imagine the excitement and joy this blind man must've felt. The blind man's eyes were opened after years of darkness. How did it happen? The blind man did not know. He just said, "This man touched me." The blind man only knew he was seeing the people and the world around him. He saw the birds, the bees, and trees. He delighted in his newfound eyesight.

Jesus, the light of the world, gives light to the blind. When I truly accepted Jesus into my heart, my blind eyes opened. I have no explanation—only that I saw my surroundings and my desperate situation in a new light. My heart came to life; hopefulness and happiness replaced my troubled body, mind, and emotions. I was encouraged and now wanted

to live. My inner spirit yearned to read the Bible to know more about this man, Jesus.

Accepting Jesus into my heart changed my life. It's hard to explain. Or perhaps it's simple. Life became livable, an amazing transformation took place, and yes, words cannot express what happened. All I knew is that I could see and I wanted to live.

When my mother saw me a year or two later, she asked me, "What makes you the way you are?" One daughter told me that she wanted what I had. Hope, encouragement, and a desire to remain in the race of life entered into my very being during mid-life.

The stirring Bible stories I learned, especially during my elementary school years, came alive. Before, they were stories I valued and dearly delighted in hearing. I was always ready for just one more story. But once my eyes were opened, these stories spoke to me in a different light. I was taught to respect the Bible in those early years, and I did, or at least I tried to as much as a young child could. My once-blind eyes now saw the light of Jesus. The stories, the bits and pieces, learned through life, now began to form a beautiful puzzle, perhaps a mystery. The words began speaking to my heart and grew into a rich and vibrant enjoyment. Reading the Bible was now like seeing and experiencing real life right before my eyes.

The words took on new meaning and spoke to me differently. Every episode helped to focus on Jesus and take my eyes off what led me to becoming single. This was like the blind man we just read about in John 9, who said, "I can see." This transformation happened when I invited Jesus to touch my heart.

The desire and determination to want to live was deeply entrenched in my soul. By God's grace, I would survive my dilemma. Hopefulness, strength, and stamina seemed to anoint my every cell. A spiritual awakening transpired, arrived, and has occupied my life since that time during my mid-life experience. This happened in a friend's living room. Like the blind man, I could now see. I was not sitting on a curb begging for alms; however, I was begging for help. My life had just been turned upside down.

When entering this friend's home, my life was in a state of disbelief and complete confusion. My best friend in the whole world—or who I thought was my best friend—had just walked out of our twenty-year marriage. For a brief moment, I wanted to run away, to die. My life had taken an unexpected turn for the worse as I watched my marriage of two decades dissolve before my eyes. The confusion, disappointment, and pain were drowning me. Unrealistic thoughts overwhelmed me. Did I turn left or perhaps right? Perhaps I should just run away and never look back. However, God wanted to rescue me.

My mother, elementary teachers, the church, and Sunday school taught me throughout my young years about a man named Jesus. I was baptized at birth, confirmed at age fourteen, and married in the same church at age eighteen.

Throughout my young years, I was taught right from wrong. Doing right was important to me. I was sensitive to matters of character: don't lie, cheat, or steal and follow the Ten Commandments to the best of my ability.

This biblical instruction was real to me, and I did try to do what was right. I think the repercussions of the fear of the Lord were forever up front, as much as a young child or a young adult could comprehend. I didn't realize this fear of the Lord meant reverence, respect, and wisdom. One Scripture says: "The fear of the Lord is the beginning of wisdom" (Proverbs 9:10). As a child, I thought this fear of the Lord meant spankings from Jesus.

I was sensitive whenever I was disrespectful toward my mom. Even decades ago, teenagers talked back to their moms, or at least I did. I had plenty of room for improvement when my sporadic stubborn streak kicked in; the disrespectful talking back was shameful, and I knew it. Pride often kept me from saying that I was sorry.

I once joined my peers as we quietly entered the farmer's watermelon patch in the dark of the evening. "Cooning" was the word we used back then. It was an awful offense to steal a watermelon from a hard-working farmer's watermelon patch, and I knew it. Well, my mother found out what I had done before I even got home that night. She heard about a bunch of kids who stole a farmer's watermelons. She taught me a stern lesson. She occasionally put the green tree twigs that grew bountifully in our yard to good use.

Did I ignore my conscience and join the crowd for acceptance? Stealing is wrong, and I knew it. My conscience told me so. I wanted out, yet I joined my peers. That inner spirit—the still, small voice—nudged me during those young years, but I did not always pay attention.

I loved the Golden Book Classics. Maybe Jesus, to me, was like one of the Golden Book characters that taught morals, values, and principles. The stories generally ended with "the moral of this story is . . ." They taught me right from wrong and the dos and the don'ts of life. The ending talked about living happily ever after.

Like these books, Mom—and teachers—made sure children knew the Bible stories. Honestly, I think the teachers loved the stories as much as the children did, so consequently, we heard them over and over. Jesus was the main character in all the Bible stories.

That day, as a middle-aged woman, I re-invited Jesus into my heart. Since that time, he has become the most important character in my life. In a marriage, life and family keep a person very busy. Jesus may not be the first influence in a busy life. But he should be first; your husband, second; and children, after.

We probably have all heard about David, the shepherd boy, who killed a lion and a bear when these animals attempted to eat one of his sheep for lunch. This young teenager was brave and eventually killed the giant Goliath with a slingshot and a stone. David was my hero. Did God set David up? Perhaps God wanted David to realize that with his help, he could do all things—even kill a lion, a bear, and a mighty giant. David was destined to eventually become the king of all Israel.

And then there was Joseph, the young teenager with a coat of many colors. He had ten older brothers but was his father's favorite son. He had dreams and bragged to his brothers about these dreams. He told them in a roundabout way that one day, they would bow down to him. His brothers were jealous because of their dad's favoritism and because of Joseph's dreams. Joseph may have even come across as a smart aleck. Through a serious of events, he was thrown in a pit, sold to Potiphar, and eventually thrown in prison. He was put in charge of all the prisoners and took great care of them. Later, he interpreted a dream for two of the prisoners, which came to pass. He was then called before Pharaoh and interpreted a dream for him as well. Pharaoh then made him a prince. He actively pursued his faith, and God took him from a prisoner to a prince (Genesis 37–50). Joseph was destined to be second-in-command of Egypt. Perhaps the prison was a preparation and training ground for what God had in mind for him.

Samson was a gigantic, robust hero in Israel who killed a lion with his bare hands. God did not want him to tell Delilah the secret of his long hair and strength, but he gave in to her. I felt so sorry for him when the enemy gouged out his eyes. I then cheered him on when God gave him enough strength and power to bring down the house on the Philistines, the real evil men of that day (Judges 16). Samson lacked discipline in his life, yet God called him a hero of faith.

Moses was another chosen man of God who led the Israelite children out of Egypt. He threw his rod on the ground, and the rod turned into a snake and gulped down all the Egyptian snakes. And this very same rod split the Red Sea in two so the Hebrew children could walk through on dry land. The story of his placement in a basket and floating in the Nile River as a baby and of his later rescue by an Egyptian princess warmed my young heart. Moses wrote the Ten Commandments as the Lord spoke them. Moses, likewise, made the list of Bible heroes in Hebrews.

I loved and treasured every story, just like those in the Golden Books. These stories found in the pages of the Bible are forever exciting, captivating, and illustrate to us what the God of the universe can do. He prepares, equips, and strengthens us during tough times for the ministry.

Surely this same God of the Old Testament can heal broken hearts and open blind eyes. The first step is to invite him into your life and my life. He is a transformer of lives. He gives salvation, power, grace, and mercy. He sees his children through their disappointments in life.

When I invited Jesus into my heart that day in that friend's living room, my life forever changed. My eyes opened. I was no longer blind. I was like the beggar man that went to the pool of Siloam to wash the anointed clay Jesus put on his eyes. He shouted out, "I once was blind, and now I see."

I invited Jesus to come into my heart and asked him to forgive my sins. I believed he died on the cross of Calvary and rose from the dead on the third day. I wanted to live and not to die, and I wanted him to fill my empty hurting heart with his anointing. I wanted, at that very moment, to live for him. In time, I learned about dying to myself in order to live for him. I learned that dying for him is a time of surrender. I said, "Thy will be done, Lord Jesus."

He took me from a desperate woman to a woman who loves others for his name's sake. This does not mean I've arrived; we never arrive. We are always growing and increasing in faith. "And the apostles said to the Lord, 'increase our faith'" (Luke 17:5). I desired the pure milk of the Word like newborn babes enjoyed their milk (1 Peter 2:2). "Be diligent to present yourself approved to God, a worker who does not need to be ashamed, rightly dividing the word of truth" (2 Timothy 2:15). As we mature, God continues to shape and strengthen his children in preparation for the future he has for them. No, I haven't arrived, yet I am farther along than I was. When we give our lives to him, we find the way to health, happiness, recovery, and, yes, salvation. Jesus becomes our ultimate hero.

Those stories between the front cover and end of the last page are called the Bible. Those stories that I truly enjoyed at one time have now become my roadmap to life. The stories I learned so early in my life now speak to my heart. The words on the pages of this book called the Bible now sustain me and give me life. Jesus, the main character of this Bible, became and still remains my hero. I wanted to live for him.

God took Joseph from the prison to the palace; he took David from a shepherd boy to a king. Likewise, God held up the walls of the Red Sea so Moses and his people could walk through on dry land. He gave Samson enough strength to destroy the evil Philistines. Trust me, God can revive and restore you and me from death to life everlasting with him. He brings healing from blind eyes to eyes that see.

My blindness no longer kept me from seeing the light of Jesus. The Holy Spirit within me is alive and well. When others asked me what happened, all I could say was that "I once was blind, and now I see." When they asked me how it happened, I could openly say, "The God of the Bible, my hero, did this."

If you are reading this and you do not have a personal relationship with Jesus, you may want to take a moment now to invite Jesus into your heart. You can repeat the following prayer after me.

"Jesus, forgive my sins and come into my heart. I'm sorry for my wrongs. Thank you for dying on the cross of Calvary to save me and give me hope. I want you to live in my heart forever. Open my blind eyes and grant me the gift of spiritual sight. I want to live for you forever. Amen."

4

The Comfort Zone—
The Season Always Changes

No sooner are you comfortable than you seem to be uprooted again. Life includes mountain top highs and low valley experiences, good times and bad. And with each event, we gain more knowledge, wisdom, courage, and a new adventure. We move forward once again, dependent on the confidence previously acquired from the earlier uprooting.

You build a wall one block at a time. Eventually, you are closer to a finished project and completed wall. The stormy weather, wind, rain, or hurricane elements do not affect this solidly built wall. If it does crack, you can easily repair it and make it stronger than ever, ready to face whatever weather situation prevails.

The various climates of life have strengthened my very existence. The seasons and years have taught me much. The climate extremes have the potential to mold us for the better and have certainly molded me into who I have become. Each season of life helps to build confidence, comfort, and, most importantly, an increase in faith and trust in the Lord. As I walked with the Lord through the various climates, I learned to trust in his security and safety, even in the storms. Although I did not know it at the time, God was in each storm and season, eventually transitioning me into safety and tranquility.

Growing up fatherless with a widowed mom on welfare to support our family was a bleak beginning. However, this tenuous start brought about a thoughtful appreciation of how families in these types of situations live, survive, and overcome. I concluded that God is our comforter who cares about his people.

The years in the military as a dependent Army wife called for uprooting, traveling, and assimilating into various stateside communities and cultures. I was also excited about the first-time adventure of living overseas. After years of marriage, my life was disrupted as I became a single mom.

I grew through each season. I sought employment, which required résumés, interviews, and stepping out of my comfort zones into a totally unfamiliar environment. That demanded courage as did filling out a college application. Doing these tasks during the midlife season called for the hand of God. As a single woman, I faced new challenges. Each step increased knowledge, know-how, and poise.

I had to learn unique acronyms, policies, and procedures while on the job. In addition, I had to set goals and objectives as part of my employment, which stretched me further still. Once in the classroom, I learned to study, concentrate, engage in book learning, gain discipline, exercise self-control, and multi-task. I had to persevere and learn and complete the ordinary, everyday responsibilities that called for a reliance on the mighty Creator. I raised active children and teenagers as a solo parent, which called for dependence on the God of strength. "I will wait for You, O You his strength" (Psalm 59:9).

I was like a baby eagle learning to fly while walking by faith and not by sight. The season called for minute by minute reflection on God while learning to see him in all situations. Daily, I considered his tenderness, whispers, and encouragement. I imagined him holding my hand and carrying me as he does in the well-known poem of "Footprints in the Sand." He goes before us and stays with us (Deuteronomy 31:8).

God is always hard at work, maturing us and expanding our abilities through the easy times and the times that could be better. Progression takes us from our familiar home and into another place. Through the scary times, interruptions, uncertain times, detours, and even the easy times, God is busy teaching and training us how to fly high in his strength and how to weather each violent or smooth experience. He wants us to learn how to navigate each situation through his grace.

Like the baby eagle, we become stronger. We acquire more strength to fly through all types of weather conditions. We learn to walk by faith and not by sight through the different thresholds of life. We rest in God's strength as he directs us to become more stable and secure. In time, we learn to build our trust on the Rock of our salvation. (See 2 Samuel 22:3.)

My transfer into a nondenominational, multicultural, multiracial church prepared me for the journey ahead. The older women of the church made sure I attended each weekly prayer meeting. My faith grew, and I began to see the light at the end of the tunnel. God's presence became real as He awakened my inner spirit and, in time, I became an intentional, dedicated Christian.

At that time, unknown to me, God was preparing me for future service. As a missionary, I entered many multi-cultural, multi-racial settings. God is always active behind the scenes of life. During this process, I did not need to know all he was doing. My trust grew, and I knew that God dearly loved me and all his children. He became the rock of my foundation.

Oh, if I could redo my previous life seasons, using the knowledge, wisdom, and experiences I have learned since then. God faithfully leads his children through easy times and the hard knocks of life.

The many firsts while facing the fork in the road called for an adventurous spirit. At a young age, we think we have life figured out, and then, at that disruptive moment, that fork in the road changes the direction of our entire lives. Through it all, we learn to trust in Jesus, and he molds us to his liking.

Yes, in the name of Jesus, we experience many firsts while we grow like a plant that has just received a healthy dose of nitrogen from the refreshing rainfall. Meanwhile, our faith increases. Ultimately, we gradually learn his plan and our eternal purpose. We soak up not only what is available, but we eventually become his hands, arms, and feet, reaching out to a thirsty and dying world. We love being available to help others.

Each new experience comes with more ease, and eventually, we become more accustomed to the changes. We realize "this too shall pass." Initially, we have the fear of the unknown followed by the fear of failure. Then we recognize God uses both the successes and failures for our betterment. "For we are His workmanship, created in Christ Jesus for good works, which God prepared beforehand that we should walk in them" (Ephesians 2:10).

He carries us into the unknown with that blessed assurance that we are not alone. He is all-powerful, present everywhere at the same time, knowing all things. As we soar, we are strengthened. With each step forward, he reinforces our faith. As we travel into the unknown, we trust that he has it in control.

Three verses on God's all-encompassing character follow:

- Omnipotent: "The light shines in darkness, and the darkness has not overcome it" (John 1:5 NIV).

- Omnipresent "You know when I sit and when I rise; you perceive my thoughts from afar" (Psalm 139:2 NIV).

- Omniscient: "Great is our Lord and mighty in power; his understanding has no limit" (Psalm 147:5 NIV).

He brings people into our lives to mentor, counsel, and teach, and he loves, supports, and encourages us. We begin to recognize our spiritual gifts and talents. Some people are intentional in growing in these areas, while others may not be as interested in doing so. Nevertheless, we all have gifts.

During midlife, I realized that God had given me a gift of encouragement. I delight in encouraging others and telling people of God's purpose for them.

First, he wants us to seek him with all of our might and to fall in love with him. He wants his light to shine through us so that others will see him. He wants to be our rock, to hold our hand, and to carry us through the journey of life with a sure foundation built on him.

I had walked many miles with the God of our salvation and now realize just how much he cares for his children. I am far from where I began and still have much learning ahead of me. I want to intentionally live the best life possible for Jesus. The stormy and smooth weather conditions bring us closer to him.

Much work was needed to write this book. A forty-year walk with God through the various seasons and storms of life helped prepare me. That twenty-twenty hindsight is worth sharing. I had much work, travail, and obedience to do before I could share my walk with Jesus with you.

He took this village girl who loved the farm into the entire world to share his love. The seasons and weather conditions of life taught me to endure, to overcome, and to encourage others. My goal is to aid you as the reader to allow God to work in and through you.

Even when we take two steps forward and one step backward, God will keep us on the path to prosperity. And as we journey on this adventurous path, we develop in the Lord. We find numerous opportunities to stretch and to prepare for what God has next for us. I'm so glad I did not settle for the couch for too long.

So as I share my story as a single woman, I can shout out, "God is good, and life is good!" He makes life happen. Do not despair but count it all joy (James 1:2–3).

5

Transitioning into a New Normal— Life as a Single Parent

"Behold, I will do a new thing, now it shall spring forth; shall you not know it? I will even make a way in the wilderness and rivers in the desert" (Isaiah 43:19).

A new normal requires many adjustments, adoptions, changes, and regulations. Transitioning into a new arena often includes new leadership roles. Variations of this may involve a shift into another arrangement or position. Transformations call for determination and perseverance. Attitude plays a huge part. When a teacher enters her classroom with a favorable attitude, the class will most likely have a wonderful day.

New tasks fill your day, consuming every minute. These tasks include taking charge of the home; upkeep and repairs; taxes and insurances; parental oversight; decisions and consents; teacher's meetings; checking out boyfriends; car purchasing, repairs and upkeep; driver's training and licensing; powers of attorney; wedding preparations; and yes, even gassing up your car—all while holding down a full-time job. The list was endless, but God's love and mercy sustained me.

While living in the Philippines, I purchased a vehicle from a missionary who was leaving the country. I loved pulling into a gas station to fill my gas tank. The attendants met me before I turned off the key.

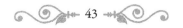

They asked if they could wash my windshield, check the oil, put air into the tires, and, of course, fill up my fuel tank. I loved this treatment.

While living stateside, I had done these things myself for twenty-plus previous years. Therefore, I just sat back and enjoyed the personal service. They likewise received the welcome tip thankfully. Often, I carried goodies to hand out to the gas station attendants and the street kids who approached my vehicle at a stop sign. Pulling into the Filipino gas station was always fun.

Many times, in the United States, I fueled my own vehicle after becoming single. This took a while to adjust to regularly. Single life means learning to adapt and to make the most of new experiences. We may not realize the list of responsibilities that each spouse usually does. We even take tasks for granted. Expressions of thank you might be few and far between. All in all, I appreciated the gas station attendants, and they appreciated the rewards.

Like my physical vehicle, I had to keep my spiritual gas tank full as well. This was now my responsibility for both my sake and those I ministered to.

Attitude can make or break a day. Likewise, changes challenge us to adjust or not as we reflect on all the prior changes and transitions we experienced. We transition from a child to a teenager, from elementary to high school to college, from the single to married life, from childless to parenthood, and maybe even from marriage to singleness.

Think about the effects of before and after. Through it all, we become familiar and resilient, which strengthens our character. Experiences make us more confident, increase our self-awareness, and advance us in areas of life. When stepping out in faith into the unseen and the unknown, attitudes can determine our progress and even affect our walk with the Lord.

A successful divorce includes the courage to switch from a victim mentality to a winning mindset. The process creates a better understanding of the challenges involved. We gain insight and a clearer understanding of what couples endure. A transition not only increases our knowledge but can enlarge our outlook on life, and eventually, when healed, we can help and comfort others who may face the same dilemma. No matter the issue—divorce, widowhood, sickness, or some other tragedy—the process of mental and spiritual transition is the same. After we are healed, God uses us in the healing process of others.

We become better at foreseeing probable outcomes. No transition has been in vain, even if it was difficult to obtain. Life works out if we keep our eyes focused on God.

Scripture tells us, "And we know that all things work together for good to those who love God, to those who are the called according to His purpose" (Romans 8:28). Of course, we have to find a way and work through painful events. Life is not necessarily smooth sailing, yet with God, we have hope and purpose.

The purpose of this book is to encourage and give hope to others who may be experiencing a similar situation or who know someone who is adjusting to singleness, to loss, or to a life of adjustments due to disappointments and hardships.

During my divorce, I was in trauma. Desperation set in, and for a short time, I felt hopeless. As the years passed, I learned to celebrate a new normal. There surely is life and joy after divorce. The divorce was not what I wanted. But we cannot force someone to stay with us if that person wants out of the marriage or situation.

I will add that celebrating the new normal or celebrating my singleness took time. So wherever you are at this moment, know that a rainbow comes after the rain. (See Genesis 9:33 NIV.) The air is fresh and pleasant after the rain and stormy weather.

My high school yearbook noted that one day, I would reach the pot of gold at the end of the rainbow. Although my senior year prophecy has been somewhat fulfilled, I still think I have more to come even after eight decades. Success does not necessarily include a pocket filled with money. For the most part, I have lived a satisfying, fulfilled, enjoyable life. I have great wealth as my wealth is in satisfaction, fulfillment, enjoyment, and contentment, which are more critical than a pocket full of cash. I feel as though I have reached the pot of gold at the end of the rainbow.

My story is about what once seemed unbearable, but my desperate times transitioned into a celebration of God's goodness. God's grace and mercy carried me to the end of the rainbow. We can see his footsteps in the sand as he moves his children forward, protected in his open arms. He is the answer to our life's challenges. He knows, he cares, and this is who he is. He is a loving God who has a wonderful future for each of our lives.

I want to encourage and offer hope to those who are enduring pain and who are diligently striving to reach the pot of gold at the end of the rainbow. Perhaps the rope you are hanging onto is unraveling quickly, yet never! Never! Never give up, even if you are down to the last thread.

God knows how to make a way, yet we must never give up, regardless of how difficult life seems. That pot of gold—happiness, love, joy, and peace—awaits the arrival of contentment in singleness. Perhaps the time for remarriage is in the future. However, this is an excellent time to draw closer to the Lord and let him show you just how much he loves and cares for you. You are safe in his plan for your life. The comfort and hardship in my younger years helped me to better understand what others experience.

The death of my young father, the status of my mom as a widow, our transition into welfare recipients, my mother's exhausting work schedule, and the polio that attacked my brother taught me about life. Several years later, my widowed mom birthed a child out of wedlock. My mom and the baby's father had become widow and widower at about the same time. Their relationship eventually resulted in an unplanned baby.

This child's adoptive parents dearly loved this baby girl. Later, this half-sister returned to our lives. She has remained a significant member of our family for fifty years.

Mom grieved throughout her life for this child. She felt someone who could have no children could give this child more than she could. My mom's heartache and forgiveness resulted in an amazing testimony as her daughter became a powerful godly woman. God's mercies are new every morning. He uses each experience to draw us into a closer relationship with him.

"Bless the Lord, O my soul, and forget not all His benefits: who forgives all your iniquities, who heals all your diseases, who redeems your life from destruction, who crowns you with lovingkindness and tender mercies" (Psalm 103:2–4).

One of mom's daily prayers was that God would introduce her daughter to her when she entered heaven. She openly shared that. Wherever she went, she looked for her precious daughter. God brought her into our lives in her early twenties. What a mighty God we serve, a God of compassion and love. God is so gracious with abundant mercy and forgiving grace to us. I want to be like this. God miraculously brought my sister into our lives.

This biblical story of the adulterous woman stands out and was vivid in mom's mind. The Pharisees came to Jesus, ready to stone this woman. And Jesus's response was perfect. He said, "He who is without sin among you, let him throw a stone at her first" (John 8:7). Don't you love this? Consequently, no stones were ever thrown. Scripture tells us that we are all sinful. God clearly and powerfully states, "If we say that we have no sin, we deceive ourselves" (1 John 1:8).

I believe God gave me the gift of singleness. I never had a desire to remarry. I wanted to focus on raising my daughters and giving them my full attention. I am and continue to be so satisfied with the tasks that God gives me to do, even in retirement. My children, jobs, college, the mission field, and becoming a counselor to mission's families satisfied my hungry soul. Forever and ever, I am thankful and appreciative. And through it all, I have reached the pot of gold at the end of the rainbow.

God's healing touch in our lives shows his glory. His grace is suffi-cient for you and me. He heals and restores his brokenhearted children despite ourselves. I continue to be amazed. That's true even now after forty years as a single. His unconditional love is sufficient for me. My peace of mind is confirmation.

My husband and I carried some customs and habits from my child-hood into our marriage. I am thankful for my family upbringing con-sisting of our church involvement and evening devotions. My siblings and I seldom missed church and Sunday school. We received a few spankings, but talk, discipline, and perhaps some ear-opening words usually did the trick.

Mom completed her eighth-grade schooling with honors and near-perfect attendance. She often spoke of the happiness of her school years. In her day, eighth-grade learning was equal to our twelfth-grade education. She wanted to continue her education, but like many chil-dren during her era, she was limited in her formal schooling because of the busy farm work.

We faced significant transitions in our early years. Through a child's eyes, some of the former times were difficult to understand. The struggles I previously mentioned seemed so overwhelming at times.

Only a few churches—Protestant and Catholic—were around. The merchants were friendly people, and the younger generations inher-ited their parent's business. A parent could send their six-year-old to the corner drug store with a five-dollar bill. A child could safely make purchases, such as ice cream or a sack of flour, at the local grocery store. People cared for our family and each other.

The God of the universe stabilized our roots. In spite of the family hardships, my childhood was wonderful overall. My mother, along with God's amazing grace and mercy, made a great life for my two siblings and me.

I struggled when I moved from a small town to a larger city to attend college. As long as I remained on campus in a confined area, the change was manageable. A semester later, I transitioned from a single gal into a wedded gal. I received my Mrs. degree at age eighteen. I then rode a Greyhound bus from Michigan to Virginia to join my eighteen-year-old military husband. I stepped out of my small town, my comfort zone, and crossed state borders to meet up with my spouse of three months.

The small steps of obedience gradually led to more significant moves. The unusual step later in life as a single took me to the other side of the world.

For example, a single woman in her late twenties might be independent with her own condominium or home. She enjoys her job, a steady paycheck, a bank account, and a vehicle loan. Her life is wonderful and moving along smoothly. Then she finds the love of her life. She decides to marry after being single for nearly three decades. Marriage or remarriage may be the best thing that happened as Genesis 2:18 tells us that it is not good that man should be alone. Proverbs 18:22 tells us, "He who finds a wife finds a good thing, and obtains favor from the Lord." First Corinthians 7:33–35 tells us that being single is better for a Christian so that they can serve the Lord without disruption. The question is, should a person enter marriage or not?

God came that we might have life and that we might have it more abundantly (John 10:10). I am certain that God wants to fulfill the desires of our hearts. Marriage can be an extraordinary adventure. I treasured and loved being married to the father of my children. I cherished this man's friendship and having a family together. Then, with little notice, I became a single. Satan is out and about, destroying marriages. He comes to kill, steal, and destroy marriages and families (2 Corinthians 2:10–11). We need to be aware of his tactics and keep our eyes on Jesus (Hebrews 12:2).

I eventually transitioned from married life into life as a fulfilled single woman and single parent. This transition did not happen overnight but took several years. Meanwhile, I focused on developing my walk with the Lord. I studied the Bible, prayed, sought counseling, and went to church and prayer meetings. I became hungry and thirsty for God's Word. My total emphasis was to deepen my relationship with our heavenly Father. God was healing me, and I began to develop an intimate relationship with Jesus and find freedom in doing God's work. God gave me the gift of marriage and the gift of singleness.

God's healing touch and a personal satisfying relationship with him created within me the desire for focused work as unto him. Christ offered me the best life possible. I desired to become all he purposed for me. I was appreciating life as a single woman and was fulfilled. Perhaps the experience of many good marriage years, even though the marriage ended in a divorce, contributed to my eventual satisfaction as a single. My single life then prepared me for the later journey into the mission field.

A dear friend, in her younger years, became single after a divorce. After nearly twenty years of independent living, she again remarried. She mentioned how difficult the transition was. She loved her new spouse and couldn't imagine life without him, but transitioning into marriage was an enormous challenge. Her second marriage, after years of singleness, called for many significant changes.

God is sustaining a few of my single friends who continue to wait for a knight in shining armor. I pray God sends a godly man to each one. It's not about looks but about what's inside the heart.

These types of life transitions—from marriage to single and a parent—take endurance and willpower. With the right attitude and God's help as the essential element, these steps are possible with bravery. It was one of the harder times of my life. The violation of trust and rejection in marriage took God and work to overcome.

A marriage violation and singleness changed me, in many respects, for the better. We eventually gain a new perspective. Trauma, healing, and adjusting to a different season in life take time. It's a process. Having Jesus in our heart produces unconditional love, and we learn to love like never before. Galatians 6:9 tells us, "And let us not grow weary while doing good, for in due season we shall reap if we do not lose heart."

I experienced five labors and deliveries. A miscarriage before the birth of my first child added a sixth pregnancy. The process from the first labor pain to the last and to birth was delicate yet painful. The more babies I delivered, the more certain the delivery expectation and process became—not necessarily the pain, but the pain management. With each delivery, I better understood the procedure. The previous experience taught me the importance of relaxing and staying calm and not panicking. Prayer and trust helped ease life's difficulties.

Military life required many moves to different military bases, communities, cultures, and environments. Transfers meant leaving friends. Unlike my younger years of attending the same elementary and high school, our children experienced the ins and outs of attending various schools. The hellos and good-byes with friends and classmates were a challenge, yet each experience helped them with the next transition.

The excitement of visiting new places added a wonderful dimension to life. Nonetheless, tears and sadness accompanied leaving friends. God, with his mysterious thoughts, always made a way. Our task was to transfer to different locations when it was time to do so. Our attitude played a significant factor in doing it well.

My transition to singleness and to being a single mom as I neared four decades of life was complicated and challenging. We were now six females under one roof, and I faced an unrelenting feeling of vulnerability, especially when pretty offspring started to date. This period was a significant transition and adjustment for me. I could write a book on those happenings alone.

I sent up many prayers for guidance, protection, safety, and wisdom for our family of six females. Many other friends prayed too, yet it was up to me to nurture the relationship with God. Children struggle to understand how a parent can just leave home. Parents are supposed to be there for their children: to help manage and protect their home, to listen to their problems, to attend school functions, to play ball, to go hiking and camping, to barbeque and prepare a special veggie omelet each Saturday morning for them and their friends after a sleepover. Children want dad to go to church with them. They want to see, touch, and talk with their father. God became the Father to the fatherless and a defender to the widow (Psalm 68:5). I was intentional about seeking him. When I was a child, I liked having my uncles or grandpa in our home. Life just felt safer. The presence of God accomplishes the same result.

Through it all, this time of singleness drew us into a closer walk with God. I was glad that God never slept or slumbered (Psalm 121:2–4). "Call upon Me in the day of trouble; I will deliver you, and you shall glorify me" (Psalm 50:15). "Then He said to them, Follow Me, and I will make you fishers of men" (Matthew 4:19). "For your Maker is your husband, the Lord of hosts is His name; and your Redeemer is the Holy One of Israel; He is called the God of the whole earth" (Isaiah 54:5).

These passages became so meaningful to me. God is our comforter, our Good Shepherd, the father of the fatherless, and the husband of the widow. I know this includes the divorced. God hates divorce yet loves the divorced person. When I first read a similar statement, I was elated.

Sunday was our family's holy day, beginning with church and a positive attitude about attending. Occasionally, the children's dad and I taught Sunday school and helped with Vacation Bible School. While living in Germany, three daughters were confirmed, along with other military children in the Martin Luther Church in Worms. One daughter attended a Christian School. My life followed my mother's example.

I wondered how God allowed my marriage to fail. After all, we were a Christian family. Since that time, my spiritual walk has grown considerably in comparison to my previous lukewarm spiritual days. Revelation 3:15 says, "I know your works, that you are neither cold nor hot. I could wish you were cold or hot." Since becoming single, church is not just a Sunday routine. I like a little church every day of the week. I read the Bible and devotions, engage in praise and worship, and listen to biblical messages or sermons, as we call them. I have taken notes as a way of life for nearly forty years. But I may or may not ever review these.

After I invited Jesus into my heart as my personal Lord and Savior, the Bible began to speak more clearly into my life. Scripture addressed many earlier unanswered questions. God has answers and remedies for our lives. He heals the brokenhearted, takes away the pain of sin, and sets us free. His healing touch and forgiveness are freely available to all who invite him into their hearts. "Blessed is the man who endures temptation." (James 1:12).

My faith continues to mature. It carries me through the nights and dark places. My eyes were opened, and I found Jesus in a new way. The awakening in my spirit is like never before. God loves you and me and has a purpose for us. "Therefore, if anyone is in Christ, he is a new creation; old things have passed away; behold, all things have become new" (2 Corinthians 5:17). One might hear me sing in the wee hours of the night. This brings peace, and soon I fall asleep, and it's morning. The morning sunlight brings joy and hope. "But the path of the just is like the shining sun, that shines ever brighter unto the perfect day" (Proverbs 4:18).

Scripture tells us that the Word feeds us milk as we are not ready for the meat of the Word. Then the day comes when we crave and want the meat (1 Corinthians 3:2). We want a deeper walk with him. We want all that God offers his children. We are ready to hear and dig into the Word.

Scripture tells us that "the fear of the Lord is the beginning of wisdom, and the knowledge of the Holy One is understanding" (Proverbs 9:10).

I feared the Lord when I was young. I did not want to show him any disrespect. My family and church taught me to respect and honor God and his Word. The time had come to invite Jesus into my heart. I longed for a good steak dinner. In other words, I longed for a deeper walk with God. This calls for a continuous study of his Word.

The parochial school Bible stories perhaps take the cake. Since transiting into a new normal of singleness, I wanted the ice cream topped with chocolate syrup, nuts, and Cool Whip. The deep pain of divorce brought me to this place in my life. Experiencing tough times draws us to God. He is the answer to healing and a closer walk with him. I want all that God offers: his entire purpose for my life. I want it all—not just a little bit to keep me going. On top of that delicious sundae, I want that cherry as well. This purpose alone is a great reason to celebrate the gift of singleness—there really is life and joy after divorce.

I now celebrate the love of Jesus. From childhood through the season of singleness, he has been faithful. I celebrate all that the Lord has for you and me. I want it all! Time is short-lived for us, dear reader. I pray God's abundant blessings on our lives and his very best in your life.

6

Spiritual Growth—Maturing in Jesus

*L*ife experiences and exposures, hardships, mountain tops, and valley lows all contribute to our spiritual maturity. Spiritual muscles become buffed and defined when we are intentional about seeking the Lord. Our heavenly Father prunes us into his likeness. When we attain a certain level of growth, pruning presents the opportunity for more growth. When a tree, shrub, or flower is pruned, the dead branches and blossoms are cut off to prepare it for the next season of productivity.

Life's occurrences—the events, environments, exposures, cultures, communities, and attitudes—can profit and benefit us. Our growth depends on our approach and attitude. Some people are comfortable with staying where they are. The person decides how he or she will respond, and these decisions have consequences, whether positive or negative.

A young man, who had spent many years in the mission field, came into my counseling office to talk. Through those years, he had learned, grown and enjoyed his job. . But he had a sense of restlessness. His life and his job were going well, yet the pleasure—perhaps the passion he had once known—was fading. He had many opportunities and achievements, yet more recently, something had changed. He had difficulty in putting his finger on his edginess.

I asked if he yet hoped to achieve anything else in life. With little hesitation, he mentioned a long-term desire: to further his schooling and obtain higher education in his current field. I suggested, "Is it possible that the Lord is moving you to further your study?"

He was concerned about leaving his present position as he still had much work to do. He felt that he needed to stay where God had placed him. Through the course of our time together, he realized that his close work with his colleagues had actually trained them to carry on without him. I asked if he thought these people could take over while he pursued his dream of further study.

Since he was committed to his task, he had never considered the possibility of leaving. He felt he could not leave God's work undone. But without realizing it, he had already trained his colleagues to the point where he could pursue his dream, the dream that God had put in his heart. He had maximized his knowledge in this position.

Together, we prayed for direction, insight, and discernment. I suggested that he and his family continue to seek God's guidance. I told him, "God has the answers to life. He is great at stirring us within and at pulling on our heartstrings. He does put desires in our hearts. Perhaps it's time to make a move. God works in mysterious ways."

Several months passed, and one bright early morning, this young man and I crossed paths. He was excited and said, "We are moving. God amazingly answered my prayer. Soon I will be in the classroom, working on the desires of my heart." This young man explored the possibility of further study and was accepted into a higher education program in his home country. He then said, "My colleagues will take over the project, so I will be able to fulfill the dream that God has put in my heart."

God had plans for this young man and prepared him at his previous position. The tugging on his heartstrings was for a purpose. With more education, this young man would be able to enlarge the program to which he had dedicated his life. But this young man was prepared to step into a new season of growth.

Sometimes we think that once in a position, we should remain there permanently. I believe that God uses people in situations while preparing them for the next place. We are always in a training ground, a pruning ground, and when a door opens for further advancement, we decide whether or not to go. God prepares and prunes us so we can bear more abundant fruit. God equips us right where we are so we are ready to move out when he tells us to go.

Mountaintop experiences are exciting and encouraging times and can facilitate maturity, preparing us for the next level, as in the case of this young man. The valley lows might be the more disruptive times, yet they can also lead to even more growth and an opportunity to become stronger. God's people can rise above, knowing the possibilities are endless with him.

I speak from my personal experience. Life is seemingly laid out like a path of stepping stones. We take one step at a time as we learn how to balance the highs and lows. We learn to rise more quickly with each incident. The stepping stones in life might not be equally positioned. Some are further apart; some, side by side, but through it all, we learn about balance and hanging in there to make the most of each God-given opportunity.

The choice is ours, and with choices come consequences. This young man realized his passion at his position was not as intense as before. Maybe it was time for a change. Change can make us more productive while we benefit from the knowledge at the previous position. This young man reached out. With his previous experience and upon his completion of the study program, he now has much more to offer. Who knows what God has next for him? Remember Joseph. He went from the pit to a prince.

Discouragement, disappointments, and disruptions sometimes set in. These disturbances can come from God. He can cause people and various conflicts to push us in a new direction. I did not know this at that time but learned it later. Disturbances can buff our spiritual muscles.

God has a way of stirring us so that we progress to the next level of life. He shakes us and pulls on our heartstrings. This stirring and tugging of the heartstrings is his way of moving us into his divine plan and purpose. With eyes and trust on him, we can move into the next phase. These phases are pre-planned by our gracious Lord and Savior. That stirring in our hearts can tell the story. Sometimes another person interferes and intrudes or causes a commotion to get our attention.

We may become so uncomfortable that we leave the situation. I eventually became ill because my city job environment became so uncomfortable.

Never in a zillion years would I have thought of leaving. But God had a different idea. Within one week of leaving my well-loved job, God gave me another valued position. Just like that, he moved me from one spot to another. Who would have thought?

The idea is to achieve a balance in our lives. Make the most of the up times and the pruning times and realize you will face low times. Reflect on the previous mountain tops and low valley times and know they will pass. The valley lows help mature us and prepare us for the next level.

Although repeating my college algebra class was no fun, I understood algebra better the second time around, which came with rewards. Through it all, I intentionally strengthened the spirit of perseverance God placed in me. I could have dropped out of college; however, God used this time to buff my muscles, to learn to trust, and to hang in there. I could have just said, "I'm too old," or "Who needs this?" After all, I was in my forties—almost middle age. That response would have been too easy.

Lo and behold, that second time around, the numbers, formulas, and answers—yes, the answers—fell into place. I definitely enjoyed that high mountain experience for weeks after. Likewise, my spiritual muscles grew.

I invite you to think about how life experiences have helped you to grow stronger and wiser and more tolerant, insightful, discerning, and hopeful. I especially like the wiser part!

When that Spirit within inspires and nudges, we are on our way. We are encouraged. Ultimately, deep within our souls, we want the challenge that comes with that next adventure. We become intentional as we mature; we see a more defined spiritual growth. We are deliberate in hearing and heeding the Holy Spirit nudges. We become more confident in trusting and walking in faith.

God intrigues me—even as I share my story, I am recalling and reliving each adventure. Age sneaks up on us. I'm glad God moved me into his plan for my life early on when this was still an option.

God healed my broken heart and placed me in a position to help others. God brings blessings out of hurtful situations even during middle life. The bottom line is that the positive and the negative in life can make us healthier or harsh, better or bitter. The choice is ours. God never gives up on us, regardless of the circumstances. He is faithful, even though we might want to give up on ourselves.

I am grateful for the encouragement and energy God offers. He showers his anointing on us, even during our down times. One season of illness after retirement kept me at a quiet low-key spot for two-and-a-half years. During this down time, I pressed into a closer walk with Jesus, a time of cultivating fruitfulness with the one we serve. I realized this fruitfulness even more at the end of the illness journey. I used this time to begin working on my book.

I pray for wisdom and insightfulness with most passing days. With each new day, decisions and opportunities come so that we can mature. Remember, we walk by faith and not by sight. God has a way of directing our paths when we are intentionally seeking him.

We can become disheartened, lose the faith, and give up when trials set in. Or we can trust that through this circumstance, we have the potential to become better. With each situation, comes a consequence, positive or negative. We can fight or flight. We fight these battles, or we run away and possibly fall off the cliff.

We can run from hard times or stay in for another round. We face the opportunity to discover and gain or decide to be livid forever. When we look back, we can appreciate and value the numerous situations God carried us through. Good ole hindsight. We become stronger and better able to handle adversity as our spiritual muscles continue to strengthen and as we learn more about the one we serve.

While I valued the challenging valley times, I was not overly passionate about them. I do prefer the not-so-complicated times, yet I realize the significance of each incident. The valley times are a part of life.

We are devastated when a spouse wants out of the covenant of marriage. Many people are affected by this disruption: the family, children, friends, the church, the office. The heartache, the pain, the uncertainty of life is overwhelming for a time. God so graciously and lovingly helps us overcome. The healing process begins, and yes, healing does take time.

Through this, we develop physically, mentally, emotionally, and spiritually. I want all of this, and I know you do as well.

My extremely tough time brought me to a closer walk with God. Throughout this time, his presence was so real to me. Life was not always easy, yet I sure value what I learned through the years—so much so that I love sharing with you in hopes that together, we can continue to strengthen our spiritual muscles. May we follow the individuality of God's destiny for our lives. We learn through our experiences that the Bible is a roadmap to wealth, health, and the answers to life. God walks before us.

I valued and gleaned from being a single mom and singleness in general. Marriage and singleness helped me to speak many languages. I understand what married life is like, raising children as a single parent, and learning to be content as a single woman. I've learned that God wants increase for us. Perhaps unbeknownst to us, he prepares us at today's job to prepare us for tomorrow's job.

Each phase, season, and stepping stone enhances our spiritual journey and spiritual muscles, and in time, we have earned a PhD in life through the mountain tops and valley lows.

Dwelling on the hurt stunts our growth. We want to leave the past behind so that we do not dwell on the former matters. That frees us to pursue all that God has for us. Attitude is vital, a significant ingredient to our progress. Hindsight is a marvelous tool as well. We made it through this, and we will make it through the next obstacle when God walks alongside us.

7

Transparency—Confronted

*H*ave you ever wondered about the masks people wear? What are they covering up? Were the people you last spoke with wearing a mask? People wear masks to cover up what is taking place within them. Is everyone we talk with genuine when it comes to expressing how they feel, or do they cover up?

Have you ever responded with "nothing" when someone asks you what's wrong? Inside, you are dealing with a lot: worry, hurt, anger, and more. However, when asked that question, you answer "nothing."

Some years ago, transparency was rather uncommon for me, even though the situations I faced were ripping me apart. I struggled to share what was going on within me. My mask was to cover up intimidation, embarrassment, defeat, and shame. My costume did a reasonably good job of hiding every damaging emotion I felt deep within my soul. I wore a mask.

I hid in the closet when speaking about my situation with my sister so little ears could not hear my dilemma. I once left my partly filled grocery cart in the middle of the aisle as I headed out the front door of the store when I spotted a friend in the next aisle. Another time, I entered a stationery store that had kits called "we sell divorce." I bawled them out for making it so easy to escape a marriage. Of course, during that time, my inside turmoil was exposed.

After the paper announced our family's business, I had a riding club meeting scheduled to meet at our home. A group of ladies were coming over to finish sewing the saddle blankets for the upcoming little Britches Rodeo. At the meeting, no one said a word about the divorce announcement in the local paper. I carried on as if everything were hunky-dory when, in the depths of my soul, I was screaming. I don't know how I managed to hold back the tears and the pain of my broken heart. My mask did a superior job of hiding the turmoil as did theirs. If, in fact, they had even seen the paper announcement.

Yes, I wore a mask. My mask wore a smile outside and a shattering painful cry for help inside. "Have you ever smiled on the outside while crying on the inside?"

I felt stuck like a vehicle in the mud. I was the victim of a crime scène, tied to a chair with my mouth duct-taped, leaving me paralyzed, stunned physically and mentally, and incapable of moving. My blunder, my failure, and my hurting head and heart hid behind the mask I wore. "How could this have happened? I have cherished our marriage, our years together."

Weeping came quickly in the silence of my home; my bedroom knew all my secrets. While out and about, I stopped crying until I stepped back into my bedroom. Weeping helps release built-up emotions, which I found in the solitude. Have you ever been so filled with emotions that you felt as if you'd burst? I needed the comfort zone of my room, a safe haven where I could relax and release all my feelings.

The secure bedroom door protected me so that others couldn't see my hurt. Once inside, I uncovered the mask that concealed my broken heart, my pent-up emotions. But does hiding our feelings and our secrets accomplish our purposes?

Fortunately for me, a new-found friend, Geraldine, came to my rescue. This confrontation and liberation happened one night after a woman's Bible study in my home. She hung around after all the ladies had left. Eventually, she got to the point. "Maggie, I have something to tell you."

She forewarned me; she was unwavering about what she would tell me. This woman and I were really in the beginning stages of our friendship. We met through Women's Aglow gatherings and Thursday night prayer meetings at the military chapel. She was about ten years older than I was, a mother and grandmother, and she was grounded in her walk with the Lord. Our husbands met while in the military, and they bowled on the same men's bowling team.

She gently stated, "I feel like the Spirit of the Lord spoke a word for you during my recent prayer time." Since I was desperate and she was a senior, I listened. She then commented, "I might even risk what this might do to our friendship, yet I am willing to take this chance."

This seasoned woman recognized what was going on behind my mask. She knew more about life than I did. I soaked up all that was spoken during our Bible study time. I was hungry and thirsty for answers to my dilemma, and yes, although others might not have known, I wore a mask. I was in the infant stages of my newly found born-again walk with the Lord.

She continued. "Since George and I care about you and your daughters, we both agree that you need to hear me out." She had me cornered. To this day, some forty years later, I remember that exact corner, the very spot. "Maggie, it's time you stop feeling sorry for yourself."

Now, remember, I was ten years younger than she, a middle-aged woman who had just recently stepped into a new born-again Christian walk. I had much work to do within my mind, body, and soul. My defense mechanisms were sensitive and familiar with kicking in. The reader might understand what I mean.

Apparently, to this woman, my phony mask did a poor job of hiding the turmoil within me. Fortunately for me, this friend noticed the confusion, the sorrow, and desperation hidden behind my mask.

"What makes you think I am feeling sorry for myself?" I replied. (Notice my defense mechanism kicking in here.)

She said, "Your children told me what's been going on in your life. They said that you spend hours in your bedroom, locked in, sometimes for long periods of time."

"What makes you think I spend too much time in my bedroom?" I said defensively.

She followed the question with concern. "Granted, Maggie, I would not want to be in your shoes. I know you are hurting. What happened to you and your children is just wrong." She continued before I could get a word in. "Your daughters told me that you even lock your bedroom door while they are left alone. They worry about you and want to be with you. They are dealing with a great deal of pain as well. They wonder if you're sick, sleeping, or what is going on. When you eventually come out, they ask if you're okay. You tell them you're fine or perhaps that you were taking a nap."

I now faced a decision. Would I graciously consider my new friend's remarks, or would this new friendship end in its early stages of development? This friend repeated herself several times and again said, "Maggie, granted I would not want to be in your shoes. We love you enough to want to help you in whatever way we can. I realize that speaking up and confronting you might jeopardize our newly formed friendship; however, speaking up and helping you in this area is worth the risk of our relationship."

My friend was right on. She recognized my despair and saw the mask I hid behind to cover up my pain. She was also sensitive to the cry of my daughters. My daughters confirmed what she saw. And if I could begin the journey forward without the cover-up, she was willing to help in whatever way she could. She was ready to sacrifice our acquaintance. The ball was now in my court. She offered to walk alongside me. From that time forward, she and her husband became my and our support system.

I was trying to understand what had just happened to me, to our family. How did I suddenly become single after a twenty-year marriage? With little notice or warning, I found myself divorced. This divorce exceeded all life's challenges. I was desperate, hanging by a thread. I had lost quite a bit of weight, likely another noticeable indicator.

My friend came to the rescue. We need friends to give a helping hand during difficult times. Jesus values relationship. His disciples remained with him through his three years on Earth. He taught them to carry on once he went to be with the Father. They witnessed Jesus in action as he healed the sick and opened blind eyes. His words brought comfort, peace, and healing. He trained and prepared these followers to go into the entire world and tell of the good news of Jesus, their friend, mentor, and Savior.

My friend was right. We do better around loyal, caring friends than hiding alone in the bedroom. Staying in the bedroom was also unfair to my daughters, who were hurting as well.

We struggled our first Christmas alone without the presence of their dad. My oldest daughters labored diligently to bring a touch of joy and happiness into our home. They, by some means, brought home a tree and decorated it with beautiful glittering lights while Christmas carols filled our house. It was a sad time without their dad, yet they attentively labored to bring about a sweet family Christmas.

When I came out of the bedroom that evening, the warmth and love of Christmas overflowed in our home. The lively tree lights brightened the dark room, and God's love filled our hearts with hope for tomorrow. God so graciously blessed me with caring daughters who brought us hope. God, in his ever-present mercy and grace, ascended within each of us. His destiny for our family included healing and a closer walk with him.

God brought special angels disguised as friends into our lives to help us as we grieved. He used Geraldine and Gerald not only to help me face reality but to remove the mask and to teach me about the gift of transparency. I now can share about setbacks, defeats, and triumphs. He knew that in time, my transparency would benefit others. My stories would teach others vulnerability and thus bring freedom into their lives.

My children cared enough to speak truth to this new friend. And my friend cared enough to speak truth to me. Yes, it was time to remove the mask and, with the help of God, to face today and each tomorrow with my eyes on Jesus. Jesus is the answer to life—a wholesome, God-fearing life.

Let's take off the mask, seek counseling, and celebrate the maturity in who we are and what life offers. We need to focus on getting to know our heavenly Father. A full life includes getting to know ourselves and our purpose.

I'm thankful for my friend who so boldly approached me that night after Bible study. She moved me out of the bedroom into the limelight of transparency. Remember, God uses his people down here to be his hands and feet.

My new dear friend helped me remove my mask. She and George stood by me and my daughters like a dedicated couple, assigned to me by God. He placed these angels in our lives to help us climb out of the low valley of hopelessness and despair. Without God's help, this would have been impossible.

8

Transparency—Wearing a Facade

Before moving on to the next chapter, I want to share a couple of stories about wearing a disguise or façade.

While in Thailand at a special dinner appearance, the Thai women used finger masks and dance to tell their stories. People wear masks during Halloween to disguise themselves. Are these masks removed after the special dinner appearance and after Halloween?

I had fun going trick-or-treating as a child. I did not realize the spiritual meaning of Halloween when I was younger, so I knocked on doors to gather treats. It was all about candy and not about tricking. Some folks openly said, "Sorry, no treats here." We wore a mask to trick others into believing we were someone else. My mask covered my disappointment from the folks who had no treats.

The church I attended as a child required a hat, dress, and gloves for women and girls. Mom made sure I passed this dress style on the outside. These accessories were not who I was. I loved a full-blown tomboy look: wearing blue jeans, climbing trees, and playing cops and robbers, and sometimes, I even beat up boys. What I felt inside did not match my outward church dress. Consequently, my focus was not always on the pastor's message. However, my grumpy disposition was not generally noticeable on the outside.

Long brown cotton stockings, fastened to a garter belt hung around my tiny waist, were a must in the cold Michigan winters. The beautiful array of pull-up colored tights like we have today did not exist.

Each morning, I carried on, but lost the battle each time. Once in the classroom, my sweet smiling face did not reflect the struggle I had just lost at home.

I wore a mask at my first official tea as an officer's wife. I smiled and greeted others while my insides wobbled. I was very proud to be an officer's wife after about six years as an enlisted man's wife. Yet, before this new season, I encountered a few sophisticated officers' wives who wore their husbands' positions on their sleeves although many wives did not. It would take time to overcome, especially if those people were unkind. Sometimes, as an enlisted man's wife, I allowed them to intimidate me.

At one point in the gathering, the brand-new officers' wives surrounded the dining room table. The host, an endearing colonel's wife, pleasantly broke the ice. Perhaps she remembered her first tea. She was a sweetheart and intentionally made her guests feel completely comfortable.

She said, "Ladies, please excuse me. I'm sorry, please excuse me." Out of the blue, she pulled off her wig and said, "This is the most uncomfortable piece of headgear I have ever worn. It pains my head." She then ruffled her fingers through her hair and announced, "This feels so much better." What a jewel! All of us burst into laughter and breathed a sigh of relief. She was so transparent. She not only broke the ice, she knew what her guests were experiencing behind their smiles that covered up possible turmoil.

We so quickly portray an exterior that differs from how we really feel. The heart says one thing, and our exterior appearance says another. Should our goal be total transparency?

God brought a handsome young man, beautiful in spirit, into my life. This guy spoke suicidal words that life was too hard and worthless. We met countless times.

In transparency, I told him, "I would have missed the privilege of visiting your beautiful state and meeting you and your beautiful family had I followed through on the low times in my life. We would not be sitting here in this counseling setting. Likewise, I can't imagine missing out on meeting my grandchildren or even on become a missionary or, worst of all, living a life without God."

He listened and took a constructive turn after his quandary. Some years later, I heard through the grapevine that this young man finished his college studies and was now ministering to others.

Another young fellow was brought into my office after he caused a commotion in his classroom. He was like a clown with disruptive tendencies in class. His masks covered up a desperate need for attention.

Another middle-aged woman avoided eye contact with others at all costs. Was there shame in her life? Some people are easy to read and others harder. The feelings and emotions of some are more transparent while others are hidden beneath a veneer.

Christians often deal with hidden emotions. Have you ever scolded your children or spoke unkindly to your spouse? But when you entered church, you acted as if your family sang during the entire thirty-mile trip?

My mom sometimes said to me as a youngster, "If people saw you when you are mad, they would not believe you are the same sweet person with the big smile." Did I mention that I was not always the most pleasant person to my family as a child?

Some people are under the impression that Christians do not and should not have storms, disappointments, and dark and down times. They smile and shout that "all is well with my soul." Yes, the mask sometimes covers up what's really going on.

Scripture tells us that the rain falls on the just and the unjust (Matthew 5:45). Perhaps as we continue in our walk with the Lord, we realize that all people, whether Christian or not, go through storms. We need some rain in our lives to grow. Trials and tough times deepen our walk with the Lord. I prefer not to deal with these tests and challenging times, yet surely I would miss out on growth without them. We live in a sinful world. Jesus was not exempt from difficult times, and our Bible heroes were not without sin.

We become real people once we take off the masks and share our trials and triumphs with others. Transparency benefits all of us. I like knowing that I am healthy, and I want to empathize with other hurting people. I value the needed stormy weather. No, storms are not fun, yet the potential outcome is stimulating.

I was often embarrassed when young. Had I known other folks had issues and hard times as well, maybe the embarrassment would have lessened or would not have been such a problem. We tend to believe we are the only ones with issues. But we should let our children know that life has challenges and can be perplexing.

Hardship creates opportunities to draw us closer to God. He uses everything in our lives; nothing is wasted. After the storms pass, the air feels fresh, crisp, and healthy. The nitrogen in the rain waters the plants and grass, and the air smells so sweet and clean. We now have a new beginning. If we sit quietly after the storm, we might even hear the grass and flowers grow. In their way, they might be dancing, laughing, and shouting for joy as the nitrogen brought them a wealth of sustenance. Life happens before our very eyes.

Later, this friend told me that transparency is like a clean window: a window one can look right through without any interference of smudges, smears, cobwebs, blemishes, or masks.

My mom often said, "We all put on our pants the same way, one leg at a time." It's funny but true. We may have been okay before the trauma, but after healing takes place, we are even better than okay. Perhaps though it all, we become familiar with walking in the shoes of others so that we understand their needs.

God faithfully demonstrates his healing power, faithfulness, and tender loving care for his children. He uses each happening for his glory. He longs to heal the brokenhearted and give us new hearts and a new spirit (Ezekiel 36:26). "The Spirit of the Lord God is upon Me, because the Lord has anointed Me to preach good tidings to the poor; He has sent Me to heal the brokenhearted, to proclaim liberty to the captives, and the opening of the prison to those who are bound" (Isaiah 61:1).

In my case, I found out that divorce was not the end of the world. In many regards, my single season helped me focus on finding a new me and helping others find a new them.

"My brethren, count it all joy when you fall into various trials, knowing that the testing of your faith produces patience" (James 1:2–3). And remember, when your friend is bold enough to confront you lovingly, drop the defense mechanisms and the mask and listen.

Readers, share your story. Transparency is good for the soul and will surely benefit the listeners. Yes, we receive that unspeakable joy (1 Peter 1:6), and the celebration of the Lord brings forth strength (Nehemiah 8:10).

9

The Janets—
Not One but Four or Humor and Forgiveness

*A*bout the same time when I became single, I became acquainted with not one, not two, not three but *four* Janets who entered my life. Actually, I already knew two of them and knew the third somewhat, and the fourth was a brand-new acquaintance. These four ladies had the same first names.

What humor that these four Janets became noteworthy and a part of my life in a matter of a few weeks. I was newly single at this time! What was the Lord speaking or permitting? Was this a coincidence?

He was working heavily in my life and was most likely emphasizing the commandment—his specific instruction—to "love thy neighbor as thyself" during this particular season. Yes, I think so. My only issue with this was that I did not necessarily love myself at that time. I was dealing with the whys and the how comes. I wondered what part I played in this divorce.

One Janet had been an acquaintance for at least twenty years. While in the military and stationed in Fort Eustis, Virginia, we had attended a church, the Newport News Church, where she was the organist. Later in life, she and her family moved right up the street from our Arizona home—a coincidence or, more likely, a divine appointment. In her front room, just a softball throw up the street from our home, she ushered me in the sinner's prayer.

Another Janet was my pastor's wife. After becoming single, I began attending a multicultural, interracial, nondenominational church. I was a member of this church for nearly forty years.

A third Janet was in charge of the paper route that my daughters had shortly after we became a family of six women of all ages.

The fourth woman was soon to be the step-mother of my five daughters. Does God have a sense of humor or what? What was he showing me? Each time I turned around, I was reminded of Janet. Each time I thought of Janet, all four of them came to mind. I think the Lord has a sense of humor. Was he teaching me, training me, or trying me?

Did I know Jesus? I knew most of the Bible stories. I was raised to do the right thing throughout my entire life, including believing in Jesus and living according to his Word. My mom, our church, and the Christian school I attended for the first eight years of my youth instilled Bible principles into me. Very often, I was reminded of the Ten Commandments. My mom regularly mentioned this meaningful commandment: "Honor your father and your mother." And we are to "love our neighbor as ourselves," another meaningful commandment. In some respects, I was a handful during my younger years. Yet I had a healthy respect, perhaps a fear, of doing wrong.

When I was middle-aged, I invited Jesus into my life as my personal Lord and Savior, which was a new concept for me. In the living room of an older friend, a God-fearing Janet, my biblical head knowledge now became heart knowledge. All my life, I intentionally wanted to do good, yet that day in my friend's living room, a deep transformation took place. My spiritual eyes were opened, and Jesus became my personal Lord and Savior. He became my husband, my life.

We had met her and her family many years earlier while stationed near the East Coast. However, as the years passed and my heart healed, this precious woman who brought me to the Lord became a dear friend. We celebrated my spiritual birthday with cards and flowers each year until death parted us.

My life since that day nearly forty years ago has never been the same. My relationship with the God of creation has continued to mature. I now say, "I am in a relationship with Jesus."

My pastor's wife was also a Janet. This pastor and his wife had ministered to our family since the time I became single. One daughter and I attended the Thursday night prayer meetings led by this chaplain in the military chapel. In time, this pastor transitioned from the military and founded a church in our city adjacent to the military base.

Let me introduce you to two more Janets.

My daughters had a paper route, which helped to subsidize our income at the beginning of our single journey with females. We delivered several hundred papers each morning before school and on weekends. The woman who taught us and who helped us get started with the paper route was named Janet. We rode the right seat in her car several times while she rode the passenger side of our vehicle. Janet was continually available to answer our questions. I struggled as I watched the girls leave home those early mornings before sunrise. The papers were delivered to our house before the crack of dawn each morning, and the girls neatly packed them in their cloth paper bags, which were always filled to the brim. The girls were then off to deliver the daily news. This early morning job taught us all the value of a solid work ethic and integrity. They usually rode their bikes, but sometimes I drove them. Eventually one daughter received her driver's license. Then my job was to pray and trust God for their safety.

My daughter stepped into the dark in those early, often pitch-black mornings. My faith increased as did theirs throughout this paper route season. No doubt, they were sending prayers to the heavens as well. The darkness of the early mornings surrounded the unknown down the street, behind the bushes and trees. Our street to this day does not have street lights. We daily had to activate the verse in Hebrews 11 that tells us that "faith is the substance not seen."

My daughters epitomized responsibility and diligent work. They learned to value their hard-earned money, which was a reminder of accountability and was an admirable trait to develop.

For a moment, they might have let their minds wander and thought about basketball or softball or their horse. These distractions resulted in a wild newspaper toss onto the roof of a home or in a cacti mass near the front door. They then needed to retrieve this wildly thrown paper—not always fun.

The girls sometimes stood on each other's shoulders in hopes of recovering the wayward newspaper. If, by chance, they failed to deliver the newspaper near the front door, a phone call was awaiting them before the girls returned home. They heard messages such as, "I can't find my morning paper!" Or "Are there no papers this morning?" Again, not a pleasant phone call. The best message was after a paper landed in a cactus. "Honey, you will need to stop by and get my paper out of the cacti garden."

One daughter worked to feed her horse. She just could not let this beloved horse go. The horse helped heal her broken heart. She and her daddy spent much time together at the corrals. With each pay day, she purchased enough food for the month to feed her gymkhana blue-ribbon victory Appaloosa. Her entire paycheck was spent on hay and oats for her precious four-legged friend.

The day came when the cost of food became more substantial than her paycheck. As hurtful as this was, she reconciled herself to this reality by finding another home for her best friend. The benefit here was that my young daughter developed many positive character traits: responsibility, interacting with others, and the value of budgeting.

The pleasure of caring for and owning her beloved four-legged friend brings a huge smile even years later. The transfer of ownership was a day of tears for our family. But the satisfaction of the sale to another horse lover made the event somewhat easier. Learning to let go is, in itself, a powerful lesson.

The older high school sister's paycheck helped with her school expenses and pocket money. Dedication and commitment as part of the job of a daily paper route became a way of life for these daughters.

Another Janet eventually became the wife of my previous husband and presented a more significant challenge for me. Scripture tells us that we are to forgive seventy times seven. Forgiving her was a bit more problematic. However, when I finally did so, God stepped in and worked out the situation. This did not happen overnight but took time.

When asked by a godly church brother if I had forgiven Janet, my answer was no. "Forgiveness is not always easy," I said. He then asked if I had forgiven my ex-husband. The answer to the second question was much easier. I could say yes, as it was less of a struggle for me to forgive a loved one. Yes, the disappointment was huge, yet love seemed to cover all sin.

Since then, I have a better understanding of the art of forgiveness. We must realize that forgiveness opens the door to healing in our lives. God enters hearts through mercy. Unforgiveness blocks God's work in our lives. Once forgiveness takes place, God heals our hearts and works intimately through our experience.

I struggled to understand this whole concept during that season. It took time to understand how a spouse could walk out of a marriage. In the same way, it took time to understand how someone could step in and take another person's spouse. Divorce alters lives and changes family structures. The girls' daddy beamed when people teased him about his many daughters. That amusement and similar joys were lost to history.

Back to the conversation about forgiveness with this brother. He quickly replied, "Maggie, I find this hard to believe. You love the Lord, and you know the importance of forgiveness, right?"

Yes, he was 100 percent correct. I knew the Word, which told me to forgive. But still. I promised this brother that I would work on this area in my life. He was right, and I knew it. My attitude needed adjusting. How can God work in our lives when our hearts are filled with unforgiveness? People who choose not to forgive end up sick or old before their time.

Consequently, I spent the night in prayer. "Lord Jesus, I know it's the right thing to do. Please, please help me be a forgiving person and forgive Janet. I know I need to forgive for my healing. My heart is devastated, and only you can restore and make me new. I want to get on with life and live in freedom. Help me, Lord Jesus."

Jesus said when you fully forgive, God's peace will rest upon you, and the Holy Spirit will comfort you. Forgiveness brings healing and health (Colossians 3:13).

Imagine if God decided not to forgive us when we failed to forgive others. Every one of us falls short. Scripture clearly says, "If we say that we have no sin, we deceive ourselves, and the truth is not in us" (1 John 1:8). Wow, this is to the point.

We know that marriage takes work, and no doubt, I was the perfect wife throughout our marriage of twenty years! (That was a joke.) Couples sometimes distance themselves from each other and waste precious time that they could spend together. We might even fall out of bed to avoid closeness with our spouse. We know that eventually, we will make up with that spouse. We can be so silly and stubborn.

Well, grace fell on me, and God heard my cry. The next morning, after a night of tossing and turning and prayer, along with the slight lecture from my church brother, an extraordinary thing happened.

As I turned on the road into my workplace, I again remembered what the Bible taught about unforgiveness. The prompting of the Spirit within me was strong and nudged me to pull the car to the side of the road and stop. My brother in the Lord was right. I needed to forgive so the Lord could begin the inner healing that I so desperately needed. The tug within my heart was earnest. Now was the right time to ask the Lord to help me to forgive Janet.

I prayed, "Lord, this is so tough. I want so very much to forgive because your Word tells us to. You mean more to me than any other person. I want a heart of forgiveness, peace, and freedom. I want to heal.

Please, Lord, help me to forgive Janet. I want to forgive her as you have forgiven me so many times throughout my life. Please, Lord, help me do so. You know my heart better than I know my heart."

As the words were still leaving my mouth, God's warmth flooded my body. As I write this story, even many decades later, the Spirit of the Lord still touches my body in a powerful, reassuring way. The Spirit of the Lord so beautifully touched my heart. His presence filled the car like an inflated balloon. A burden lifted off and out of me. A sense of freedom and joy filled me all at the same time. And then, in my spirit, it was as though the Lord said, "Maggie, I know your heart and the hurt you felt within. You have done the right thing by wanting to forgive Janet. Your healing has begun."

God knew the sincerity of my heart, and he knows your heart too. He touched me at that moment. He will do the same for all who sincerely seek him. The weight of unforgiveness left me, and the gladness of forgiveness flooded my entire being from head to toe. In that incredible moment, forgiveness happened. That encounter with the Spirit of God brought peace and joy—an exuberant joy—and health and happiness. The tears flowed freely. With forgiveness and freedom, I now had the ability to move forward.

Yes, let the healing begin. Dear readers, his grace is sufficient for you and me. Yes, the art of forgiveness. The art of letting go. The art of moving forward.

The Lord wants to confirm that trust in him brings us freedom. He wants to bring healing and restoration. Each morning, when my daughters ran their paper route, my task was to pray for their safety as they ventured into the darkness. God can bring bright lights into dark areas, whether in a heart or in the dark of the early morning streets.

Each of the four Janets brought me closer to the Lord in one way or another. How awesome is that? What the enemy set out to use for my destruction, the light of the gospel used to display the glory of Jesus.

10

Delivery of Divorce—
Traveling to See My Husband

"My brethren, count it all joy when you fall into various trials, knowing
that the testing of your faith produces patience. But let patience have
its perfect work, that you may be perfect and complete, lacking nothing"
(James 1:2–4).

*T*rials have the potential to strengthen us spiritually. We are then
in a position to help others as they face their trials. Few people,
if any, pass through life without facing some testing and tribulations at
one time or another. Tests have the potential to strengthen us.

I was served the divorce papers several months before the summer
school break. I was a teacher's aide at the local elementary school during
this time. It was now May, and school bells ceased their ringing until late
August. Summer break was in full swing. In a few days, I would journey
by air to visit my husband. Leaving his home months prior was unlike this
man, so I wanted to see if he was all right.

I had purchased my plane ticket once my income tax return was in
my hand. I now had a ticket and hoped to see my husband in just a short
few weeks.

Maybe a personal visit would encourage him, I thought. He met me
at the airport, and within ten minutes, we parted ways. This unexpected

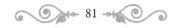

short visit was one more opportunity for God, in his reliable way, to pick me up and carry me through the disappointment.

My trip included a rental car. God provided strength to catch the bus to the rental car lot. In my shattered state, God pulled me together. With a change of plans and in the driver's seat of my rental, it was time to make a few crucial decisions.

How would I spend my next six days? During those moments, my world felt as if it were coming to an end. The Mighty One supplied me with an incredible amount of his amazing grace. It was difficult, yet God held me in his arms. He was with me and gave me strength in my time of weakness.

"O God, You are my God; early will I seek You; my soul thirsts for You in a dry and thirsty land where there is no water. So I have looked for You in the sanctuary, to see Your power and Your glory. Because Your loving-kindness is better than life, my lips shall praise You. Thus I will bless You while I live; I will lift up my hands in Your name" (Psalm 63:1–4).

My answer came after a short roadside nap. An estimated six-hour drive north would take me to my adopted Southern aunt. Yes, that was the answer. The excitement within my spirit was my confirmation. I was heading north.

I was stepping out and into new territory. During the past years, my task was to ramrod the family while their dad took care of our travels. My new normal had begun. "Enlarge the place of your tent, and let them stretch out the curtains of your dwellings; do not spare; lengthen your cords, and strengthen your stakes" (Isaiah 54:2).

I reviewed my situation on my drive northward. *What happened to our marriage?* This man was the most attentive, responsible husband and father — my memories of the past were happy and, yes, some sad. I was thankful for both and for what God had done in my life through the seasons.

The enemy was actively seeking to destroy families, my family, in this case. "Be sober, be vigilant; because your adversary the devil walks about like a roaring lion, seeking whom he may devour" (1 Peter 5:8). The Spirit of the Lord never misses an opportunity to carry us through the most challenging situations and to offer peace. We might miss the chance, but God never does. He is the God of the universe.

I was on my way to visit Aunt Katie, and joy filled my heart. She often said, "If I had a daughter, I would want her to be like you." In turn, I esteemed this dear Southern woman. God brought her and her husband into our lives years prior when we were all stationed at the same military base.

I kept driving in anticipation of seeing Aunt Katie's big smile and open arms. My heart filled with many sweet memories spent with this dear friend with the snow-white hair and distinguished southern accent. We met before I was a young mother and she was a grandmother. She was always available to help with my young children.

Joy filled my heart, and had I not been in a rental car, I would have been dancing on the street corner. It was not the best idea to dance while behind a steering wheel, so I just sang. I visualized happy melody notes escaping from the roof top and out the windows of the rental to the tune of "Amazing Grace, how sweet the sound, that saved a wretch like me. I once was lost but now am found was blind, but now I see."[1] Over and over, my refrain filled the air and my heart. God's amazing grace showed up many times since I invited him into my heart. Aunt Katie was not on my mind when planning this trip; in fact, I did not realize I would have six days before returning back to Arizona. Again, the Lord took my sorrow and turned it to joy.

"You have turned for me my mourning into dancing; you have put off my sackcloth and clothed me with me with gladness" (Psalm 30:11). God heard my prayer and was attending to my needs once again. He reinstated hope and joy and filled my weary soul. The thought of Aunt Katie's embrace made me smile as I drive down the road. She was a great listener, a secure and safe place to pour out my story of heartache. Her heart—and her ears—knew how to offer compassion and care.

---

[1] John Newton, "Amazing Grace," public domain.

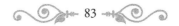

My mind wandered to a few months prior to that moment when God opened my spiritual eyes, and I saw the light. My understanding of God, his peace, and his hope entered the depths of my soul like never before during this spiritual awakening. I remembered how she prayed. I followed along, repeating each word carefully in what she called the "sinner's prayer."

My weary spirit lifted after that. My stance took a change for the better. Hope, encouragement, and God's presence entered my every cell. I experienced a hunger and thirst for God's Word. I eagerly read the Bible and was amazed at the contents therein. The Holy Spirit was alive and well within my soul. Previously I knew of God as my Bible hero; now I was learning to know God as his born-again child.

My travels continued north as hope and encouragement filled my heart. My wounded heart and hurt at the airport disturbance melted as the warmth of Jesus's healing hand touched my soul.

The thoughts of God's love and healing just caused me to sing louder. He knows about the tears that stream down our cheeks, whether gentle or like an open faucet. "You number my wanderings; put my tears into Your bottle; are they not in Your book?" (Psalm 56:8).

God, in the confusion and disappointment of that ten-minute airport visit, now provided sufficient strength to carry on and poured a dose of abundant joy within me. At the same time, he directed me to my adopted Aunt Katie's home. How does one explain his presence since I invited Jesus into my heart? He brings people into our lives who care and who offer love and friendship. When our eyes are focused on his, life works out. "And the peace of God, which surpasses all understanding, will guard your hearts and minds through Christ Jesus" (Philippians 4:7).

My daughters were so excited that I was going to see their dad. They sent along cards and notes. One daughter said, "Mom, please bring Daddy home with you." I wanted to honor her priceless request. I could only trust God had a plan for our lives and a method for good and hope. I was launching out in trust in God, letting go and letting him lead my new life.

Life on a single pathway was not always easy to travel. Some days were brighter than others. Some days, the rain fell slowly and soaked the earth.

The path was rocky and filled with thorns, scorpions, and dust. Other days, joy filled the path with a few sprinkles here and there. Some days, the ground remained relatively dry, and I sensed all would be all right.

My nine-month part-time teacher's aide employment was close to my home, so I biked home every day for lunch. This lunch period provided me with time on my knees to fill my cup with his goodness. This time helped me make it through one more day. I intentionally sought the Lord. He was my answer to healing.

When the church doors opened, I was there. When there was a women's Bible study, I was there. When the church's small group met, I was there. And eventually, I offered a weekly Bible study in my home. My cup required filling each day, often several times a day. Determination kept me moving forward. The older women at my church cared for me. God, in his immeasurable mercy and grace, was working in my life and in the lives of my daughters. He poured hope, happiness, and endurance into each of us. The single mama chores were bearable. God, somehow, someway, made a way for this daughter.

Bright and early each morning before our school bells rang, our stereo system filled our home with praise and worship songs, songs we were learning in our new church environment. The Spirit of the Lord filled our hearts in preparation for one more day. Joy substituted the sorrow that could so easily take over. "Those who sow in tears shall reap in joy. He who continually goes forth weeping, bearing seed for sowing, shall doubtless come again with rejoicing, bringing his sheaves with him" (Psalm 126:5–6).

We missed our daddy and husband more than words could express. We hoped each day that the sound of his truck would resonate as it turned into the driveway and that, moments later, he would walk into our home. The empty chair at the dining room table was a sad reminder. Our hearts would always carry much love for this man, whether he was with us or not.

A sister in the Lord said that Jesus would now be my husband. I, in all honesty, did not know what she meant. God as a husband was a new concept to me. My young years in the Christian school and church taught me many biblical stories, yet I had much more to learn and understand as I continued my Christian walk. "For your Maker is your husband, the Lord of hosts is His name; and your Redeemer is the Holy One of Israel; He is called the God of the whole earth" (Isaiah 54:5).

Our lives include making decisions, and each decision has a consequence. We are responsible for our choices. Unless we chose to change, no one can make us. The school was in session, and I chose to do the best I knew how. Moving forward was a much better option than staying stuck. My daughters were also trying to understand what was happening. Parental separation is difficult to comprehend.

The blurry tearful eyes cleared after a few songs. It was time to keep my eyes on the road and the map. I was venturing into new territory. During the past years, my task was to support the family while their dad took care of our travels. My new normal had begun. I was beginning to move away from my familiar space.

God had a way of turning my sorrow and spirit into joy. I worked at intentionally finding something to be happy and thankful about each day. God was healing me, even though the healing and happy mixed with tears that filled my heart and the interior of the rented car.

A spiritual awakening resembles blind eyes seeing the light. Experiencing this concept caused me to weep yet not for sorrow's sake but for joy's. I was beginning to know about God not just know of him. The Bible passages began to speak to my heart, to my spirit. Joy, hope, peace, and contentment filled the empty spots—the Word and God's presence settled in and absorbed every empty place like a thirsty sponge. God had resonated in my heart. He was showing me the way. "The steps of a good man are ordered by the Lord, and He delights in his way" (Psalm 37:23).

Aunt Katie was not at home when I arrived. Her home was dark, yet the small dim light hanging from the open carport ceiling welcomed me. Its brightness contrasted with the surrounding darkness. God's sun was shining.

There you have it. "This little light of mine, I'm gonna let it shine."[2] Like the Star of Bethlehem that the wise men followed, the star was shining brightly. It led the path for the wise men to the baby Jesus. The light from Aunt Katie's carport brought well-being and peace. I had arrived.

The crickets were singing in full tune, and the moonlight made its way through the thickly wooded area surrounding her home. This familiar place was so soothing. I was home. God provided a safe trip to the north and a place of lodging and comfort for the next few days. He was busy working behind the scenes. My task was to trust. Yes trust. I was learning about faith and trust.

I reclined in the seat of this rental car for the night. The day was long, and with little effort, my tired eyes closed. I was safe. I was home. Surely Aunt Katie would be driving down her long driveway before too long.

The sunlight and the chirping birds in the wooded area around Aunt Katie's home woke me. Now, where was my Aunt Katie? I walked the grounds and then decided to visit her neighbor, a friend from our military years. We embraced and talked like women tend to do. We carried on as if we had never parted. Soon, the phone rang. Aunt Katie was on her way home. Together, we waited for Aunt Katie to return from her visit to her aged mother who lived several hours away near farmland.

Aunt Katie's voice on the telephone elevated when her neighbor said I was there. She assured us that she would hurry home. Aunt Katie knew the farm roads like I know the back of my hand. Her heavy foot weighed on her car pedals during our earlier times together. Soon Aunt Katie's car was coming down her long driveway toward her home. Our embrace was one of the best of friends. We talked for hours and shed tears of sadness and joy. Aunt Katie loved my husband. He, too, was much like a son to her. After much talk and catching up, we decided to tackle some needed yard work. My aging Aunt Katie was limited in what she could do, but I was not.

---

[2] "This Little Light of Mine," unknown origin, public domain.

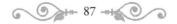

Soon her old gas lawnmower was whirling and not missing a weed or blade of grass around her home. We tackled her kitchen, and with great delight, Aunt Katie glowed at the sight of her shiny clean cabinets with the dishes placed neatly inside. She could see the bottom of the sink again. Her overflowing clothes were washed, ironed, and neatly placed in her closet. Together, we tidied up her modest three-room home. In her younger days, she was the energetic work hand, and now age and declining health limited her activities.

The days went by quickly. Soon my rental car and I would head south again. Spending time with my dear friend was always a huge blessing as we reminisced about the days of yesteryear and just enjoyed each other's presence. Could we ask for more?

I knew why the Lord brought Aunt Katie to mind. She needed help with tidying up her home, and I needed help to strengthen my soul. We were a perfect team. This woman had been a second mom to me since my younger years.

My biological mom and Aunt Katie had met years ago and became lifelong pen pals. My mom was grateful that Aunt Katie was in my life and available to help with my children. My first child was born when I was nineteen, and the rest followed one after another. Aunt Katie helped me during my husband's two Viet Nam tours. She encouraged me to take a few community college classes during his second tour. She insisted on caring for my four-year-old daughter while I attended class a few times a week. Her adult son stayed in touch even though his widowed mom lived in another state.

This hindsight demonstrates how God took care of our family. Throughout these years, I became acquainted with her family. She had many brothers and sisters. We called her loveable aged mother, "Granny." Our correspondence through the years lessened, yet we squeezed in an occasional phone call.

To this day, I stand amazed at how God had arranged this time together. Yes, together one more time. We shared moments of tears and sadness during this visit. It is sad when families break up. We then focused on the more positive memories that blessed us both.

My life was full of energy, even surplus energy. At times, I was sure I could move a mountain if need be. Our time together flew by. I needed to think about my return trip, as I had one more stop before returning to my children.

To my amazement, one more incredible surprise awaited me before our good-bye hugs. God was in the business of blessing, restoring, healing, and affirming his love for me—yes, and busily working behind the scenes. This huge, extraordinary surprise topped all.

I needed two nights of lodging closer to the airport before returning to my southwestern home. Aunt Katie's sister called just before I headed south to my original destination. Aunt Katie told her about our visit and that I was leaving in the morning to be closer to the airport before heading back home. Aunt Josephine remembered me, and before I knew it, Aunt Katie had arranged for me to stay with her. She just happened to live where I was going. She was delighted, and yes, so was I—I could stay with her.

Do you believe in divine appointments? God had it all figured out. What a perfect example of not being anxious about tomorrow! I knew this sister and her hubby. They had been married for many years and were parents of more than a dozen children. They called this a baker's dozen or thirteen. While I stayed with her, I would have to share a bed with one of her grandchildren, who was visiting at the time. God had pre-arranged my lodging. Scripture tells us to "Be anxious for nothing, but in everything by prayer and supplication, with thanksgiving, let your requests be made known to God" (Philippians 4:6).

Like Jonah and the whale, when Jonah went overboard, the whale was there to catch him. Now Jonah probably didn't know the whale was waiting on him, but God knows our need before we do. Aunt Katie's sister was there with open arms. God's love is always there, waiting for his children. Aunt Josephine's arms resembled those of her sister's—warm and welcoming.

I had one more visit with the father of my children. He lived close to Aunt Josephine's. Amazing! He was just down the road within a fly ball over the back fence. Who would ever have believed it?

Aunt Josephine had outlived many of her thirteen children. Like Aunt Katie, she was well along in years. Her heart was tender and precious. She opened her home for a wayward child in search of her children's father. The time with Aunt Josephine was of great value. She loved our Lord and Savior and was instrumental in strengthening my faith and reinforcing that blessed assurance.

My visit with my husband and the father of our children only lasted a few minutes. We shed tears and had an emotional conversation. I then returned to Aunt Josephine's where I spent the night. The next morning, I caught a flight heading home. Mission accomplished although not entirely with the outcome I had hoped. But God knew.

No, my children's father did not accompany me back west. Overall, in a subtle way, the trip was fruitful. I am thankful for the years with this man and certainly for Aunt Katie and Aunt Josephine. God had powerfully revealed himself. Through it all, my faith and trust was strengthened. I saw how he made a way for me as I stepped out in unfamiliar territory.

I had the satisfaction of trying to resolve the issues with my husband. Now I asked what the decades ahead would offer this single woman. In good conscience, as I look back, I would not have wanted to miss out on the years that followed. So I did not dwell on the lonely times and always encouraged myself in the Lord.

Scripture talks of the various seasons of life. I gave little thought of seasons during our military years. I was busy raising our family. And yes, my grandparents were up in years, but I did not think about those passing years or about the aging process.

One daughter once mentioned, "Mom, I don't mind having birthdays, yet, when I have a birthday, you also have one. And you are twenty years older than I am."

At the age when I became single, men went through a mid-life crisis, and women went through menopause. This information was new to me. I began to study this topic. What was this mid-life crisis in men and women? When will menopause take place? I vaguely remembered my mother's experience yet never gave much thought to reaching this season in my life.

God gave me the gift of finding the positive in most situations. This gift did not happen overnight. Life is a process from entering elementary school to high school graduation and beyond. One year, one class at a time. In my case, we married shortly after graduation. Babies followed, one after another. "Behold, children are a heritage from the Lord, the fruit of the womb is a reward. Like arrows in the hand of a warrior, so are the children of one's youth. Happy is the man who has his quiver full of them" (Psalm 127:3–5). God faithfully filled our quiver and blessed us with the gift of five daughters.

Life includes hard work, determination, and usually some blood, sweat, and a few buckets of tears. Sometimes, one has to fail to succeed. The years of happiness, fulfillment, and growth have outnumbered the times of failure. Time passes, and attitudes change. An approach of fortitude and gratefulness aids in living a happy life.

As I entered the next season of life as a single person, I realized I had a decision to make. The ups and downs of life can make us bitter or better. Living better is better than living in bitterness. We accept or refuse life. Forgiveness is the key to healing. I remember exactly where I was standing when I chose to go on and try living from my experiences, no matter the challenges.

I sometimes faced a shortage of finances, which helped in decision-making. I willingly took on the problematic outward tasks. I learned to change the flat tires on the girls' bikes. Life in Arizona included cacti, and cacti needles punctured tires. I learned and taught my daughters how to change a flat tire on a car. Soon, I was on the roof of our home, servicing our swamp cooler, which helped cool our home in the heat of summer. I learned to paint our house inside and to seal the block on the outside. These fixer-uppers gave me a sense of joy and triumph, and in many respects, I became an intentional learner. God turned negatives into positives.

I am a firm believer that when God gives us a home, car, and other material possessions, we have the responsibility to care for them. That day came when I could openly thank God for the twenty years of marriage. I was ready to accept these changes and make a go of life. I understood better what happened when a marriage went wrong. I was grateful to have children from the years of my marriage. These children have produced many grandchildren. I understand what being a single mom entails.

"When I was a child, I spoke as a child, I thought as a child; but when I became a man, I put away childish things" (1 Corinthians 13:11). We learn to accept the consequences and prepare for the next season. God emphasizes forgiveness and restoration. We learn that his grace is sufficient.

My marriage taught me about life as did living as a single, especially as a woman. I value being a single woman, a whole and unique person, and God did it all. A relationship with God is like no other relationship. The possibilities for me as a single person are enormous. Now I understand this life is not for everyone. It just happens to be right for me.

We experience the blessings and those which could be better as we go through life. The wonderful news is that each one, whether good or not-so-great, contributes to our physical, emotional, spiritual, and even financial maturity. Sometimes the pain is an excellent motivator to take the high road for all that God offers.

God desires to enlarge our tent stakes, "Enlarge the place of your tent, and let them stretch out the curtains of your dwellings" (Isaiah 54:2). He is the lifter of our head and the healer of broken hearts. If you've invited him into your heart, you know what I am saying. If you have not done so, invite him in right now and ask him to take over your life.

In good conscience, I would not have wanted to miss out on the four seasons, decades, of my life following the divorce.

11

A Fateful Trip—
The Beginning and the End

When I initially found myself single, life was complicated. The break of trust in my marriage was devastating. God used his hands and feet on Earth to guide me during this dark time. Once I accepted Jesus into my life, I wanted to live my life for him like never before.

Today, people around me might see me and think that my life is a piece of cake. While life can resemble a piece of cake, the ingredients need to be properly measured and combined before the cake tastes delicious. This set-up and my healing process date back forty years.

In 1979, I was a client, seeking answers from a Christian counselor. One session a week was by far too seldom. So I decided to sit at the feet of understanding whenever this counselor's office door was open. My hour appointment flew by. I was in desperate need of talking and listening to words of wisdom. I needed answers, directions, and guidance. I needed help.

Embarrassment and great shame entered the pit of my soul. Defeat and rejection assaulted me; my self-worth and humility were lower than low. The world around me had grown enormously and overwhelmed me; I felt so minute in contrast to the vast universe. The trees grew taller. The moon and stars were tiny like the crown of a stick pin. The stars lost their warmth, luster, and life. Heaviness weighed down my bosom. My feet were wobbly; my legs unsure of the next step. My limbs buckled beneath me. I often fell to the floor. My head swam like a fish in a pond. The tears flowed like waterfalls.

I was now single; my high school sweetheart was no longer with me. What happened? Help me, Lord Jesus. I had known of you since I was a child. I was so lost and confused. I was a young woman in the prime of life, the mom of five daughters ranging from elementary to middle and high school ages. We missed the man in our lives.

My life had fallen apart. I was numb, and at a total loss. Did I turn left or right? Did I run away, maybe even take my own life? I wanted to die, yet I knew this was not the answer.

The security and love of a father were not available. The empty dining room chair brought tears. Each day, we longed for his return.

This Christian counselor was listening and praying as I spoke. My talk and thoughts made little sense, rambling. I felt mentally unstable, emotionally a wreck, and physically weak. I had recently backed our car into a telephone post because I was so distracted.

The military and high school youth saw my husband and me—our whole family, really—as role models. These teens freely dipped in our cookie jar. They spent happy times and chats in our home and on the military post and hometown streets. What would people think?

Well, this scenario, thank God, was behind me. However, I wanted to offer a sense of where I was when singleness set in. To anyone who finds themselves in similar shoes, I want to shout this: "*There is hope.*" Our Great Physician, Jesus, heals broken hearts. He lifted our heads and restored our sanity. "Heal me, O Lord, and I shall be healed" (Jeremiah 17: 14). "He heals the broken hearted" (Psalm 147:3). "God will wipe away all tears" (Revelation 2:14).

When a friend heard of my dilemma, she said, "It's time to place Jesus first and your husband second." I thought that if a wife and mother cared for her family, this was putting Jesus first. She gave me this verse. "Trust in the Lord with all your heart, and lean not on your own understanding; in all your ways acknowledge him, and he shall direct your paths" (Proverbs 3:5–6).

Meanwhile, I repeated the sinner's prayer led by an acquaintance of earlier years. Inviting Jesus into my life was a new concept for me. I had been baptized, confirmed, and spent years in parochial school. But I did not know about asking Jesus into my heart. Or maybe I did and forgot. In either case, I do not know. But through the eyes of a child, I did know him. I was one of the people he saved. He performed miracles while he walked the earth for thirty-three years. As a child, my knowledge and understanding were limited, yet I was taught to honor, obey, and respect him.

When I repeated the sinner's prayer and invited Jesus into my heart, this awakened the Spirit within my heart. Jesus and the Holy Spirit no doubt were in my heart since I obviously wanted to do the right thing. But since that time in the living room of this woman's home, the Holy Spirit truly became evident within me. The Bible now seemed to speak to the depth of my heart when I read it.

My relationship with Jesus since that time has matured remarkably. My daughters continued to grow in their faith journey as well. They realized that God was "the way, the truth, and the life" (John 14:6) and "a lamp to my feet and a light to my path" (Psalm 119:105).

I now better understand what Scripture says about older women in the church. They are to teach the younger women. Perhaps the journey of knowing and understanding will result in a smoother ride for you, the reader. Otherwise, I would have no reason to write my life story. Yet our pain is of great value.

My failures helped mature me. The bumpy and random potholes in the road of life can make or break us; they can defeat us or lead us to victory. Some potholes in the road called for me to take a deep breath and shout for help. Before my eyes, hope and help came. Without the bumpy road, my walk with the Lord might have remained too stagnate.

These challenges contributed to my overall character. I value those shaping times, as painful as they were. Tough times can help shape lives or make one bitter forever. The choice is ours.

My widowed mother's journey aided in shaping my life, teaching me to hang in there and make the best of situations. Life experiences, I believe, can educate us, maybe even more than reading a book. The good news is we, in turn, can teach, comfort, and mentor others, once we have traveled this road.

I am so glad and grateful that God is never too busy to take time with his children. I'm also thankful for the valuable life lessons he has taught me. He delights in holding our hands and showing us the way. Actually, he has held my hand through the years—for eight decades—whether or not I realized it. That adds up to a lot of hand-holding.

I hope to share and ultimately assure you that God is the answer. I want to encourage the readers, especially the single ladies. No matter your stage or season of life, yes, God is the answer. I have learned this as a single of forty years. Jesus fills that hole in our hearts that no one else can—not even a spouse. Why do you think so many married people are lonely? God never intended for your spouse to fill his position in your life.

Jesus first, spouse second. I see him in so many things: the salvation miracle, the birth of a child, a tax refund, mowing my lawn, a super sale, and getting out of bed each morning. The list goes on, and I desire to help others to see how Jesus works in our daily lives. Our every breath involves him.

He is available for everyone; I am not alone in my experiences here. What I'm saying is that I see Jesus in all areas of my life, from large to small. Likewise, I see life as filled with divine interventions. I don't believe in coincidences. I hope you will relax on the ride and take time to smell the roses. I hope you will see Jesus orchestrating all areas of your life just as I do.

I am incredibly thankful for the years of marriage. We had many great years, yet we did not reach the twenty-five-year mark. It took time for me to become content as a single, and it took tenacity to make life work. Jesus sprinkled kisses and hope into my life once I invited him into my heart. This same hope is for everyone.

When a spouse wants out of a marriage, believing the grass is greener elsewhere, the other spouse can't do much. We then have to learn to let go and to live life to the fullest. This realization takes time—how long depends on the person.

I want to encourage singles and really, everyone, to never give up—to never, never, never give up. A single person can experience an extraordinary life and much joy after a divorce. At the time of the divorce, we tend to think our world has fallen apart, which is a genuine feeling. Sometimes singles quickly enter another relationship before taking time to heal and to realize their identity. I understand this as finding yourself alone, maybe with children and perhaps little to no income, is scary.

Our identity can be in our marriage. Maybe we were married before we even knew who we were or before we were whole and could stand alone as an individual.

Scriptures addresses the basis of remarriage. I know many couples who have remarried. They worked hard to make this second marriage work. Following a divorce, people often take problems into the second marriage. They both bring a U-Haul filled to capacity with previous experiences, traditions, rituals, financial debt, insecurities, trust issues and children who are confused over what has happened. But they need time and patience to find out more first about themselves, their make-up, and their identity. They need to wait on God to bring the right person to them.

Life was busy, and I was content. In the process of healing and finding out who I was, I focused on my identity in Christ as a single and as a daughter of the one we serve in heaven.

From childhood forward, I was blessed with a vast amount of energy. During my life, I often needed to put this infinite energy to good use. At times, I could have easily thrown in the towel, yet this energy level and God would not let me quit. I learned that God had a plan for my good and a hope for the future. I did not want to miss where God was taking me.

"Be strong and courageous. Do not be afraid or terrified because of them, for the Lord your God goes with you; he will never leave you nor forsake you" (Deuteronomy 31:6 NIV).

12

My Résumé as a Wife and Mother— In Search of a Job

M y résumé listed a few formal classroom studies; nonetheless, it listed plenty of noteworthy volunteer activities in the community, which filled the page. These activities included interacting with people of all ages.

Our Army career of twenty years was behind us, and so was my marriage. I had embraced my husband's military endeavors as he progressed from an enlisted soldier to an officer and later, a military pilot. This military advancement came from determination and the countless opportunities for instruction. Our cooperative military efforts conveyed an impressive résumé for my husband. In addition, our large family brought us great fulfilment. Our daughters were born in military hospitals except for one who was born in a civilian hospital while her dad was on an extended aircraft testing trip.

My prestige as a wife dependent on the military activities led to many pleasurable military and community volunteer opportunities, both in the States and in Germany. My experience as an enlisted wife and then an officer's wife involved the know-how of both spectrums. My family, homemaking, and supporting the needs of each member through the years was my pride and joy. This included involvement with Girl Scouts, coaching softball, camping, sewing, and other volunteer work, which greatly contributed to my happiness and satisfaction. I also

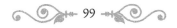

managed a thrift shop for officers' wives and co-managed a boutique while living in Germany. These military entities offered personnel and their families an opportunity to sell and purchase items.

Other volunteer commitments while in Germany included coordinating fundraisers and implementing my Girl Scout troop's rapid transit trip to Switzerland to visit the World's Girl Scout Chalets. Everyone needs to pay close attention to rapid transit with the local train system. When a fast-moving train schedule says 1:01 p.m. pick-up, the train will come at precisely that time. In addition, I directed a Girl Scout Summer Camp.

Together, my husband and I assisted with the Army Dependent Youth (ADY) activities and chaperoned out-of-country touring and ski trips. We coached girls' softball, which demanded commitment, coordination, flexibility, responsibility, patience, stamina, scheduling, and a few other needed character traits. The work-outs, preparation, exciting games, and cheerleading called for endurance.

We were active campers and skiers in Germany and in neighboring countries. I was a hands-on school volunteer, and my homemade burritos were best sellers at the rodeo. I was involved in additional volunteer activities far beyond formal classroom opportunities.

I was engaged in the labor force to subsidize our finances at various times throughout my married years. Sometimes, I watched other children who were dropped off at our home. With five already in my care, one, two, or three more were not too noticeable. The care of a few extra children provided us with a week's groceries. The various volunteer jobs also helped me stay connected with the outside world.

I was now a single mom facing a new season in life. The unexpected fork in the road called for pursuing a full-time job. The part-time teacher's aide position within the local school district was perfect, except it was now time to find a full-time position.

My résumé was full of positions that required stamina, adaptability, hands-on activities, and other notable character traits. Raising children required all of the above and more and included ample trial and error. My work and all these activities were worthy of a spot on my résumé.

So I mustered up boldness and determination and applied for several full-time city positions as they opened up. The thought of facing a city's interviewing committee was scary. I met this committee on two separate occasions with the second interview more relaxing than the first. The city was in search of a full-time sports coordinator and a full-time recreation coordinator. My attitude was "what I don't know I can learn."

The phone call finally came through. Other individuals with degrees now filled these positions. Shortly after my interviews with the city, I became a full-time warehouse clerk with the school district and achieved my goal of finding a full- time job.

A few months into my full-time warehouse position, I received a very unexpected phone call. As always, God was working behind the scenes. The two previous jobs that I so boldly and bravely applied for set me up for a delightful surprise. My résumé included exactly what hiring personnel were looking for. The same lady who previously interviewed me was now on the phone. She remembered me. Yes, our heavenly Father was working behind the scenes.

Caller: Hi Maggie, this is Susan, the person who interviewed you for the two city recreation positions a few months ago.

Maggie: Yes, I remember. How are you, Susan?

Caller: I'm fine, Maggie. And how are you?

Me: I'm fine as well, thank you.

Caller: Maggie, we hoped you would apply for the upcoming community center position. The announcement made the local paper. Did you see it?

Me: No, I didn't notice. I stopped watching the job opening posts. Since my interview with you, I moved into a full-time warehouse clerk position for the school district. I like this new position. The benefits are very nice as well.

Caller: Maggie, there is an opening in the senior adult area as a recreation coordinator. We'd like you to come in for an interview. We still have your previous application. We will set up an interview with you today over your lunch hour.

Me: Thank you, Susan, for thinking of me. But I am happy at my new position with the school district. I have been with the school district for almost three years between my part-time and now full-time positions. In addition, I have accumulated a few weeks of vacation time. Thank you for thinking of me. I'm fine where I'm at.

Susan ignored me and informed me that an interview board was ready to meet me over the lunch hour.

Susan: Maggie, we will look for you at twelve thirty.

The board remembered me from my previous interviews. I had now interviewed with this group of people three times. This meeting was to convince me that this new opening was perfect for me. They wanted me in this position as the senior citizen recreation program coordinator. *Maybe they felt sorry for me because of the last two interviews*, I thought. I choose to believe, however, that they instead truly thought I was the right applicant for this position. After all, my civic community volunteer activity did fill the entire résumé. It showed I worked well with all ages, even for no pay.

The interview dialogue went well. The board expressed their confidence in me. They felt sure I was the person for this position. They believed that I could learn about any areas that I was not familiar with. I thanked the committee for the interview and again mentioned that I was happy with my full-time position at the school district. My new colleagues and I got along well, and I had already earned vacation and health insurance benefits.

Even so, they called me! Perhaps God prepared me through the years through my military, family, and volunteer responsibilities. They had confidence in my ability. I had toiled over filling out that application and was trying to put down everything that might impress them. And they called me. God was working in someone's heart.

Yes, God was behind the scenes. His Word says, "There are many plans in a man's heart, nevertheless the Lord's counsel–that will stand" (Proverbs 19:21). When we pray, do all we can about a situation, and it still doesn't work out, God seems to have something different in mind. Our timing does not always synchronize with his.

Susan asked me not to say no and to set this matter on the back burner. She encouraged me to take my time to think this opportunity over. She said that they could wait on me for a few weeks. She emphasized, "Take your time. Just do not say no right now."

"But he said to me, 'My grace is sufficient for you, for my power is made perfect in weakness.' Therefore I will boast all the more gladly about my weaknesses, so that Christ's power may rest on me. That is why, for Christ's sake, I delight in weaknesses, in insults, in hardships, in persecutions, in difficulties. For when I am weak, then I am strong" (2 Corinthians 12:9–10 NIV).

They talked about pursuing a college degree during that first city interview. Maybe it was time for me to prioritize my goals. I desperately needed finances to make ends meet. The interviewer casually mentioned that one day, perhaps the city would only hire college graduates.

I had often thought about pursuing a college education while my husband was in the military. Family life kept me busy. Eventually, I would take that next step. During the interview, the reality of college was suddenly that much closer. I was in my first semester when I chose to get married instead. I did, however, finish one semester before joining my military husband, so I had that underneath my belt. Possibly during that brief college talk, in one of the interviews, God planted a seed in me. The words stirred up what had previously been dormant in my life. Sometimes it takes a while for the seed to sprout.

In time, I accepted this city position as a senior citizen recreation coordinator. This decision called for all of my praying friends to do just that. Pray! Our heavenly Father wants us to visit with him about every situation in life. He knows us from the inside out. We are to seek him for direction, followed by listening to him, stepping out of our comfort zone, and moving when it's time to move. He wants us to fulfill our maximum potential. The benefits with the city—sick leave, vacation, insurance, and retirement—were appealing even though I was receiving these benefits at my current job. Yet the thought of college gave me something to think about.

Here is a simple prayer that I have often prayed through the years: "Lord, please open and close doors, according to your will. I don't want to go down a path that you don't have for me. If I am reluctant to enter, give me a push if that's what it takes. I desire to be where you want me to be." This job opened up for me, and I walked into this position and became a city employee with the Parks and Recreation Department.

My family and I were in the midst of wedding preparations. In a few weeks, my twenty-year young daughter was scheduled to walk down the church aisle to wed. I needed time to finish sewing projects for her upcoming wedding. The trial-and-error sewing ventures through the earlier years led to a practice-makes-a-perfect outcome. These attempts resulted in pursuing more advanced sewing projects, such as a wedding gown and dresses for the bridal party. I had a lot to complete before my daughter's big day.

Susan did mention that I had time before I set foot in the office. She did, however, want me to stop by for an hour or two for a few days before the outgoing city senior coordinator left the position.

The college reimbursement incentive came up during my early days of employment. The employee received an 80 percent reimbursement upon the completion of each class. I paid for classes up front, and when completed, finances were available for the next go around. God knew before I did that a college degree was a prerequisite for what he had in mind for my future. Pursuing a degree in my early forties was perfectly okay.

Meanwhile, before going back to the college classroom, I had to focus on professional and personal skills. God knew earning an undergraduate degree would take time. In addition, I still needed to heal from the divorce, and I had much to learn before he would move me into the next part of his plan for my life. He even knew that the city would employ me for a total of fifteen years. Isn't this all amazing?

"In everything give thanks; for this is the will of God in Christ Jesus for you" (1 Thessalonians 5:18). "For I know the thoughts that I think toward you, says the Lord, thoughts of peace and not of evil, to give you a future and a hope" (Jeremiah 29:11).

13

Learning and Leaning— The Art of Letting Go

*L*et's face it, we have all heard the truism, "It's not a matter of if something happens but when." And when it does happen, we will hopefully not fall in a bottomless pit of despair. We learn about balance and remember God's faithfulness in our previous experiences. Balance, stability, strength, and endurance depend on focusing on Jesus.

Mountain top experiences exhilarate us; however, we are not always on a mountain top. They fill us for a time, and when the Goliath hurricane and desert storm hits, we won't completely sink. We hopefully learn to focus on Jesus to keep our perspective.

Life is that way; situations happen. Scripture tells us that "rain and trouble fall on the righteous people and the unrighteous people." (See Matthew 5:45.) But the just people have Jesus to lean on to help them in the recovery process. During his three years of ministry on earth, many people, leaders, and priests persecuted Jesus. So why wouldn't they persecute me? And he was sinless. The loss of a job, a financial struggle, marital issues, a divorce, the inevitable car accident, and other problems—life is full of circumstances that can throw us for a loop or even topple us over.

We frequently struggle to give these situations to God. We might even get mad at him or leave our faith when problems come and life goes wrong. But when we focus on God and allow him to take control of our

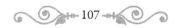

lives, the weight of the condition eases; we pray and wait for answers and healing. We will find the strength to deal with these situations and to even overcome them. God wants to offer healing, relief, and peace. When we give our sorrow to the one who knows us better than we know ourselves, we can depend on him for help. He is our refuge and strength (Psalm 46:1), the burden carrier (Psalm 55:22), and the Creator of our entire being: mind, body, and soul (1 Thessalonians 5:23).

Once, when I was experiencing uncertainty in my life, a spiritual mentor provided godly counsel. "Maggie, your task is to 'seek ye first the kingdom of God,' and all of these things will come about'" (Matthew 6:33). We eventually realize that we can let go of issues that we may or may not have control over (1 John 1:19). Our attitude improves as we then focus on the Great Physician (John 5:1–9) who can help us when we insist on being in control of the situation. He can restore us when we release these challenges and can lead us to his healing touch and power.

When we ride in a car as a passenger, the driver is in control. We can't both sit behind the steering wheel. If I tell the driver how to drive, I am trying to control the vehicle as a back seat driver. Telling God what to do or how I want it done puts me in the position of a supervisor. He does give us free will. We can do anything we want, yet the Bible is our road map with instructions on how to navigate through life.

It was now essential to give up control and accept my new status as a single person. The benefits outweighed the challenges with an enormous payback. But learning to let go does not happen overnight. Many more lessons about letting go followed. God positively strengthened our wimpy backbone. We continued on our journey down the road before us. God wants us to climb higher and farther with him. We always want to keep learning.

Scripture tells us to trust God and obey him as we give our lives to God. Since life is a process and God has a plan for each of his children, we must not get stuck. We need to step out of the box or get off the sofa to do all we can do to reach God's goal for us.

The goal post becomes closer when we run toward the prize. Paul put it this way: "I press toward the goal for the prize of the upward call of God in Christ Jesus" (Philippians 3:14). With each life experience, we have the opportunity to gain needed attributes, such as perseverance, self-control, courage, endurance, determination, discipline, trust, confidence, and improved decision–making skills. Our faith and trust increases immensely. We learn to dream big and advance into God's ultimate purpose for us. We forget what was behind us, and we move toward the goal before us.

I journeyed through many seasons of life and saw the power of God. God wants increase in our lives and sometimes stretches us in the process. So much in life is just waiting for us. Once I realized this, I did not want to slow down. I wanted everything God had for me and not one iota less. I got off the sofa and started from where I was. As I walked in faith, I learned about trust while gaining insight and answers to life. God has an answer for life's traumas. Much life is ahead for you younger readers.

Perhaps the reader can apply some of the hard lessons I learned in life to themselves and learn from my experiences. We can also take advantage of the traumas, Goliaths, and desert times that others and that we experience along the way. These incidents can help to further God's kingdom work. So many opportunities are available to help with the healing process. My desire and goal in writing this is to encourage each reader to let go and let God take your hand and show you the way. When I first became single, I had absolutely no idea what was available and ahead of me. That is why I'm excited to share my story.

I once was young and now am older; therefore, my get-up-and-go has slowed way down. If I were younger, I would still be doing the work God had for me as a mission's counselor on the other side of the world. But at eighty years of age, it might be time for me to settle down. However, I can still offer a helping hand and have opportunities in the world. Healing happens when we stay busy helping and comforting others. The more we give of ourselves, the more we seem to receive. It really is more blessed to give than receive (Acts 20:35).

The sky is the limit when you are available to help others. If you can't reach the stars, maybe you can reach the moon. I like shooting high enough to avoid hitting the ground. Life becomes less stressful and smoother when we hold hands with the Creator. He has a great destiny for you and me, and you will love it.

Each disruption in life is an opportunity for learning that can help us spread our wings and fly. Life becomes more comfortable when we lean on God and learn his ways. We learn to enjoy being unique, single, and whole. A merry heart does well like medicine (Proverbs 17:22).

Singleness after marriage can be satisfying when we let God guide us. Scripture tells us, "The unmarried woman cares about the things of the Lord" (1 Corinthians 7:34). I realize that singleness is not for everyone. However, until fully healed, staying busy and single for a time may be an answer. God is very capable of granting a spouse to the single person who desires this. His timing is always the best, and healing from divorce takes time.

It is important for a single to be content, happy, whole, unique, and able to stand on their own two feet before approaching a second—or even a first—marriage. Wholeness means knowing who you are in the Lord. We are a peculiar people, a royal priesthood; in other words, we are God's special children who he dearly loves (1 Peter 2:9). All marriages take work. Therefore, we need to know who we are before we enter another relationship. We want to avoid carrying surplus baggage into a relationship. We want to leave that U-Haul filled with backgrounds, traditions, experiences, exposures, habits, and unhealed issues behind us. Life often consists of working through issues. In other words, take your time before saying "I do."

We serve a God who gives second chances. We know who we are in him in our uniqueness as individuals. Yet we are to walk in his footsteps. Occasionally, I wonder why it took me so long and why it was so difficult to let go of issues after becoming single. But after a struggle of wanting my way, I finally let God begin the healing process. This doesn't mean I gave up on my marriage or that I agreed to the separation. Instead, I came to the point where I realized I needed healing, and whichever way the marital situation went, I trusted God and what he wanted to do in my life. I prayed, "Thy will be done, Lord Jesus," and I just expected God to return my husband. In reality, I was still expecting "my will" to be done. I was still a back seat driver.

You and I have free will. It takes two to be in an agreement and to want a marriage to be reunited. If I wanted this marriage to be rekindled but my spouse did not, we were not in agreement. We were expressing our individual free will. It was time for me to give this situation to God and to say, "Lord Jesus, this is in your hands. Whatever happens, I know you will heal and take care of me and our children. I will let go, and if we are reunited, it must be the will of each of us. If not, I will be in your hands and trust in you."

This statement was hard as my expectation was that God would somehow, someway, change my husband's mind. By letting go, I relinquished my will, and God was now beginning to heal and strengthen me. I focused on healing and caring for my children and myself. Letting go was a process. I would be happy if he did return, and if not, I would make the decision to live life without him and become happy.

I share more truths I learned along the way in this chronicle. The seed of "letting go" germinates in the darkness, in the soil deprived of sunshine. The seed dies to itself in order to live and become fruitful. We learn to let go and let God take over. We do not blame God if our spouse does not return. We trust God for healing and to guide us into the next phase of our lives.

We, then, with high expectations, experience God's faithfulness and the blessings of letting go of each illusion that held us back for years. Letting go lowers our blood pressure and slows us down. This ultimately stops our head from spinning as we gain assurance and authority in the Lord. We mature, and exercise our spiritual muscles so that they become stronger. We realize that only God can take care of matters that are beyond our reach.

"The steps of a good man are ordered by the Lord, and He delights in his way" (Psalm 37:23). If we can get a grip on this, it will help guide our lives. Believers will be able to live—not just exist—until they die. The previous Scripture was the first given to me after I became single. As a new born-again believer in Jesus Christ, I was somewhat perplexed about how to trust the Lord and put my rational thoughts behind me. In time, it became easier to relinquish control and let God take over.

My life became more peaceful once I learned to let God work things out. I was thankful for those years of marriage, our military journey, and especially for the blessing of my five daughters. All of this increased my awareness of married life to include both the joys and struggles. I better understood what a single parent experiences. Most importantly, I gained insight into many biblical concepts.

Today, after years of spiritual growth as a born-again Christian, trusting is easier. This faith journey increases with each day. When we allow God to step in and see his consistency in caring for our every need, we can let go of our fears and anxieties. I will admit, however, this faith journey did not happen overnight but took time.

We give the situation to God, and he begins to work in us and free us so that we are not stuck. We are no longer a back seat driver. When we realize that each person has free will, we know that whatever happens, happens. But when we try to push our will onto others, we steer the car. We are totally in charge of the car instead of allowing God to drive.

To say, "your will be done, Lord Jesus," means I give up my will, regardless of what my will is. When we give God complete control, we are saying, "Whichever way this goes God, I accept that." God wants families to come together, yet God has given each person a free will. It takes two wills in agreement to reunite the family.

Yes, giving God full control is easier said than done. I was good at saying, "Your will be done," yet I expected the outcome to be according to my will. I trusted that we would reunite. After all, I prayed, and my family, friends, the church, and many prayer warriors prayed. I had the result all figured out.

By letting go, I was relinquishing my total will. At first, for a brief moment, I wanted to die. But this was senseless as I had five beautiful daughters; they needed restoration as well. "Lord, I want to live for you and for the children you have given me. You have so greatly blessed me with the beautiful gift of children."

Many times, I said, "Maggie, give it up. Let God intervene." Over and over, I repeated this until that day came. I remember exactly where I was standing and what took place to make that decision. It took strength, endurance, desperation, and a broken spirit that encouraged me to give it up. I was standing in the middle of a school courtyard, working as a teacher's aide. I had dropped many pounds. The sparkle in my eyes had dimmed, and my hair became frosted nearly overnight. I was a sad sight. Possibly if I had released control sooner, I might have been well on the road to recovery.

The strength I gained from managing the household while my husband served in Viet Nam on two yearlong occasions had weakened. Military wives stand firm and somehow muster up the courage to keep the family together while their spouses are absent. Military life contributed to my resilient nature. I was sure with each passing day that our family protector would return. God knew differently, and it was best to let the much-needed healing and strengthening process begin. At some point, we just need to put our hope and trust in God's hands and fully hand over the situation to him. I needed to get out of the way and let God do what he needed to do.

Often, I tell the story in jest that the Lord was talking with Gabriel and Michael and telling them that Maggie girl down on earth was about to find herself single. God knew my upbringing would aid in the healing process. His healing hand would touch my life and place me in a position to comfort others in similar situations.

This episode and season in my life would help and give hope to others going through tough times. Yes, he knew what was ahead. He would not let me die and wanted me to live. He had great plans for my life that included times in an international airport, a 747 aircraft alone yet in his presence. I would need endurance, strength, trust, and faith. He whispered in my ear, "I am with you. Do not be afraid. You can do this, Maggie."

He waited patiently until that day when I could say, "Lord, your will be done. If our family is reunited, I would love it. If not, I know you will take care of my daughters and me." You bottle my tears (Psalm 56:8). They are precious to you. You guide my way. "I will instruct you and teach you in the way you should go" (Psalm 32:8).

14

Singleness—The Word Is Out

Once the word was out that I was single, men began to track me down before the ink was even dry on the divorce papers. Divorce and marriage announcements were posted in our local newspaper. So the word was out for the world to see. Men constantly made persistent phone calls to my home and office. They pursued and wooed me.

A few of these men looked me up and down. They said, "How could a man leave you?" Some of these men calling on me were acceptable; others, not at all. Some were married; others were single or divorced. Some were prominent, honest, and seemed sincere. I questioned the motives of others. I knew a few of these men; others, I did not know.

Once, my doorbell rang at midnight, and after numerous rings, this person returned to his car and drove off. That was scary. The bottom line was that I was not looking for a replacement for my spouse. And even if I were, I needed to wait for a year or two until after I went through healing.

At this point, I was only interested in pursuing a relationship with Jesus, my Creator and the Creator of everything. The time came for a closer walk with the God of the universe, and his name is "Wonderful, Counselor, Mighty God, Everlasting Father, Prince of Peace" (Isaiah 9:6–7). He, and only he, could give me complete peace of mind. I desired an intimate relationship with Jesus of Nazareth, the one who knew me before I was born, the Creator who knew me inside and out.

Paul tells us, "He who is unmarried cares for the things of the Lord— how he may please the Lord. But he who is married cares about the things of the world—how he may please his wife" (1 Corinthians 7:32–33). In his infinite ways, God heals and brings peace and satisfaction. I see singleness and serenity as an extraordinary gift in my life. A life of celibacy takes discipline and a positive attitude. Now I know this lifestyle might sound unusual and even unhealthy or a bit strange. However, that was the way it was, and I fully recognize this was a God-given gift, a wonder in itself.

After enjoying marital intimacy, living a life of self-restraint was a wonder in itself. Abstinence requires self-control, discretion, and God. I think we just might add discernment and insight. I had to make wise decisions about dating. Why would I go hiking on the other side of the mountain with a man I scarcely knew, on a first date no less, even if hiking were my forte? Why would I consider watching TV with a man in his home who looked me over from head to toe as if I were a meal? Perhaps I sounded like a killjoy, which was perfectly okay. With years of marriage and intimacy, I was familiar with how privacy works. I was human. Sex, within my marriage, was for intimacy, pleasure, and procreation.

When I became single, I was in search of the Creator—the one who told us that he would never leave us or forsake us, the one who said he loved us with an unconditional love. Our bodies are holy temples; the Holy Spirit lives within us. Now I sound preachy! I am just openly sharing my convictions according to my understanding of the Bible. "Oh, do you not know that your body is the temple of the Holy Spirit who is in you, whom you have from God, and you are not your own" (1 Corinthians 6:19). God is a loving, caring God.

Teenagers may be timid about admitting they are virgins. In a similar way, a middle-aged single woman would feel this way about living a life of sexual restraint. Please know I am not condemning anyone. Cohabitating may mean one or the other has a difficult time with commitment. Without commitment, it is easier to leave the relationship. Even with commitment, people leave marriage, yet they are more likely to think twice before doing so. But when we fall, he forgives us.

I have experienced my partner leaving his commitment to me. It was a challenging situation to be in and to overcome. I am forever thankful our heavenly Father gives us the opportunity to do something different and that he gave us a second chance.

Meanwhile, my total satisfaction was focused on being about my Father's business and caring for my daughters. Maybe if I had never been married, my story might have been different. However, I am nearing forty years as a single, seeking our Creator during that whole time. No, I am not weird. I want to insert a smiley face here about right now.

He lives and reigns within my heart and your heart. What a privilege. "And if Christ is in you, the body is dead because of sin, but the Spirit is life because of righteousness . . . the Spirit of Him who raised Jesus from the dead dwells in you" (Romans 8:10–11). "In Him, we live and move and have our being" (Acts 17:28).

My marriage and my singleness both consisted of gratifying years. I value the insight gained in each season. The stimulating seasons continue to benefit me, even more so through the years as a counselor. Both seasons have included much happiness, and certainly, at times, life could have been better. My years of marriage offered the gift of a better understanding of a marriage relationship when I counseled married couples. As I previously mentioned, remaining single is not for everyone. It just happens to be right for me. We are each uniquely made, which is a beautiful exclusive gift in itself.

There was a certain man I did not know and had never seen before. Maybe he knew my high school daughters and heard about our family situation through the grapevine. This man sat down and scooted beside me while a daughter and I were sitting on the high school gym bleachers, watching another daughter's basketball game. The daughter sitting next to me quickly positioned herself between us. This same daughter scurried between us as he followed us to my car. As young as she was, she instinctively knew that she should be protective of me.

I often felt vulnerable. When a newly divorced woman is trying to make sense out of what has just happened, she might be confused when men actively pursue her. On the other hand, she might be comforted to know that she is attractive to someone, and it may even increase her self-esteem. When abandoned, a recently divorced woman may be dealing with feelings of low self-worth. I also know about these emotional challenges.

I continually prayed for a hedge of protection around our home, the home that now housed six vulnerable single females of various ages. (See Job 1:9–10.) I prayed that the angels in heaven would surround our house and asked for one to stand at each entrance. I still repeat this prayer today on occasion.

Scripture tells us, "The Lord will destroy the house of the proud, but he will establish the boundary of the widow" (Proverbs 15:25). My daughters were very protective of their mother, and their mother was likewise protective with each of them. They used to say, "Any man that pursues my mom will have to go through an examination and five interrogations—one per daughter!"

Well, after turning down date requests, I asked God to stop these inquiries. I was uncomfortable with my usual reply, "I will let you know." I knew from the start that I was not interested in pursuing a male relationship, other than with the Healer of my broken heart—the Great Physician who understood my grief (Jeremiah 30:17; Proverbs 4:20–22). I only wanted God in my life, the one who sincerely and lovingly knew my heart (1 Samuel 16:7; Psalm 26:2).

Even though I was divorced, I still hoped that, eventually, the father of my daughters would return. I was willing to take him back until he said, "I do" to another woman. That door then closed. One very eligible single man told me, "You just don't get it. I send you flowers. We bike many mornings before our work day began, and you still don't get it! Did you think I was doing all of this for no reason?" I saw this man only as a brother and was only interested in friendship. I guess I was what you might call naïve. Later, I was invited to his wedding as a guest.

Well, God heard me and honored my plea, and telephone calls and visits mostly stopped. I was so happy about this. Can you imagine being happy because no men are pursing you? It definitely was not that way in high school. God, in his unique way, honored my request and ended the pursuit. Possibly the word spread, "That woman is *not* looking for another man." I think it's time to insert another smiley face.

Perhaps these men had a nudge or an unseen vision of the colossal angel Gabriel or Michael in armor with a sword in their sheath, standing boldly at the office or front door of my home. Or maybe they breathed heavily into phone conversations. Maybe Gabriel just shook his head as if to say, "Not this one. She belongs to the Creator of the universe. He has great plans and a purpose for this single gal."

This story may seem funny, yet it is factual and happened at the beginning of my journey as a single. I was simply focused on pursuing a relationship with God.

You probably wonder why I'm sharing this rather personal story in such vivid detail. I do hope you readers find this story somewhat humorous. Well, I believe there is life after divorce and even another marriage for some people, but first, the person must heal. The length of time for healing can vary. It took longer for me than perhaps for others I know. The relationship within the marriage may be one factor that affects this. Some people may want out the day after their wedding.

Secondly, we need time to find out just who we are in the Lord. We must realize just how much the Creator of the universe loves us. I did not seek a divorce, yet this healing period was an excellent time to allow the Lord to touch my life as I have never experienced it. Pain has a way of drawing us to God, perhaps like nothing else. The pain of a divorce, the rejection, and the break of trust all need substantial healing. Becoming single through death, the loss of a loved one, the loss of children, or the loss of a home can traumatize a person to the depths of their soul. Ultimately, God is the healer. This might be a time to step out of the boat to explore the qualities, gifts, and talents from the Lord. Some people are interested in pursuing these gifts, while others might not be. There is only one of you, and God has special gifts and talents for each one.

As single individuals, we have the opportunity to find out who we are. We discover our uniqueness. We all need to be able to stand alone, to become whole, and to know who we are before starting another relationship. We need to know who we are for ourselves and who and what God created us to be.

While in the military and as an officer's wife, the military police saluted me—or maybe, they recognized the sticker on our automobile when I drove onto the base. I was important because of my husband's status. That ceased once I became single. But when I drove up to the entrance of the international school in the Philippines, the guards saluted me, or, again, maybe they noticed the sticker on the car. In any case, I was overjoyed because I was sure the Lord was behind this and winking at me. He was showing me and reinforcing that I was his precious daughter. Perhaps in his own loving way, he was encouraging me and showing his approval that had nothing to do with a sticker.

Scripture tells us that "without a vision, people perish" (Proverbs 29:18 KJV). A Jesus vision helps direct our path within us. "A man's heart plans his way, but the Lord directs his steps" (Proverbs 16:9). Singles need to find themselves before leaping into another relationship too quickly. First, try focusing on a relationship with God and become involved in church, small groups, or a Bible study. Seek counseling, preferably Christian counseling. "If God is for us, who can be against us?" (Romans 8:31).

Just for the record, I truly like and respect men. Please know I am not against men. I like to hear from them and converse with them, and I value the male perspective. A man's view helps me to evaluate my female sensitivity and to strive for balanced decisions in matters of life and the world.

A colleague helped me shop for my first computer. I knew virtually nothing about them. In time, all employees were given a personal computer for their work desk. But for a time, I was the only one that knew very little, if anything, about this computer. Many nights, I burned the midnight oil at the office after work, trying to become acquainted with this machine. I was intentional about learning, and finally, I did manage to grasp the basics. At times, I went home in near hysteria. I was sure I blew up the entire city system. Once I started college, all homework needed to be done on a computer or a typewriter. It was either pick up the needed computer skills or work with the annoying carbon paper and deal with white out on a typewriter. Since then, the laptop has become my cherished friend.

I also consulted with a male friend when purchasing a car, home, a home cooling system, and even a microwave. Remember, I am now eighty years of age, so although I was not born in the horse and buggy days, it was shortly after that. I knew their wives, and often, they were involved in the conversations. My objective was to find the right equipment when I knew very little. I also searched the consumer's publication. We can now search the web for answers. A man even taught me how to white roof coat my house. I learned a great deal through the guidance of my male friends. One friend helped me with finances too.

Throughout the years, I learned to take care of the essential tasks. While working for the city, the purchasing procedure called for three estimates. I carefully follow this rule in my personal purchasing. We learn as we grow, and we grow as we learn. The consumers taught me how to buy a car. The dealer mentioned that I did a great job. Some years ago, I purchased a home. With the home purchase, I experienced buyer's remorse. In time—with lots of time—I worked my way into being happy in this home and profited when it sold. I did not learn these skills overnight, yet in time, I did learn. My children have picked up on these important skills as well.

I also was and still am intentionally seeking and developing a spiritual relationship with God and his Word. This intentional living is a discipline as well. I want to know him and pursue him. I will continue this until I pass into glory. In good conscience, I do not know how to live without him. A newly single woman and sole parent faces many responsibilities. So I needed time and involvement with a church and church family. God brings people and opportunities for mentoring, guidance, and walking beside you. The single, however, must get up and go out, as hard as this may seem at times.

Healing and adjustment take time, and a rebound relationship is not the answer before you know who you are in the Lord. We tend to blame God for our divorce and misfortunes, especially if we are Christians. But remember, we live in a sinful world with right and wrong. Wrongs get us into trouble. The good news, however, is that God is available to pick up the broken pieces of a tattered heart, to help us stay sexually pure, and to run from a rebound situation.

With our eyes and hearts focused on him, healing is inevitable. And there is even more good news. If you desire to remarry, God can fulfill your dreams. Most of all, remember adjustment takes time. Through it all, the single might come to be satisfied.

Employment, college, workshops, and church are excellent ways to meet people. Mental and emotional healing takes time. Volunteer work is another great way to meet others. When we give of ourselves and help others, we begin to feel healthy inside. We forget about the trauma, and in time, before we realize it, we are on the path to healing and wholeness. Residents at the nursing home, the hospitals, or even shut-ins are waiting for someone to visit them. You might become a softball coach or teach Sunday school. It's amazing how a kind gesture can boost our morale.

We sometimes even see that others are in worse shape than we are. We get and give an extra dose of love, and that feeling of helping others motivates the happy endorphins. These feel-good hormones can help keep us on track. Now I know this isn't for everyone, but the idea of staying busy and useful does wonders for the soul. As a retiree, I still visit hospital patients to keep my endorphins active.

Healing requires a close walk with our Creator. We are learning to trust him and look to our heavenly Father for needs and direction. We must take the initiative to become involved with other mature people. God is the lifter of our heads.

Becoming a single in the middle of life is difficult, yet this is also a time to tighten our relationships with our children. They need structure and a stable parent. They might become traumatized when their parents are no longer together and can even blame themselves for the breakup of the family. Children will stabilize once they see mom and dad stabilize.

In my opinion, entering a new relationship other than a relationship with our Lord and Savior is not the answer. God can bless you and bring a new spouse into your life if this is the desire of your heart. Meanwhile, take the time to heal as this is essential for both the single and the children.

God can fulfill our every need. One day at a time, one step at a time, we trust, heal, and learn more about God Almighty. Become intentional in a walk with him while you develop into a whole person as a single.

I will end this chapter with a little humor. When working with the older adults during my first years as a single, a senior lady said. "Maggie, you need to start looking for a man before you get too old as men like younger women." These seniors just said whatever was on their minds. I loved and valued working with this age group as a senior citizen recreation supervisor. They enjoyed teaching me interesting life issues.

15

Back to College—
In the Classroom as an Older Adult

Who would have thought I would enter employment that I loved and that this employment would take me into the classroom and pay my tuition fees? God loves you and me and has the best waiting for us.

I began to talk about attending college with a colleague after a short time at my city job. This was a big move. Was I ready to step into the classroom? College required commitment, determination, discipline, and time. My plate was already full as head of household, full-time employee, and mom of five active growing daughters. Was there room for one more item on this plate? Several years went by before I could even imagine stepping in the classroom. During this time, I was still in the process of healing from the divorce.

However, after much talk and time—perhaps a few years—a colleague began to challenge me. "Maggie, you are all talk. We've heard this school talk for a long time. How about some action?" Yes, my colleague was right. I talked a lot while trying to muster up the courage to begin both a stimulating and scary study expedition. I was adjusting well to being a single parent. Time, adjustment, and a busy life aided in my healing. This healing and adjustment period was not just about me but about my daughters as well. And a part of me did not know if I could buckle down and tackle the books.

I asked myself a hundred times over. *Could I add college to my already busy schedule*? Finally, the day arrived to set foot onto the campus grounds of the local community college. I followed the signs to the administrative office.

The thought of class pre-requisites was chilling. I knew I had much to learn. I was okay socially; formal education was another issue, yet I felt exhilarated.

Thankfully, each college contact welcomed me with a smile and an inspirational word. The counselor and administration staff instilled certainty and kindness and left me feeling hopeful and positive. My confidence increased with each step. The college staff had a way of building and boosting my self-assurance.

God's favor, grace, and blessings all worked together and made it happen. I entered this world with positive thinking, persistence, and patience. I hit the panic button on occasion but usually not for long. Well, it certainly could have been worse. I often thought, *You can do this, Maggie*. I knew that, within my every cell, God had opened this door of opportunity. My employer provided the finances.

My placement scores reflected a significant need for a brush-up course in math and English skills. The English scores, however, were better than my math score. The best place to start was with remedial classes. I recognized a few math problems on the pre-entrance test but forgot how to find the answer. The entire test was a guessing game. I handed the unmarked placement exam back to the proctor. She said, "Maggie, you know, by handing this placement assessment back without any answers, you will automatically be placed at the bottom level of the math class." I agreed and just handed it back with a smile.

The math proctor was a very soft-spoken middle-aged gray-haired woman. She was youthful in appearance and smiled with both her mouth and her eyes. She became one of my biggest cheerleaders. Her warm smile and heart won me over. She always seemed to be available and sat behind the study hall tutor's desk or nearby. She offered suggestions and guidance and became an excellent coach and cheerleader. Oh yes, Mrs. Jewel was a godsend. I will forever be grateful for her encouragement and availability. I think she was one of God's angels disguised as a college freshman coach and cheerleader.

I kept thinking that if I worked from the bottom up, I would not mess up in the middle of the required math classes. By God's amazing grace, the back-to-college days began amid full-time employment and caring for my family and our home. I started the journey to becoming an accomplished college student. In just a few classes, my memory about how to find the math answers returned. I easily aced the class, I am happy to report. My English teacher also mentioned that she enjoyed my stories.

Those first brave steps into the college classroom led me to becoming a lifelong learner. Initially, I did have to work on that big elephant that filled the room—managing my time. Where do you begin when the plate is so full? I learned about eating an elephant. Yes, it takes one bite at a time to eat an elephant. When the elephant is big, you take many bites and take a long time to eat.

How does a student with a full-time job focus and finish one assignment and then the next? The journey began and so did the tears of joy, disappointment, and wonder. However, God's gift of perseverance and purpose helped me stay focused. With focus and courage, in time, the elephant began to shrink. I started the journey to focus on discipline, determination, and the ultimate decision that I would be busy for a time.

The beginning years at our local community college crept by one class at a time. Yes, one more completed level, seldom two, during each semester, and then repeating college Algebra made for an added detour. Starting at the bottom of the math prerequisites called for more perseverance on my part than I had anticipated. College algebra had me spinning my wheels. Repeating the class was discouraging.

Oh no, not a repeat of algebra. Help me, Lord Jesus. At the end of round two, I realized just how much this second algebra class pulled the pieces of the puzzle together. No, I did not receive an A, but I did pass with a strong grade. Fortunately, my younger years taught me to persevere, to hang in there. From early on, this determined spirit was ingrained in my every cell. I was familiar with blood, sweat, and tears. My pillowcase became acquainted with and hid a few algebra and college student tears.

In time, I received my associate's degree—what an exciting feeling! Then I was off to earn my bachelor's degree. The steps were small yet steady. This first marathon race ended in total victory—so many classes, miles, and years, filled with mixed emotions, some tears and much joy and satisfaction. Even today that pomp and circumstance tune brings tears, tears of reminiscing and joy.

A few years later, I began my graduate program. The miles again were significant: a seventy-five mile jaunt to class and home again, one-hundred-and-fifty miles round trip. After a few classes, I dropped out for a season. Classes were now interfering with work. What I didn't know at the time was that God had the best plan up his sleeve, an easier shorter route. In just a short time, I would be in a different setting.

Unknown to me, he would lead me to the big city. The one-hundred-and-fifty miles to class and home twice a week was now shortened to an eight-minute trip to an accredited university campus. More details follow in the coming chapters.

A Scripture that spoke to my heart through the years is: "If the ax is dull, and one does not sharpen the edge, then he must use more strength, but wisdom brings success" (Ecclesiastes 10:10). My ax was beginning to sharpen. Even today, this Scripture speaks volumes to me.

This was the start of a life of formal learning, which eventually took me to the other side of the world. Notice that I said "start." God had more work for me before I embarked on the visits to the other side of the world. Let me tell you more about this side of the world first.

I was surprisingly accepted to join a Barnabas Ensemble Team to travel to Africa in 1993. Graduate classes surely would have interfered with this trip, so I took a leave of absence from the graduate program, which worked out nicely. You will read more on this particular trip in an upcoming chapter.

I had many opportunities after my divorce. Yes, I received many telephone calls, drop-ins at my place of work, etc., but God had other plans for me. Think of what I would have missed had I taken on one of the men that expressed an interest in me. I believe in some unknown way, God kept me from entering another relationship.

Scripture talks about the younger women marrying again, and I am certainly in favor of what Scripture says. That desire was not given to me and was not for me. One might ask, "How do you know this if you never gave dating a chance?" And that's basically true. I did not give dating a chance. I had worthy male friends, yet dating and marriage a second time around was not for me. Maybe I did not give it a chance as it was not in my heart. My covenant was for my married partner and our children, and I have never regretted my decision. As I mentioned previously, I believe God gives us our desires. I loved my first marriage, which was exceptional, except for the last few years. The positive part satisfied my view and desire to be married.

Life as a single was busy and eventful. My employment and study time offered great satisfaction. My daughters needed healing in their lives, and I wanted to be there for them. Remember, I grew up without a father. I knew the sad feeling of not having a daddy around. My mom held our family together. She and I just decided to remain single.

God sent a couple into our lives to mentor us. They were with us many years until both went to be with Jesus. Their presence blessed and fulfilled the lives of my daughters and me, and we forever miss them and are grateful for them.

Now people have mentioned that my children could have had a wonderful, God-fearing stepdad, and yes, I certainly agree. I know many amazing stepdads sent by God. I believe God gave me this gift of single-ness, which I do see as a gift. Singles are free to "go into the entire world" (Matthew 28). Remember, as a young child, after the missionary spoke to our elementary class, I wanted to become a missionary. This desire was ignited in my heart for many years and then became dormant for many years.

This desire again was awakened once my life changed. I believe God let this missionary desire go dormant while I was a wife and mother. Somewhere along the line, after becoming single, this desire awakened. Unbeknownst to me, God was preparing me for the mission field. I was in need of study and a degree to fulfill the missionary requirement I hoped for. This sequence of events and how my single life came together is nothing short of amazing.

How do I begin to express in words the feeling of this accomplishment? A single mom completes her college education. Her children graduate with diplomas from high school, and several graduate from college. This achievement is all due to God and his unconditional love, mercy, and grace for his children.

In turn, I wanted to openly honor my Lord and Savior with this degree. This adventure and accomplishment were to honor and glorify the one who made it all possible. At the same time, I had the opportunity to openly honor my mom. She encouraged me and prayed for and supported me all the days of my life.

As a young widow, she, by the grace of God, kept her family together. She often spoke of her school days and how proud she was to have completed eighth grade. Her beautiful diploma and near-perfect attendance certificate hang in a prominent place on my wall in a frame.

More importantly, I saw God's faithfulness in this college pursuit as well as how he took care of my home and children. When I was down, he lifted me through his Word, family, and friends, and even my wonderful community college coach. The gracious proctor encouraged me with an occasional comment or a simple gesture, a wave, a touch on the shoulder, or just by saying, "You've got this, girl."

I started college in 1983 and completed all my required classes and graduated in 1990 when I was fifty years old. By this time, all the girls had graduated from high school. We had college graduates and wedded daughters and even grandchildren in the family. Life was a test, yet God made a way for us. He planted a determining and tenacious spirit within each of us.

Shortly after receiving my BA, the Retired Teachers Association invited me to their monthly meeting, which met at my workplace. Many teachers knew me when I was a teacher's aide at their school. These now-retired, vibrant teachers loved their children. I watched their students on the playground, in the lunchroom, and sometimes tutored them in the hallway near their classrooms.

I admired and appreciated the steadfastness within each teacher in this particular elementary school. These educators held a special place in my heart and obviously appreciated their positions and their students.

As I entered the meeting room, I recognized most of the teachers. To my surprise, the president of the association called me to the front of the room. He proceeded to say many kind words about me before he handed me an honorary teacher's membership. He mentioned that I received my BA and that each of my five children graduated from high school and that a couple had graduated from college. He mentioned that this was not always the case with single moms. The Lord so graciously lifted my spirits with this kind gesture.

God made a way—an unexpected way or perhaps a predictable way—because God is just like that. We wonder when and how in the world a situation will work out, especially when we find ourselves single.

As we put our hand in God's hand, he sees us through life. He takes over if we allow him to do so. We realize that when he says, "Ask and we will receive" (see Matthew 7:7–8), he follows through. He is always available, trust me.

My story hopefully will encourage you to keep going through the ups and downs and even the could-be-better-times in life. God has a wonderful plan for you, the reader, as well. He will give you experiences, opportunities, and joys and will even stretch us during times of hurt and hopelessness. You and I are important to him. Psalm 139:14 tells us that you and I are fearfully and wonderfully made. This entire chapter of the Bible is worth memorizing. It describes his unconditional love for you and me.

God offers the opportunity to step out of the boat and into the classroom of life. He promises to guide his children through the calm water, the blustering wind, and the rough waves. He strengthens us when we are weak, and through his grace, we become strong. He wants to take you and me safely to the shoreline.

16

The Driver's Seat—My Need for Control

I once had to be the driver of the car that I traveled in. I felt that I had to operate this vehicle with my own two hands at the wheel and my own two feet at the pedals and my eyes looking down the road ahead and viewing the side and center mirrors. I had a great need to control this vehicle. This hang-up surfaced after my divorce.

During the divorce, in a sense, I lost control as I could not keep our marriage together. To compensate, I gained power by becoming the driver of the vehicle and not the passenger. I especially noticed the need to drive in a carpool situation. Consequently, I had to learn to release control or forget about joining the carpool. I needed to monitor others, and I struggled with trust.

I had to learn to sit back and enjoy the ride, which I did while married. I could snooze or snack, read or relax, watch the scenery, and even play games with our children. A passenger in a vehicle has plenty of benefits. "Have I not commanded you? Be strong and of good courage; do not be afraid, nor be dismayed, for the Lord your God is with you wherever you go" (Joshua 1:9).

Those were busy years with family activities, graduations, college, jobs, marriages, and grandchildren. In time, my maternal nest totally emptied. The endearing name of "grandma" filled the air. I learned to downsize the portion of food I had previously prepared for a large family. Leftovers for one or two meals were great, but now leftovers lasted a

week. Single life presented itself with countless opportunities for change in the quest for a new healthy, happy, healing endeavor.

Those years involved a regimen of obstacles to overcome, and by God's grace, my daughters and I worked through the many ups and downs. We were all growing, developing, and maturing over the years. Life moves on, whether or not we are ready. I appreciated my job, the people, projects, and the many events that came along with life. I had opportunities to volunteer.

I learned more about city policies and procedures, and my array of work-related responsibilities increased. The college interactions were stimulating and thought-provoking. I was learning to study and focus and to never, ever give up. It was an amazing time of faith and trust and maturing in my walk with Jesus.

Sleep came quickly each night, and I was blessed with sweet rest. No grass grew on the bottom of my feet during this season, yet for the most part, this season was such a delight. My deep-rooted pain from before was healing, and I could see that with God, there was life after divorce.

My dream as an elementary school child of becoming a missionary was still somewhat dormant within my spirit. With the innocence of a child, I was a big thinker. Yet through the years, the Scripture fastened to my bathroom mirror—Isaiah 40:31—told the story. I wanted to soar like an eagle. My mom taught me this Bible verse, and I heard it again in church and Sunday school. After becoming single, the desire to soar like an eagle strengthened by leaps and bounds. During this time, I was waiting on the Lord to renew my strength. "They shall mount up with wings like eagles, they shall run and not be weary, they shall walk and not faint" (Isaiah 40:31).

During those busy years, a refreshing night's sleep renewed my strength. God gives rest to his loved ones (Psalm 127:2). I was so happy to fit in the category of "his loved ones."

Our heavenly Father became my revered love and was central to me. I concentrated on "working as unto God" in all areas, particularly with my family, my employment, and even in college. This meant thinking hopefully, having a positive attitude, and being grateful for even the least little thing in life. Let's just say that my overall disposition was improving. I wanted to be a fully committed Christian.

My relationship with Jesus was flourishing in contrast to a few years earlier. As a single, I had more time to focus on Jesus. Let's face it, I desperately needed God. When we marry, we focus on family and on the things of the world. After inviting Jesus into my heart, my life began to change. Each day, I was transitioning into a new me. The ride was not always smooth as I faced plenty of various obstacles in life.

Yes, Jesus was always an influence in my marriage, but somehow, as a single, it was different. Raising a family and being a wife keeps women and mamas very busy. Life as a single is also busy, but that love he gives us makes life right and fun, and we learn to appreciate and dearly love the families he gives us and the people he brings into our lives.

When we are stuck, we can't move. This is like sitting on the fence, deciding which side of the fence to jump off. Sometimes we sit immobilized until our hinnies hurt. Let's face it, fence sitting is stressful and uncomfortable. We waste precious time, resulting in anxiety, which causes headaches, delays, and even missed opportunities. However, we can't sit there frozen forever. With the Lord as the leader of our lives, we might be more likely to take a risk. However, as we overcome many obstacles and hurdles in life, we find freedom.

We pray and seek direction. Brainstorming with a trusted, mature friend is helpful. Scripture tells us that "where two or more are gathered" God is in the midst. (See Matthew 18:20.) God speaks into our lives through his Word, the Holy Spirit, and friends if we take the time to seek him. We can take action once we make a decision.

I was now routinely asking God to open and close doors, according to his plan for my life. And yes, my ears were not always open to hearing; sometimes I was impatient. Waiting on the Lord is crucial. We learn to trust those reliable nudges from the Holy Spirit.

Experiencing peace and joy usually accompany a right direction. And of course, a wrong path can take us around the mountain a few more times. I have experienced right roads and detours and sometimes even getting lost. All in all, I am thankful for the second chances in life.

Wanting to mature takes work. We don't go to bed one night and wake up changed the next morning. While overnight change may be possible, this did not happen with me.

On our undergraduate university orientation day, among the dozen-plus pupils, two students lived in my area. The professor happened to ask where everyone lived. Was this a blessing in disguise? Carpooling was now an option. I had to deal with this attitude of taking charge and taking control. This undergraduate program would take two years of travel, two times a week, about one-hundred-and-fifty miles round trip. Did I want to drive by myself or join the available car pool? I could make a choice to sit and relax during two out of three trips.

Many firsts and changes had taken place during the past ten years. Was I ready for just one more? This decision called for a change in my life, one more turn for the better. I would face one more hurdle that would take a lot of work. I had one more opportunity to get rid of another hang-up. The undergrad students who lived near my home responded and agreed quickly and eagerly. *Hmmm, how will I answer?* How could we carpool?

Unknown complacency within a marriage can take over when two people are sharing responsibilities. It is great when couples pitch in together; Scripture even tells us that two are better than one. Regaining normalcy in life as a single takes persistence in transitioning from one stage to another. This new season calls for endurance to stay above water and to swim to the other side.

We become at ease in our comfort zone, our space, and our security blanket. One of my daughters functioned better while her security blanket tickled her nose with her thumb comfortably tucked in her mouth. In time, this blanket became tattered and torn, and her thumb, red and raw. Time to make a decision. "No, honey, this blanket needs to stay home while you are in school."

I had been holding on to my safe spot as the driver of the vehicle. Now what? This choice and challenge awaited an answer. Was I ready for the test of sharing the steering wheel while sitting in the passenger seat or embracing the comfort of the back seat? I visualized carpooling and all that went with it. I needed to make a decision.

I now had the opportunity to stop straddling the fence. As mentioned, straddling hurts our hinnies and causes stress, anxiety, headaches, stomach aches, and even high blood pressure. It was time to "just do it." Just give up that steering wheel. Yes, easier said than done.

God knew my days were long, and when we think about two years, that is a long, long time. The decision was mine. I could join the carpool or drive alone.

Taking turns and chauffeuring each other is an answer to prayer. Consider an eight-hour day at work, followed by a seventy-five-mile drive to class, followed by four hours of lectures, and a return trip after class at ten o'clock at night. Traveling the highway at almost midnight with companions is an answer to prayer, I thought.

Again I faced one more hurdle. Our kids today would say, "This carpool is a no brainer," and they are right. Carpooling was the way to go, but...oh, those buts. I would have to let go of fear in order to develop. Hang-ups can be so embarrassing, and sharing about them can be even more uncomfortable. "Oh, Lord, help me with this problem. I already know the answer! Give me the courage to make the right choice."

Life is filled with choices and challenges. When we learn to let go of personal baggage, we lighten life's load and journey. Why is this so hard? Think of all of the things we make do with in life. We leave home and venture out. One day, we wave and throw kisses as our children step into the school bus for that first time. Or when they leave for their first time at camp.

Our military husbands go off to war. Soon a year passes, and they return. Our children leave for college; eventually they get married. Some children move out of state; some move back home. We say good-bye to family and friends who die. Why do we struggle with giving up habits and disruptions that are a total inconvenience, troublesome in many respects, and a disruption in life?

Now I needed to work on something else as I let go and learned to relax in the passenger seat or the back seat or travel alone for two years. The process of letting go helped me develop my faith and trust. I began to reap the benefits of freedom.

Thank goodness, with time and thought, and yes, prayer, my need to be in control as a driver was behind me. I learned to relax in the passenger seat or back seat and partake in female chit-chat. We three ladies were exciting, fun, and shared the commonality of the army life. Moreover, we reviewed during the ride and prepared for class. With each trip, the two years grew shorter. That Circle-K Slurpee stop on our way home added to our routine and comradery.

The hang-ups can limit our opportunities to venture out. Did this happen overnight? No, it took a few trips, and with each trip, I released my need to be in control and learned to trust. The two years flew by. My turn to drive into the congested city traffic rolled around every third trip. With the benefit of relaxation, less gasoline, and the development of unique friendships, I experienced a deeper trust in God and even in myself.

I thought, *No need to worry. God is in control and teaches us through a process*. We learn to soar like an eagle. I liked that, and I bet you readers do too. This process was one more prerequisite for what God had in store for me.

In time, I was handed a credential for a job well-done. It was a great occasion, a time of that beautiful feeling of accomplishment in more than one way. I was soaring like an eagle and free of one more hang-up.

I was now a college graduate, feeling as if I had conquered the world. I presented my diploma to God to do with whatever he had in mind. I thanked my mom personally and through her local newspaper. Mom always prayed and had great faith in this middle child.

Proverbs 3:5–6 tells us to "trust in the Lord with all your heart, and lean not on your own understanding; in all your ways acknowledge

Him." I often referred to this Bible Scripture. This verse is an excellent verse to ponder. Perhaps our timing may not be the same as his, yet he always comes through.

Upon receiving my undergraduate diploma, I now reached the ten-year mark as a single, and my nest was almost empty. Who would ever have thought that God knew of this journey before I entered my mother's womb? He wanted this daughter to soar like an eagle: to be strong without fainting as I gained strength with each hurdle.

17

Elizabeth's Office Visit—Atonement

E lizabeth entered my office with my desk positioned between us, thus creating a barrier. She sat quietly as she looked me over. She didn't speak and appeared to be lost in thought. My office remained quiet for what seemed to be a long time.

I was trying to remember this somewhat familiar face. *Where have I seen her before? Who was this person, this older refined woman?* She knew me since she came to see me, or maybe she didn't! Who was she?

She mentioned something about the Senior Olympics to the receptionist. My mind was racing to recall who she was. What was her real reason for this visit?

Just moments before, the front receptionist had phoned to tell me that a woman was here and had asked to see me in my office. "I'm here," I replied to the receptionist. Footsteps echoed down the long hallway to my office. She passed six other offices before reaching my office.

I purposely requested the end office located near the back door entrance after this new addition to the building was completed. This spot gave me easy access to the older adult recreation area. It was a perfect short cut for the seniors to stop by my office and avoid that walk down the long hallway. Visitors had convenient access to my small office. It also afforded a firm sense of privacy.

My visitor plodded along as she took the long way to the front door. She finally arrived and seemed to be in a daze. Her feeble body was inflexible as she stepped into my office. I initially thought, *I will suggest that she join the sit-down senior exercise group.* I always encouraged older adults to join the various senior programs. Many seniors participated in the exercise class, held three times a week.

"Welcome. Please come in and have a seat," I said with concern. I pointed to a chair.

She stood quietly at the doorway for what seemed like a long time. Finally, she entered and sat down on the outer chair. Her eyes were fixed on me. After a few moments, she propped her cane at the edge of the chair. Perhaps she was contemplating a quick departure if necessary. She finally settled in, yet moments passed before she spoke.

I chit-chatted. "What a beautiful day we are having. It's a nice day to be out and about."

Elizabeth nodded in agreement yet seemed distracted. She appeared paralyzed and just stared at me. I sat still and waited for her to speak.

Finally, after a few moments, I said, "The receptionist said you wanted information about the up-coming Senior Olympics. You have questions and wanted to speak with me personally. I'm glad you stopped by. Have we met? Are you new to this area?"

I did sense that we had previously met; she seemed familiar, yet I couldn't remember how I knew her.

She finally said, "My name is Elizabeth." She continued, "I have lived in this town for most of my life. You and I casually met some years ago. My opinion of you at that time was not the best. I had listened to a one-sided conversation about you and believed your husband and his female friend. Since then, your name keeps showing up in the local media. Even through years have passed since your divorce, I am reminded of those incidents. Seeing and hearing your name in the media reminds me of listening to a one-sided story. All this made me want to meet you. Maybe my sense of guilt about remaining silent years ago and possibly even contributing to your family break-up still troubles me."

This older woman now had my undivided attention. I was curious and wanted to hear more of her story. I wondered how I would react if

I knew someone who was unfaithful to their spouse. Would I approach the innocent party, or let it ride?

I felt some relief at her words and was glad to hear her side of the story. I was also glad for the healing that had taken place in the lives of my children and me. Likewise, the Holy Spirit was alive and working within me as I listened without remorse. I even felt compassion for this woman.

Many years had passed since this incident. God's healing touch filled my every cell. God had definitely worked miracles within me and my children since the break-up of our family. He confirmed his work within me. I just felt sorry for this elderly woman who had carried this burden, perhaps for many years.

Her words were sincere and straightforward. Her visit and mind were occupied with purpose. As she spoke, her eyes stayed focused on me. She was looking me over. Was it my makeup? Or maybe she was just wondering, "So this is the woman."

Like a flash of lightening, in a moment, I recognized this elegant senior woman. The years had passed since we met, and our appearances had both changed with time, yet she resembled the woman I met years ago. Yes, I knew this lady despite the aging process. My memory was doing an excellent job of recalling. This prominent woman had hosted a party for her workers that I had attended with my husband. Suddenly, I saw myself standing alone in her small yet elegant apartment at the edge of her kitchen counter, feeling entirely out of place. A wide range of emotions swept over me. My husband was not as attentive as he had been in earlier times. That night, he spent time with other friends, people I did not know. That would have been fine had he invited me to join him, yet I was not included.

I just wished I were at home and wanted to leave. Down deep, I felt something wasn't right. I did not fit in with this crowd and felt like a misfit. The guests and my husband were in one room, and I was in another.

It's incredible how an event from years ago can suddenly sneak into your mind like a movie scene. The good news was that God had touched my heart since then and healed me from this hurt and other hurts of the past.

I chose not to let the memory of that night affect me. Old things had passed and newness restored my heart. "Therefore, if anyone is in Christ, he is a new creation; old things have passed away; behold, all things have become new" (2 Corinthians 5:17). Yes, I remembered that night, but God's goodness reestablished my soul.

Suddenly as I grounded my thoughts, I wondered, *Was this woman, by chance, here to speak of that night*? A whole lot of laughter and commotion had been going on in that other room. Did they miss me or even know my whereabouts?

In reality, I experienced both the role of an enlisted man's wife and an officer's wife during my twenty years as a military wife. On many occasions, I mingled with people in all stages of life, which my extroverted personality relished. Hand in hand, my husband and I joined in the troop conversations. If we were momentarily separated, we were mostly within close distance of each other.

This graceful woman suddenly broke into my train of thought. She carefully voiced her heartfelt words. I felt her effort, and her pain was evident as she spoke. Her voice and body trembled, her eyes teared up, and her words conveyed her sorrow. With sincere regret and sadness, she began to apologize. "I am so sorry. I am so sorry," she repeated with her teary eyes centered on mine. She was visibly grief-stricken, and the words poured from her heart. "I didn't know," she repeated. "I didn't know. I could have perhaps stopped or discouraged what I saw."

I wondered what she was trying to say. She continued, "I listened to one side of the story. I should have known better." She expressed regret, perhaps because of her behavior and maybe because a family broke up. At one point, she said, "You're so beautiful, so radiant. How could this have happened? How could I have only seen one side?"

She then quietly sat and stared without saying another word. She had lived with guilt and a noticeably heavy heart. Her words were so complimentary. "How could he leave you?" she asked.

The pieces of this puzzle were coming together. Elizabeth wanted time alone with me in my office to speak about the concerns of her heart. Who knows how long she had been troubled by this incident? How many times had I been guilty of similar regret? Yet God is a God of forgiveness. He wants us to experience his forgiveness, peace, and love.

This visit really blessed me. Regardless of the size of your regret or mine, God is bigger. He longs to bring forgiveness and heal our deep hurts, shames, disgraces, guilt, and our sins, regardless of how big or how small. His love for us is so great that it took him to the cross.

That sensitive, attentive conscience within, which I refer to as the Holy Spirit, actively nudges us. We know and feel the prods. We then decide: Do we want to give in to the lifesaving nudges or blast out words, actions, and offenses that we know only too well will cause remorse? God has given us a free will. Shout out or be compassionate.

We know what his answer to life is. We sometimes go against his will and follow our free will. The consequences can be devastating. A simple sentence, the statement can be expressed in many tones, which tells the story of the heart. We can also intentionally choose words that encourage and teach with no regret. "He who believes in Me, as the Scripture has said, out of his heart will flow rivers of living water" (John 7:38). "Keep your tongue from evil, and your lips from speaking deceit" (Psalm 34:13). "My heart is overflowing with a good theme" (Psalm 45:1). "My heart also instructs me in the night seasons" (Psalm 16:7).

Elizabeth's heart pain was intense. I felt her regret, yet I thought, *Good for you, Elizabeth. Not that you went along and may have encouraged this happening, but that you followed your heart, that Holy Spirit nudge, and expressed your apology.*

Elizabeth may not have known of the Holy Spirit. However, I'm sure she felt much better after her visit with me. Although she may still have some regret, she released her guilt. She broke the chains that had bound her. She listened to that nudge.

God graciously and generously wants to heal your pain and my hurts. His healing touch takes away our pain. I, for one, am thankful that the Lord had me at a place where my response to Elizabeth was one of acceptance, forgiveness, and empathy. Perhaps earlier, I might not have been so accepting. God's timing was at work. This visit and our time together were healing for both of us.

Expressing the right words is a healing ointment in itself. Likewise, using the wrong words has the potential to destroy. Here was a woman with great sorrow in her heart. This matter was of concern to her. Her last days on earth were nearing. Her heavy heart needed healing. Only God can free us from the burdens of sin. He then uses his children to reach out to others. We've been there and walked in the shoes of pain. We understand, sympathize, empathize, and can even lead another to the Lord.

I thank God for a testimony of his goodness in the lives of my daughters and me. This testimony displays a miracle. God is the Great Physician. He brings people into our lives to help us, to mentor, and to comfort; we, in turn, are then in the position to mentor and comfort others.

Divorce is devastating. It can bring about a complete testing of our faith. This disruptive time can tear us apart. And then we discover God has a way of picking us up and putting us back on our feet. He then makes good out of the devastation. God wants to draw you and me into a relationship with him. We go through a process of healing that takes time. We have an opportunity to experience a deeper walk with God and depend on him. We discover who he really is when we invite him into our lives.

We even take life for granted. We can be at a place where we think we know him. When we invite him into our hearts, head knowledge becomes heart knowledge; it is the most exciting happening in our lives.

Had I not gone through my painful time, I might have missed out on learning more about the depths of his love.

Elizabeth was getting up in years and was intent on taking care of unfinished business while she still could. By clearing her conscience and knowing that my family had found peace and were doing well, she, no doubt, had some comfort. The regret that she spoke of was history, and our family was moving forward.

The bumps and bruises take time to heal, and when we invite Jesus into our lives, the process goes a little more quickly. We then have the opportunity, by the grace of God, to overcome the adversities in life and to heal.

Elizabeth mentioned the Senior Olympic program when speaking with the receptionist, perhaps as a way of getting in the door. Yes, she did sign up and pay for the activity, yet she never showed up. A no-show may have been her intent from the start; however, in many respects, she was a blue ribbon winner. Her courage and fortitude took her to the finish line and brought victory into her life. This was another way to look at her atonement.

Elizabeth was instrumental in speaking kindness into my life. God had graciously crowned this daughter with his healing touch through her compliment. A sincere approval brings healing to the ears; an appreciated dose of good cheer, healing to the heart. God wanted her healed, and perhaps he wanted to reassure me that he knew the hurt and pain my family and I experienced. Maybe he just wanted to remind me of his blessed assurance, his special love for his children.

"I know the pain you experienced, Maggie. Remember that others also experience great pain, and you are now my hands and feet, my voice to reach out to them. As I have used others to help you in your time of pain and to bring healing, I have prepared you to be there for others who are also in need of a healed heart."

God's light shines through his children, and I would like to think that on that particular day, the light bulb was bright. One might say it was perfect timing on God's part as he gave me an extra dose of his love and poured love into Elizabeth's heart. Perhaps she experienced his peace and satisfaction and the feeling of "all is well with my soul."

I thanked Elizabeth for bravely following the nudges of her heart and for taking time to stop by. Her willingness, boldness, and actions were much appreciated. I pray that now her heart rests in peace. She wanted to see the other woman—me. She willingly humbled herself and told her story. She might have taken years to muster up enough courage to follow through with this visit. But she did it. On the other hand, had she not waited so long, she may have had fewer sleepless nights. I pray that as a result of our visit, her sleepless nights were turned into peaceful nights.

She ran the race. When we exhibit the fruit of God's Spirit and run the race set before us, we are winners. The training ground calls for perseverance, discipline, and self-control. This is where we develop the attributes of the fruit of the Spirit, which is even better than a blue ribbon (Galatians 5:22). We then have fought the good fight. We then are in the perfect position to help others win their race (2 Timothy 4:7).

"Our Father in heaven, Hallowed be Your name. Your Kingdom come. Your will be done on earth as it is in heaven. Give us this day our daily bread. And forgive us our debts, as we forgive our debtors. And do not lead us into temptation, but deliver us from the evil one. For Yours is the kingdom and the power and the glory forever. Amen" (Matthew 6:9–13).

18

Stepping Out of the Boat— Fear of the Water

"Be still and know that I am God" (Psalm 46:10). This verse speaks directly to my heart. In time, I learned to slow down and listen for God to say, "Go!"

The phrase "no pain, no gain" is certainly true when it comes to life. One of my daughters regularly works out and often encourages me to go to the gym as well. As a Silver Sneaker, gym membership is free for me. For years, I loved to walk to help me feel healthy. I even participated in Senior Olympics, so why do I avoid the gym now? I don't know!

Maybe it's because of my daughter's reminder that my body will hurt at first but will get used to the movement and stretching of my muscles. When we apply that to a spiritual analogy, we begin to develop and define our muscles as we face new challenges. We feel healthy and invigorated and begin to see results. We mature spiritually when we are intent on doing so. We will need to stay in the Word, take time for the Lord, and feed ourselves spiritually each day in order to stay healthy.

The imagery of mounting up with wings as eagles is on my list of favorite pictures. I want to mount up and soar for Jesus. God wants you and me to soar. Rising for Jesus is for everyone. We need spiritual guidance when dealing with the obstacles of life.

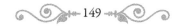

My life has been full of much adventure, contentment, and joy; however, some experiences have also come with discomfort and even pain. Even so, the triumph after the pain is worth the struggle.

As I mentioned, I experienced leg aches as a child, sometimes called growing pains. I stood on a stool to wash the dishes after supper, crying and complaining about this leg pain. The pain came in severe spurts for a time. Eventually, the pain lessened and disappeared. The next time my mom measured my height, I was taller. I liked that word: "tall." Spiritual maturity can also come with pain and in spurts.

In the same way that my body grew taller through the season of leg pain, I have grown in knowledge and wisdom of the Holy Spirit through the various trials of life that have come my way. I love studying and getting acquainted with Scripture. I like growing in the Lord more than I like going to the gym. Both working out at the gym and growing spiritually benefit us.

As a youngster, I spent time at Christian camps and 4-H projects and displaying my blue ribbon projects at the county fair and, occasionally, at the state level. After high school graduation, I applied for out-of-town jobs, including at Mackinac Island, a resort located a considerable distance from my home. My application was not accepted, because I needed to leave in the fall to attend college. I then found a job in Houghton Lake, which was still a ways from home yet not as far as Mackinac Island.

The journey of life is a process of one or two steps forward and, occasionally, a step backward. These steps took me from being a single and a busy parent to eventually traveling and residency in various countries and cultures. Holy Spirit nudges prompted me to get out of the boat and experience the water and the waves.

My wounded heart healed once I became acquainted with Jesus. My quivers—my many children—were eventually ushered into college and marriage, and I transitioned from many children at home to an empty nest. "Happy is the man who has a quiver full of them; they shall not be ashamed, but shall speak with their enemies in the gate" (Psalm 127:5).

Through the pleasurable and the unpleasant times, I purposed to weather the storm and swim to the other side. We can make it to the shore if we do not give up. Most importantly, when we invite Jesus to be our captain, success is assured.

While a single mom, I also worked as a part-time teacher's aide. I eventually became a full-time city employee and, after my nest was empty, went on to state employment and to a mission's counselor, providing stateside and overseas counseling services.

My employment began at an elementary school and eventually transitioned to a full-fledged family and child therapist mission's counselor in Papua New Guinea, followed by a mission's counselor in the Philippines. From the start of my employment to retirement, I faced the unknown. So why would I avoid the gym?

From the beginning to the present, my work history is a forty-year-plus journey. I labored attentively and intentionally. During those years, my spiritual muscles continued to become buff. My journey consisted of sunshine and stormy weather and growing from each weather condition.

Writing this story required much time, energy, and working the brain. My appreciation for authors, needless to say, has increased immensely. To do life well takes time, effort, and the Spirit of God. No matter what you do—mowing the lawn, painting a home, taking a test, writing a book, or even going to the gym—it all takes time and determination.

So many extraordinary life opportunities wait for a single, even as a woman. God uses ordinary people to do extraordinary exploits. The list is endless, and once the journey begins, it becomes addicting. My daughter tells me going to the gym can be addicting. I know she is right. At one time, for a full year, I diligently went to the gym and did achieve a more fit body.

Blessings come when we spend time in the Word of God. God offers infinite ventures. We grow spiritually in the Word and grow muscular in the gym. We become stronger, secure, and more stable in our Creator.

When we offer ourselves to God as a living sacrifice, he hears our appeal. He will answer the cry of our hearts. "Here am I, Lord, send me" (Isaiah 6:8). He knows our hearts. He knows our names as they are written on the palm of his hand (Isaiah 49:16). He knows the number of hairs on our heads (Luke 12:7). You and I are the apple of his eye (Zechariah 2:8). He cares for us (1Peter 5:7). People might forsake us, yet God never does. (Hebrews 13:5).

This is my testimony: God is the answer to life and all its problems. He is there for us. There is life after divorce, just as there was life after my father's death for my mother. Life is waiting.

During difficulties, God is available for us. He wants to heal broken hearts, pick up the pieces, and give us a brand new heart (Psalm 147:3). This journey might be slow but sure. When the uncertain times come—and they will—we cannot give up. Scripture tells us that the rain falls on the just and the unjust (Matthew 5:45).

No doubt, we have all experienced storms and sunny days in our lives. Anyone who responds with a "not me" is not being real. Our experiences, whether they are positive or negative, have the potential to bring us closer to God. "It is good for me that I have been afflicted, that I may learn Your statutes. The law of Your mouth is better to me than thousands of coins of gold and silver" (Psalm 119:71–72).

19

The Thirteenth Year— What Goes Up Must Come Down!

*J*esus suffered and had no sin within him and yet underwent persecution. He was spat at, whipped, beaten, mocked, and rejected. He was kind, caring, loving, and healed the lame, sick, and the oppressed. And he is available to heal you and me. A healing journey takes time and takes rolling up our sleeves. Life makes more sense when we invite God into our journey. He takes us ordinary folks and does the extraordinary in our lives. The hurts from a broken marriage can then be used for his glory.

I write this book from my experiences to spread the hope and joy of knowing him. Victims can become victorious. Our hurts offer the opportunity to comfort others when they go through challenges. When we invite God into our hearts, his work begins inside and works its way outward. He is the potter, and we are the clay (Jeremiah 18:1–9; Isaiah 64:8).

Without the scar of my divorce, I would not be who I am today. That scar forever reminds me of the Great Physician's work. He is the healer of broken hearts and the lifter of our heads. Consequently, I want to shout the good news of our heavenly healer.

Once we take the initiative to go wherever he sends us and do what he puts in our hearts, changing become more comfortable. We become more secure in our movements. Just like when we work out in the gym, we become more flexible when we continue to move in the spirit.

When I watched children at the elementary school playground, many of them needed someone to talk with and to care about them. After working as a teacher's aide, I grew mentally, emotionally, and spiritually and was ready for my next job. God healed me and opened the next door for employment, and I was more prepared and able to adapt. At just the right time, the city called me.

My work around the teachers, my colleagues, and children helped build my confidence so that I could accept another area of employment. In addition, this time helped me get my mind off my own problems. God used this group of helpers to minister to me while I was on the road to healing. God knew I needed the teacher's aide job before my city job. He knows more about us then we know about ourselves.

My next position brought even more healing. Tears of joy and tears from hurt produced a stronger character overall, just as focused work outs on the gym equipment developed muscles. I picked up more skills and readiness for the next advancement.

We start with baby steps, and they become bigger. We then learn to run. This process does not take place overnight. Remember, no pain, no gain, just as with working out at the gym to develop our physical muscles. I had much to learn, and thank goodness, God gave me a desire to do that.

I was asked to serve on a state committee. My boss encouraged me to accept this position. The city provided me with a vehicle and cash for meals in advance. His nudge to take this position was more urgent than mine was. The comfort of my office was my security blanket. I had no need or desire to leave the city. But God had different ideas for me.

I arrived in Phoenix safely and managed to navigate the underground parking. The stairs to the upper level took me into the center of gigantic skyscrapers. The courtyard sign directed me to the entrance, where the receptionist promptly pointed out the elevator to me. Another polite receptionist directed me to the meeting room near the top floor. Some people refer to these floors as the nose bleed section.

I asked where the stairs were. She chuckled respectfully and informed me that the stairs did not go that high. The elevator was the only way up. The idea of flight or fight entered my mind. I was afraid of elevators. If I ran, my journey would end in defeat, and I would return to my office in southern Arizona. What would my boss say? He had such faith in me and wanted me to have more opportunities.

The fight meant that I would get on that elevator, watch the doors close, and push the buttons that would take me to the top. Instead of perspiration, pure sweat covered me, which could not be wiped dry. I hoped the wetness would not drip down my legs. I was facing a serious problem. But the fight was intense and mighty within me. I was terrified of what was next. But I knew that I had to "just do it."

The receptionist assured me that the elevator was safe and that it would zip to the top in record-breaking time. Soon, I was near the sun. I went up many floors until I safely landed in the meeting room— the meeting room that I previously thought was on the first floor. My plan was to walk into this skyscraper and take a left or a right into the meeting room. Despite my fear, the thought of returning to my old office without attending this meeting was painful. I would be admitting inevitable defeat. So I pushed past my fear. My impact on the committee likely suffered as my mind was focused on the return trip down. After all, it's true that what goes up must come down.

My boss was pleased with my short but positive report when I said, "I made it." He knew progress was important and that it was time to expand. He was pleased and so was I. But I did not share the details of the flight-or-fight reaction. He did not need to know about the moment when I tried to decide to take the elevator up or return to underground parking, get in the car, and head home. This new city employment opened many firsts for me. God put me in a setting that required focusing on him.

A colleague gave me the nickname of "Magi," like the wise men. He saw God restore my once-broken heart and give me much joy. One day, he asked me to pray for his sickly body, and he recovered. My eagle wings were becoming stronger and spreading. The strength and spread of these wings was preparing me for my next flight, for advancement.

I was not aware of this at that time. Later, I better understood what was happening with twenty-twenty hindsight. God was teaching me during this occupation to trust him in every situation, even when riding an elevator.

This fifteen-year job offered many firsts. Eventually, I drove to state conferences and flew to out-of-state workshops. I learned to use public transportation after landing at an airport. No doubt, to an outsider, it looked as though I traveled alone, yet my omnipresent companion remained safely lodged in my heart. In time, I relaxed more on those trips. The elevator rides became more comfortable, even to the nose-bleed section.

I stayed in hotel rooms between the first and the top floor, all with varied experiences. Once, on the first floor, the sliding glass door to the room was open. Yes, my internal panic button went off. I checked under the bed, in the closet and the bathroom, behind the shower curtain, and behind the large window drapes.

God most likely was thinking, *That's my girl, always mindful of her surroundings* or maybe, *Oh ye of little faith*. Little did I know what the future would bring. Little did I know what great things he had ahead for me. Who would have ever thought?

After I had been at my employment for about thirteen years, I travel to Africa with the Barnabas Ensemble Team. We were a group of eleven singers, dancers, and a pastor. I joined them to do whatever odd jobs needed to be done. My expertise was in the area of raising children. At my present city job, I learned to be organized and to operate a PA system and implement programs.

In this position as an all-around helper, I managed the sound system, cooked frequently, and washed clothes—in the bathtub!—and ironed them, all with joy in my heart, I might add! I wanted the team to look their best. I was also invited to sing and dance at times. This three-week tour changed my life.

This trip sprouted the seed planted in elementary school when a missionary spoke in our school about her experiences. Nearly forty years had passed since that time, but this African trip again awakened that desire to become a missionary at age fifty-three.

Marriage, military life, raising children, and my newly acquired occupation were all essential in the preparation process that would one day make me a missionary. My employment and college helped in the development process in this missionary endeavor. "As iron sharpens iron, so a man sharpens the countenance of his friend" (Proverbs 27:17). I needed to be around people who could increase my skills.

Every step forward was essential in the journey. Management, colleagues, work environment, and time with the older adults increased my knowledge. Attending workshops, conferences, state committees, and volunteer experiences enlarged my spiritual muscles. God was grooming me to be his hands and feet here on earth.

I enjoyed the African people, their culture, and the communities. The trip was not always easy; yet life in general is not easy. Some days in our lives are better than others. The Africans and our team alike heartily participated in the ministry of song and dance—what a fulfilling and rewarding time. Upon returning to my job, a sign was posted on my office door that read African Queen. Since my office had been ransacked, I felt the sign was an insult and an attack. The custodians and I just cleaned up the mess in my office. The three-week trip strengthened my spiritual muscles. I had come to appreciate life, people, and other cultures in a broader way.

In hindsight, this was the start of my preparation by God for my future—unknown to me yet known to him. God has a way of stirring his people and moving them forward. We mature mentally, emotionally, and spiritually, increase in knowledge, and are soon ready for expansion. God gives us strength to stand and prepares his children for that future position.

I realized this as the years passed. Hopefully, we are stronger and wiser in each of life's seasons. Ecclesiastes 10:10 tell us, "If the ax is dull, and one does not sharpen the edge, then he must use more strength; but wisdom brings success." This noteworthy verse explains that you and I learn if we are willing. The decision is ours. Every choice has a consequence, whether positive or negative. We can choose to become better or bitter. Opportunities to grow are available if you and I take the initiative.

We need to be open to new prospects: a college class, a short mission's trip, or a visit to the nursing home. We want a sharp mind (ax) as a dull ax takes more strength. We can sharpen the mind by seeking new experiences. Every time we go to the gym, we strengthen our muscles. Stepping out of a comfort zone might mean a trip to the other side of the world. It's up to us. When you and I step out, God steps in. I want to be ready to say, "Here I am, Lord, send me."

God wants his children, including me, to fly and soar like an eagle, as I previously mentioned. Through the pleasurable and the challenging times, we learn to weather the storms of life. We learn to get out of the boat into the water, wind, and high waves. And yes, we learn to swim by the grace of God to the other side. We can make it to the shore when our eyes are on Jesus, and we do not give up.

Yes, the journey begins with one step, one stroke at a time. Psalm 119:71 says, "It is good for me that I have been afflicted, that I may learn Your statutes." In the gym, we buff our physical muscles. In God, we strengthen our spiritual muscles, which does not require going to the gym. But it does require spending time with the Lord.

It was good for me to be afflicted in life and after the return from my first African trip. Notice my wording: my first African trip.

20

A New Season—Moving Forward

"For this is God, our God forever and ever; He will be our guide even to death" (Psalm 48:14).

*T*he idea of leaving my city job after fifteen years became more comfortable as time passed. I had always contemplated transitioning from an employee to a volunteer in this older adult program. God placed me in this position that used my gifts and talents. We brainstormed, created, coordinated, and enlarged the community programming for older adults.

My specialty was challenging these folks to become involved and encouraging them to use their gifts and talents. These opportunities satisfied their hearts and mine. I saw how this population flourished as they involved themselves in the various volunteer tasks and programs. Together, we introduced and worked together to implement an endless array of senior adult programming.

The members took great satisfaction and ownership in their community involvement, which enhanced the activities. The socializing benefits added to their contentment and well-being. Friendships bloomed at the gathering areas and extended into telephone connections. People blossomed like carefully attended plants. People began to look out for each other. The widows even looked out for the widowers.

This position was the best place in the world for a newly divorced woman. I enjoyed the friendships with hundreds of older adults and, in some cases, their offspring. In turn, they valued my friendship and loved spending time with my daughters whenever they were around.

God poured his anointing oil inside my heart and head. I loved this age group and my job—what a huge blessing. We spend days and years away from home, pouring our time and energy into our livelihoods. What a delight to have a job we dearly love. This position as the recreation supervisor of the city's parks and recreation program perfectly fit my talents and gifts.

But it was clear the time to leave this position was nearing. God's plans and ours do not always synchronize. We eventually realize that he knows best. Working with this population was God's plan for fifteen years. He orchestrated it so that I would be employed long enough to develop and to be ready to step through the threshold of expansion into a new way of thinking that, at that time, was foreign to me.

Unknown to me, God had prepared me for the next phase of my life. My task was to shift into a new season in faith and obedience. What I did not know was that this employment was a prerequisite for what God had in mind. God only gives us a piece of his puzzle for us. Yes, only one sneak preview at a time.

Is it reasonable for anyone to love the older adults like I do? I often asked myself. *Is this normal?* I repeatedly asked myself during the preparation period before I walked out the front door, *Are you sure, Lord?*

God blessed my work and time at this center beyond words. My heightened energy level and endless creativity, ideas, and innovation flowed like a rushing creek after a rain storm. The fun indoor and outdoor recreational, educational, social, health, and travel ideas were plentiful for all walks of the older adult's life. With the assistance of senior volunteers, we built Christmas floats and entered them in the annual city Christmas parades. Travels took us throughout the state and even out of the state and the country. Most of these programs have continued some twenty-five years later.

The older adults sometimes sought counsel regarding personal issues. They needed an attentive listener. My ears were available when they needed to talk. One woman in her eighties entered my office to speak about wanting a divorce and her desire to end her lifelong marriage. By the time she heard her own argument and voiced her frustration, she decided divorce was not the answer. Consequently, she left the office in a better state of mind.

I had a limited understanding of seniors at this time. I thought older people had worked through their various hardships and differences by now. Here I was, less than half the age of these folks, and they came to me for support. These seasoned folks, nevertheless, had much to offer, and I had much to learn. Surely, God had brought me here. I was looking forward to this new chapter in my life.

My grandparents never argued and did not display their differences and difficulties in front of me. They expressed enduring love and affection to each other, even through their glances. I thought all grandmas and grandpas had their lives together!

These years of employment included learning opportunities and connections with personal mentors, advisors, and coaches. My task was to be willing to sit patiently with my ears attuned. This skill did not happen overnight as I was an on-the-go person. My mom used to say that I had ants in my pants.

Several couples with long-lasting marriages informed me that commitment held their marriages together. They stated that emotions and feelings can easily bounce all over the charts and distract you. Age has nothing to do with what's in an older person's heart. Some people are young at eighty-five while others are old at sixty-five. I let the older person come to their own conclusions. If they needed direction, they would ask.

The older adults commented that marriage means commitment, sacrifice, faithfulness, and the need for a closer walk with God. He is the only one that can fill that hole in our hearts and that can adequately sustain us. We cannot expect our partner to do what only God can do. I think these years offered me a PhD in both older adult issues and my own personal affairs. I was aware of some of these matters since I had experienced marriage.

Sometimes God, unknown to us, uses other people to relocate us. Character conflicts among employees can play a large part in whether to remain at a job or to leave. My body had physically reacted to my indecision and unresolved conflicts. My two-week medical leave included an array of medical tests. The physician's tests found no medical reason other than stress. The decision to leave my employment improved my physical and mental well-being.

My task was to obey God and follow him in faith. God had miraculously put me into this occupation; evidently, he now had another position lined up. Just like our bodies grow when we feed them, our spiritual lives grow when we steadily feed on the Word. My walk with God was growing by leaps and bounds since I had become single, which was a priority during this season.

God faithfully showered his presence and anointing power on me over the years. He would not leave me stranded. Philippians 1:6 tells us that we can be "confident of this very thing, that He who has begun a good work in you will complete it until the day of Jesus Christ." Once I made plans for retirement, I experienced great peace that helped me to let go. Yes, occasionally, doubt wanted to sneak in. When negativity sets in, we have the option to let go of it or to let negativity take over our thought lives.

Often, I visualized my brain as a big sponge. It can quickly soak in views, harmful or otherwise. We have the option to allow negativity or to say, "Nope, not this time!" When we give thought to rebuffs, the sponge fills quickly.

Once I submitted my letter of resignation to the Human Resource desk, the cleaning-out process began. After business hours, I stayed to empty out my office filing cabinets and desk drawers, which were filled with fifteen years of paper work. The office bulletin board of clippings and special notes also needed to be removed.

The colleague who challenged me to step into a college classroom dared me to stand on my desk while she snapped a photo. I did, and we laughed together. "A merry heart does good like medicine" (Proverbs 17:22). My heart was again becoming happy.

The city council passed a timely ordinance before I retired. Employees now had the option of exchanging sick-leave hours for vacation hours. The exchange yielded a substantial payday for me. I saw this ordinance embedded in what God had for me. This surprise gift was a God-given confirmation. My future lay safely in his hands. All was well with my soul.

The seniors honored me with a very nice retirement party. The restaurant was packed. The city also held a retirement party for several employees retiring at the same time. Positive wishes were plentiful. Bittersweet messages filled the air. The older adults and I were so thankful for the many valued years together.

The final day arrived, the day of my last meeting with my colleagues and friends. I would speak a few final words. Before this meeting, I believe the Lord had laid a word on my heart. I followed through, and after a few words to my colleagues, I presented my successor with my admired title plate of Recreation Supervisor. This gift to my successor surprised each person present. I was also surprised at how well this transition went. The Holy Spirit nudge was more important. Of course, I took my nameplate with me. God only made one of me, one of each of us. No one in the whole full world can replace you or me. Seemingly, all was now in order.

This was a God thing as I had appreciated where the Lord had positioned me during the past years. My departure went smoothly. The decision-making process, preparation, and peace did happen. It was time to leave my familiar territory into the next unknown season of my life. I was ready and waiting on God for the next step. He knew.

A retirement check would follow me in a month or so, and I was grateful to the senior who taught me how to pay off my home and vehicle earlier than I had initially anticipated. Financially, I would make it. My mind contemplated options and thoughts of the future. We pray, wait on him, and explore promises and potentials. Perhaps it was time to pursue my graduate degree.

The years and all that I learned in this job gave me increased confidence that God would guide me. At age forty, he gave me this fifteen-year employment on a silver platter. I started as a novice and walked out as a professional or, at least, proficient.

I had matured in all areas of my walk as a committed Christian. I had become more familiar with Scripture. I had a better understanding of God's call on my life. Jeremiah tells us that God has a plan and a purpose for us. If it's written in Scripture, it must be true.

Through the years, I intentionally immersed myself in numerous professional and spiritual workshops, conferences, and prayer meetings. I attended many women's conferences, single's workshops, and healing workshops. I was deliberate about feeding my hungry and thirsty soul and enhancing my relationship with God for myself and for my precious daughters as well.

I grew mentally, emotionally, spiritually, and even financially through the years. I also became comfortable with myself as a single, parenting my children at various ages and stages in their life. This season offered opportunities for development in the most significant area: trust in God.

This Scripture spoke to me through the years. "When I was a child, I spoke as a child, I understood as a child, I thought as a child; but when I became a man, I put away childish things" (1 Corinthians 13:11). God grew us up and healed our wounds. Through it all, peace became my barometer. When there is peace, I know all is well with my soul.

I wanted all that Jesus had set before me. I needed to stretch myself; that was significant. Spiritual growth is a lifetime practice and process. It's not only church on Sunday. It's church—a personal relationship with Jesus—on Monday, Tuesday, Wednesday, Thursday, Friday, and Saturday. Sometimes we don't realize our maturity until after the fact. Other times, we might sense increase as we follow God.

I continued to think about pursuing graduate work. Perhaps there was a grant for single women. I was offered two jobs during this indecisive time. They were not me, yet it was reassuring to have these offers. During that time, I focused on how to better myself. God surely had it all worked out, even if I did not realize to what extent at that time. My task was to wait for him. He was busily working behind the scenes, even before I sat on that fence. He kept me at this job for years before releasing me.

My married daughters were filling their quivers. Grandbabies were now entering our world. Some daughters had college degree certificates hanging on their walls. God diligently took care of us. Our hardships teach us how to care for and comfort others. We walked in the shoes of struggles, healing, and renewal. "He heals the brokenhearted and binds up their wounds" (Psalm 147:3).

Yes, I became more used to the thought of leaving this city job after fifteen years as time passed. I'm thankful that God stirred me at my job so that I would obey him. I love this story, a story that God so graciously offered this recreation supervisor.

Our relationship with him is what life is all about. Living for him until we die is even better than just exciting.

Yes, Lord, you can send me. I am ready for whatever you have for me and for wherever your agenda takes me because you have my best interests at heart. "Let all those who seek You rejoice and be glad in You; And let those who love Your salvation say continually, 'Let God be magnified'" (Psalm 70:4).

21

Hindsight Really Is Twenty-Twenty— Saying Goodbye

I had so much to learn and work out at this city job. And now the years had quickly slipped by, and I knew in my spirit that it was time to let go, say good-bye, and make a change. God had me there for a season, for such a time as this. My personal and professional skills had improved. Even if my skills still needed work, I was better prepared than when I had started; much work was now behind me, and more was yet to come. I was ready for progress to the next stage. I had no answers other than trusting that everything would be all right.

My office was now empty. The special touches that so joyfully and warmly made it inviting were now put away. The office was waiting for the next privileged senior supervisor. I was leaving this job that had vastly changed my life. My love for older adults began at the start of this employment. God positioned me in the right spot. His anointing included enthusiastic joy and adoration for this older age group. I certainly wanted to reap from their wisdom and life experiences. It was the perfect position for a newly single thirty-nine-year-old parent who had just received her walking papers in a shocking family divorce.

The mutual adoration of the older adults and I for each other increased as we spent time together. I treasured them, and they, in turn, valued me. Some of these folks had also experienced grief and loss through divorce and death. The program participants consisted of widowers, widows, and caring couples. The journey through life consists of treasured times and times of grief and sorrow. These veterans offered and, in turn, received care, compassion, concern, and pleasure from others.

It was the most beautiful place to develop in my professional, emotional, and spiritual growth. This position was part of God's process to train me and to eventually take me down the road he had for me. Hindsight showed me that God uses us right where he plants us, and during this time, he is preparing us for the next planting.

This opportunity with the city and the older adults was more significant than I ever anticipated. He convinced me that as we journeyed down life's lane, I was making progress. Perhaps at that time, I was more extroverted than I am today. Today, I enjoy the quiet time. Most of my life included energy that exceeded a mountain climber's endurance. Back then, the time to relax in the quiet of my own company was rare.

When I took a trip to Tucson, a one-hundred-fifty-mile-plus journey to and fro, one daughter asked me who I went with. I mentioned I had traveled with my very best friend. She asked which friend, and I responded, "Me." It took time to know who I was after my divorce. What I learned after fifteen years of city employment came with plenty of blood, sweat, and tears, and, yes, much exuberant joy. God anointed the joyful side of me.

The part-time teacher's aide position before this job called for a high dose of energy and enthusiasm, especially during playground duty. Staying abreast of the many elementary children in need of a stretch and a shout away from the classroom setting was not for the faint of heart. My role as a parent of active daughters prepared me for the playground. Life with my family included plenty of recreation, sports, and outdoor action. Basically, the teacher's aide position was just as stimulating, only with many more kids.

This new job with older adults was likewise stimulating as, together, we offered creative and careful programming. We developed many programs: social, educational, recreational, travel and touring, swimming, and sports. In many cases, senior volunteers oversaw the entire operations.

The older adults provided group leadership once the programs were in full swing. This process taught me the art of delegation and how to become a more skilled supervisor. The competent senior adult leaders and I planned and implemented the first Senior Olympics activity in the state. I learned that by allowing volunteers to take ownership, programs could multiply in quality and substance.

My work with the older adults helped to prepare and shape me. I learned to be a leader, to supervise, to coordinate, and to set goals and objectives. With the aid of the older adults, we carried through like troopers.

A more painful responsibility and not without some blood, sweat, and tears was writing and preparing a monthly newsletter. Retired seniors, including former English and writing teachers, aided in proofing my work before releasing it to the local newspaper. Occasionally, when the newspaper hit the newsstand, a misspelled word jumped out as if to say, "Ha, ha, you missed me." Plenty of personal pain accompanied this particular responsibility.

During my time in this position, I enlarged and emerged into a professional. I learned so much and gained insight, wisdom, and knowledge. This position was a win-win situation since the skills I learned, unbeknownst to me, prepared me for future work. God so faithfully provided mentors throughout this learning process. Pleasure and pain seemed to go hand in hand.

My appetite for acquiring and absorbing information was apparent, perhaps motivated to some degree by my need for this job. This position was the perfect place for me in the pleasant and even painful areas. The older adults offered plenty of wisdom, knowledge, and insight. Often a widowed pastor's wife and I spent valuable sharing time. Her stories inspired me and nourished my hungry soul.

I craved learning all that my employer and these older adults could teach me. My job was to take time to listen, to soak in what they shared, and to sort through the bits and pieces of their advice. I viewed these acquaintances as mentors. My life knowledge seemed to increase with each interaction.

The possibility that I would leave this much-loved job was mounting. That required an enormous undertaking from the very first thought to walking out the front door. Eventually, leaving became a reality. That God-given peace was and continues to be my barometer.

By now, I had earned my undergraduate degree and obtained numerous office and leadership skills. My self-worth and confidence in God had grown, and his chosen mentors lent me a hand as I healed from the divorce. I was maturing spiritually as I learned about trusting in God. God knew what I needed to continue my journey across another threshold even if I didn't.

To think my original plan was to work at this job until retirement and then shift into joining the older group activities. I had planned to switch from a supervisor to a participant. The decision to leave was mine. Or so I thought.

Those first thoughts of leaving this treasured occupation were mind-boggling. Each day at this job resembled a fresh start with no ho-hum days, and every two weeks, I received a payday as a bonus. God placed me in an endearing setting, and yes, I was even paid for this gem of a job. No doubt, the God of the universe had nudged the city supervisor some years earlier to interview me twice and then, later on, to remember me when this precise position opened up.

In reality, God was moving me into the next phase of my life, the next position he had for me. He purposely stirred my environment, uprooting me. God knew that I loved and valued this city job. Had I known this ahead of time, the decision to leave surely would not have been as painful. I would have eliminated the uncertainty of figuring out what in the world was going on.

This uneasiness about the position was a God thing. We learn from trusting and heeding the Holy Spirit nudges throughout the process. I, perhaps, was more focused on how much I treasured the job instead of on where God was taking me. Of course, I did not know this while facing the unfavorable job situation. Now, as a senior citizen, I have learned from hindsight and the seasons of my life. God is concerned about your life, too, dear reader.

If we resist changes, we can be sure that God will motivate us to change in another way. The doctor suggested, after yet another visit, "Perhaps it is time to leave this job."

"Whoa, leave this treasured position. I don't think so."

The city programs and the seniors flourished. We were an exceptional team, yet something changed. The annual winter visitors returned with energy, vigor, and vitality, ready to dive in. These visitors added to the exciting programs while they enjoyed the companionship of the year-round residents. Between the snowbirds and resident citizens, we had prospered.

The volunteer leadership team set up many programs: aquadynamic, track and field, pinochle, shuffleboard, special events, crafts, and travel—you name it—with a ready-set-go approach. Our recreation programs grew by leaps and bounds. Both young and older adults hung out at the community center. In this respect, the center characterized a teenage center, full of commotion and conversation.

God waited to offer me his best. If we would only realize his timing is perfect. He knows what's down the road. My task and yours is to wait patiently and to trust that something good will evolve even from life-changing situations. I'm glad and thankful to know this in hindsight and in retrospect.

Making decisions and saying good-byes would definitely be simplified if we only remembered the previous lessons we had learned. Eventually, the dark tunnel leads to a ray of light ahead. Transition can be a challenge, yet these times strengthen your trust in God.

I did not think I should leave, yet coping with the daily challenges kept me at the doctor's office. God uses certain strategies when it's time to transition. In my case, extensive chest pain kept me from being my best. I needed rest and the couch.

A year or so before leaving this employment, I took a three-week leave of absence for my first mission trip to Africa. Ministering in the various villages and cities of Ivory Coast and Ghana changed my life. I wanted to become a full-time missionary right there on the spot, but the timing was not right yet, according to my inner nudges.

This trip awakened my childhood desire to become a missionary. Life had taken a different course, or perhaps God had planned a specific direction. I believe God wanted me to experience the joy of the previous seasons of life first. He knows our future, and he had more work to accomplish within me before I was ready for the mission field.

Before this mission trip to Africa, I had completed my undergrad work and begun a graduate study, but after a few classes, I had taken a break due to office pressures. God has wonderful goals for his children. Yet God uses us right where we are in preparation for what lies ahead. While traveling through life's difficulties, I wasn't sure what was happening, yet good old hindsight gives great perspective.

When reviewing the seasons of life, the story becomes much clearer. At times, life's pressures and demands take us in a different direction. God, no doubt, anointed me to work with the older adults in this season. The genuine love for both the people and the job was evident as was the endless energy and the delivery of a prestigious state award in our senior adult programming.

This city job fit me perfectly: my personality, my giftings, and my creative juices flowed like a river after an Arizona flash flood. During those years, I attended many funerals, sometimes when no one else was there. Photos of the senior participating in these events were often on a table beside the casket—photos with an Olympic medallion hanging around their neck, a photo of a happy participant in one of our Christmas

Parade entries, or another photo on a bus trip. These tributes spoke of their active lives after retirement.

The seniors found so much joy and exuberant fulfillment in constructing an annual Christmas parade float. They showed off their abilities as their prize-winning float traveled the boulevard in our city of nearly 85,000 within a ten-mile radius. It was mind-boggling to realize this was the first parade entry for many seniors. As they walked the main street with great enthusiasm, their bright smiles told the story.

As a child, I participated in plenty of parades. Later, I so proudly and loudly played the cadence on my snare drum as my high school marching band entered all the parades in our small township. Oh, the joy of processions! While in the military, the Army parades touched my inner soul as tears wet my cheeks.

My heart warms as I recall the parades during my young years. I proudly rode my small bike brightly decorated with red, white, and blue crepe paper woven carefully through the tire spokes. We kids followed closely, zig-zagging in and out of the parade formation with much laughter and smiles. The American flag was fastened tightly with tape on my handlebars stating, "I, Maggie Volz, love parades, and I love America."

The roadside cheerleaders loved the presence of older adults. The joy on their faces touched my heart as tears filled my eyes. Their laughter and proud smiles spoke of their roused enthusiasm and hope for the large crowd of aged folks. The sidewalk spectators greeted and cheered the walkers. The walk down Main Street was a highlight for all participants.

The excitement made everyone's day, including mine. I jokingly threatened, "You walkers and float riders must excitedly greet the spectators at least fifty times while walking the town boulevard! Count or transfer pennies or stones from one pocket to the other. Do whatever it takes to reach fifty greetings."

They laughed energetically as they shouted out each greeting. Happy tears flowed down the cheeks of the walkers, spectators, and me. What great memories! God is so good!

Another highlight comes to mind. The annual Senior Olympic Games program was a yearly event throughout my fifteen years as the senior citizen recreation supervisor. Together, volunteer seniors and I accomplished the first Senior Olympics in the state.

The event included the city government, a proclamation, and support from town merchants for designer T-shirts and medallions. A chairman and grand marshal were selected each year, and invitations reached all the senior centers in the surrounding area. The event boasted distinguished speakers and guests. The Senior Hall of Fame wall located in the city's senior center displayed the front-runner chair people for older adults along with me. What an honor!

Our bus trips, whether they lasted one or several days, took us in and out of the state and country. Seniors teamed up with their friends, such as a buddy who perhaps would not have otherwise been able to travel. Often, I bunked up with a senior lady in need of a roommate or a little extra care. The adult children of these senior travelers were supportive and grateful for the opportunities their parents had to travel.

Our older adult activities kept seniors active, vibrant, on the move, and perhaps even more physically and mentally fit. This ideal program developed friendships and telephone buddies. Retirees had a reason to get up, shower, and get ready for a day with peers.

Yes, leaving this job was very challenging indeed. I often asked myself during the mental process of letting go of this position, "Can I really leave?" I had asked the same question some years before when it was time to let go of my marriage. Eventually, through the grace of God, letting go was possible in both of these situations and in others.

Letting go involves trust, faith, and a belief that God is in control of the situation. He knows what's ahead. If he arranged this job, surely there's another surprise ahead. And now, God chose to stir up the work environment to transition me out of this job and into the next phase of my life.

Through God, we experienced successful programs and happy older adults, and at the same time, I flourished. Maybe God knew that his older children, these seniors, also needed healing and someone who cared about them.

Of course, I had no idea of this at that time. I was and will forever be a committed Christian in progress. He carried me through the challenge of getting back on my feet after becoming single. At one point, I was sure there was no life after the divorce. And oh my goodness, I found there is not only life after a divorce but a celebration of singleness.

A new job may call for a new beginning at the bottom of another organization, yet in reality, it isn't the bottom. It's just a new level as we continue on our way up.

Therefore, we enter his presence with boldness. (See Hebrews 4:16.) We continue learning, becoming stronger, and gaining confidence in the Lord as he reveals himself to us. We drink milk for a time, but we eventually need a nice juicy steak. Our errors turn into valuable learning experiences.

Sometimes we take a defensive stance. Sometimes we think we know best. Maybe in a few cases, we might, but that is our human side. However, we can listen and learn from the incident, whether we are right or wrong.

God set me up. He knew about this job while I applied for the other two jobs. My role was to trust him and to realize something better was up ahead. He knew that this position with the older adults was right for me and not the other two positions I applied for. And now, fifteen years later, he was setting me up one more time.

Yes, it was a set-up. Had I known another valuable, treasured, ground-breaking adventure was waiting for me, I would not have waited so long to make the decision and then had to go through the challenging process of letting go. God had it all figured out. Perhaps he just wanted me to let go and to trust that he had my life under control.

Today, I know that challenging times create the opportunity to mature us and help us fix our eyes on our Creator. I mean, the doctor found nothing wrong with me other than stress. Perhaps when the doctor said, "Maybe you need to leave this job," God was speaking into this decision: a hint or motivation to help me as I let go. He knew the benefits of the job he had for me down the road.

Meanwhile, while tidying up my office, the flashbacks and reflections of my years there bombarded me. Although this position brought such happiness to many older adults and me, this healing place was important in preparing me for the next season of my life.

One of the senior women had caused a lot of friction on the job. But she mentioned on several occasions that my personality—not my knowledge—made things happen. Later, she confessed that she had purposely made life difficult for me. I was fully aware of what she was doing and did not need her to tell me. Yet through it all, God put a special care in my heart for her. She needed his touch. I visited her while she was very sick. She mentioned, "I was pretty rough on you, yet I appreciate how you care for the seniors. When I get out of the nursing home, I want to adopt you."

I said, "I'm available." Well, she did get out of the nursing home, but she forgot to adopt me.

A gentleman up in years and a previous tour guide helped me earn the qualifications to coordinate state and out-of-country travel. My level of patience was strengthened as I sat through his rather lengthy training periods. Senior ladies taught me fun activities, such as making cactus jelly and zucchini bread, which my daughters and I found delicious. We also went caroling while visiting our shut-ins, followed by hot cocoa, which warmed the hearts and bodies of many.

My mind raced through numerous activities. A Grand Canyon trip and our first night's lodging in the northern part of the state turned out to be a fun, memorable time. We shared many stories and great laughs. The moon shone brightly on the grassy area below the upper hotel room. Surprisingly the next morning, not one blade of grass was left uncovered by an unpredictable snowfall. The adventure brought laughter, fun, peace, and excitement. We had limited warm clothing with us; after all, it was early spring.

Our bus pulled into a nearby grocery store. The manager of the store listened to our animated story and went to the back of the store to pull out a box of last year's hats and gloves. He offered all of us his merchandise at a super bargain. I have so many stories where God's hand directed me. He cared for all our needs before we even knew of those needs.

On one of our trips, we ran into a nun and a priest who were dressed in street clothes although they did have their cross necklaces hanging freely around their necks. They joined our sing-along at the restaurant and questioned us as to where we were going. We had reservations. They had hoped to find a place to lodge.

At midnight, a knock came at my door. Yes, there was no place in the inn. You guessed it. I shared my bed with this nun that night, and a senior man shared his room with the priest. Needless to say, I slept with one eye open. I was too trusting; thankfully, the Lord always had me surrounded with his angels. Perhaps the Lord saw me as a teenager who needed a 24-7 watch.

The energy level of all our travelers was so high that lunch at a Canyon roadside snowy picnic area was delightful. The group devoured the tasty food and snuggled up in the toasty warm clothing. The gloves, hats, laughter, and fellowship warmed us up—inside and out.

How could life and a job possibly top this fifteen-year position? God knew it was time for expansion even though I had many wonderful stories and memories there. What an honor and privilege to have been involved with this older group.

I was about to walk through the front door for the very last time. I did not look back. That blessed peace and assurance that passes all understanding now accompanied me. My heart overflowed with memories and a sense of accomplishment and satisfaction.

Thank you, Lord Jesus, for this grand healing and healthy season in my life; you have stretched me and heightened my learning ability. That incredible peace assures me within and whispers, "It is well with my soul."

Yes, indeed, saying good-bye was huge. Peace and more peace filled my every cell as I was about to leave. Confidence, security, and fulfillment followed. Everything would be all right. Little did I know how everything would be all right!

We—you and I—are his beloved. His love for us is immeasurable. The director wished me well as he walked me to the front door. It closed behind me. Yes, it is well with my soul!

Little did I know that another opportunity was about to open the very next week.

22

A Step in Faith—
One Door Closes, Another Opens

"Behold, I stand at the door and knock. If anyone hears My voice and
opens the door, I will come in to him and dine with him, and he with me."
(Revelation 3:20).

*T*he word "sensitivity" comes to mind. God comes "after the earth-
quake a fire, but the Lord was not in the fire; and after the fire a
still small voice" (1 Kings 19:12). When Jesus reigns in our hearts, we
become sensitive to his Spirit within us. We strive to sense His still,
small voice. I missed that voice plenty of times. At times, this voice
within me gave a nudge, and I elected not to follow through, maybe
because of fear or rebellion, or perhaps I just wasn't sure it was really
him. Consequently, I missed God's blessing, as well as failed to help the
one in need of God's touch.

The times I did bravely obey and saw how God blessed me in this
respect made me not want to miss out on the next nudge from the
Spirit. "Oh, taste and see that the Lord is good" (Psalm 34:8). Within
the depths of my soul, I wanted to be obedient. Maturity and sensitivity
gives us more confidence to respond to the nudges. God reinforces our
obedience as we see the results of previous action.

Paul says, "For what I am doing, I do not understand. For what I will
to do, that I do not practice; but what I hate, that I do" (Romans 7:15). I

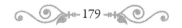

want everything God has for me. When we don't pay attention, he may stir up the waters and make life miserable. That's what happened to me. I ended up at the doctor's office and had to take sick leave. It took some coaxing for me to leave my much-loved work with older people. And then one day it happened.

I consented to God's offer—do or die. My love for older adults remained unfaltering. However, the worries I faced each day at my position were relentless. Had I known God's plan, the decision to leave and turn in my resignation and retirement papers surely would not have taken so long. God uses people and situations in our lives to motivate us. Although my faith grew by leaps and bounds, yet I had more leaps and bounds to grow. We never receive all the answers at once.

When the Spirit nudges us, we need to take notice, which is a great reason to pay attention to the still, small promptings. We need to take time to rest and refresh ourselves in the Lord's presence. This sounds simple, yet Jesus says, "Because of your unbelief; for assuredly, I say to you, if you have faith as a mustard seed, you will say to this mountain, 'Move from here to there,' and it will move; and nothing will be impossible for you'" (Matthew 17:20).

"You of little faith" (Matthew 6:30). "Now faith is the substance of things hoped for, the evidence of things not seen" (Hebrews 11:1).

The Lord loves to open and close doors in the lives of his children. Finally, after straddling the fence, I jumped off and took a step forward. Peace like a river poured over me, which was my confirmation that it would be all right. I could leave this wonderful city job with a clear head. Within a week, I would have a new opportunity.

I received a phone call a few days after retirement from the City Parks and Recreation Department. The caller asked if I had another job yet. This agency hoped to reach me before I accepted another position.

God provided me with on-the-job training in my role as a senior adult recreation supervisor. I was now prepared to go to the next job. I would need every skill I had learned through the years in this new position. Every new job position uses prior skills and gives you the chance to acquire new skills. We can become too comfortable at a job and miss out on what God has for us next. Our muscles work better when we continually use them.

"Enlarge the place of your tent, and let them stretch out the curtains of your dwelling; do not spare; lengthen your cords, and strengthen your stakes" (Isaiah 54:2). Jeremiah 28:8 reminds us that "God has a plan for our lives."

We should leave the safety of our boats to experience the water, wind, and the waves. The storms teach us to swim, exert energy, and take us to God's next level for our lives. Stormy and windy times help us appreciate the calm and sunny weather. Sometimes we encounter smooth sailing in preparation for the turbulent times. We grow through rough seas and blue skies, and both situations broaden our understanding and knowledge. Maybe unknown to us, God wants to prepare us for the next level.

We made arrangements to travel to Phoenix for an interview. I purchased an attractive black suit with gold buttons and dark hose and black shoes. I was ready to go, prepared to interview for a state position.

My friend, Geraldine, was my traveling companion. This was the same lady who had approached me after our women's Bible study more than a dozen years prior who had confronted me. She had told me, "Maggie, you need to stop feeling sorry for yourself." Her openness and challenge to me made us best friends.

She and her husband, George, cared for my daughters and me for life. They were committed and forever available to give the six of us a helping hand. She voiced her belief of a word she felt the Lord spoke to her. Her spirit was open to hearing from God. Perhaps this word saved my life. This couple felt that God gave them a mission—the mission to care for my family, ages seven to thirty-nine.

Had this dear friend not followed through with what she believed was a nudge from the Holy Spirit, I might still be in the trenches of self-pity. It took courage to speak those words. She stepped out and spoke what she felt came from that still, small voice within her. "Listen to counsel and receive instruction, that you may be wise in your latter days" (Proverbs 19:20 NIV). If you listen to advice, one day you will be wise.

The morning to travel to Phoenix came quickly, and together we ventured out for our two-hundred-mile trip. The car headlights guided us to metro Phoenix. We first made a stop at Geraldine's son's home. I changed from my blue jeans into this newly acquired black suit with the gold buttons. We then found our way to the interview site located near the state capitol. Geraldine sat outside the office door, praying while I entered the room for my interview.

My time with the city taught me about office management, goals, objectives, and organizing and implementing programs. With the assistance of older adults, we produced hundreds of active programs.

My job offered financial assistance so that I could attend college, and because of this, I hold a degree in my hands. God provided for me. My interest in community civic volunteerism lasted for years. I became a volunteer and a regular visitor at the nursing home. In addition, a pastor and I were steady ministry partners in an Alzheimer's ward.

Seniors from my area of work occasionally called and asked me to stop by their hospital room. I learned the city culture, how a city is run, and about the city manager and the city council duties. I increased my understanding of the process, procedures, and productivity of our agency.

Most importantly, I learned who I am in the Lord and just how much he loves me. God blessed my endeavors. The city and the older adults accelerated the healing of my hurt heart from my failed marriage. God put me in a nurturing atmosphere. This readied me to broaden my horizons and qualified me for the next stage.

The interview went well. This new position offered expansion for me once again. From early on, God was at work behind the scenes. He advanced me from the teacher's aide position to a city position, from remedial math to achieving a degree. God provided the funds for college tuition, and I learned that once again, he could be trusted and that he has our best interests at heart.

He was actively putting my life together for what he planned for me and for his glory. I also put in the effort on my part. I persevered. We learn to play the piano by practicing, energy, and determination. One must leave the sofa and attentively apply oneself. God brings people into our lives that care and mentor us.

Geraldine and I reviewed the pros and cons of work in Phoenix. Would I consider this job if they offered it to me? The con list was maybe two to three times as long as the pro list.

Geraldine and Gerald were my best friends. Their call to support my family was evident. They were on an assignment, given by the one we serve. Their goal was for my daughters and me to do well. They followed God's direction to care for us. A move to Phoenix meant two hundred miles would be between us. I would miss our weekly lunch dates and the time spent sitting together during prayer and Bible study.

These two best friends were angels selectively appointed by God to care for their three children and their families and for me and my family. Geraldine's husband carried a special place in his heart for my seven-year-old daughter. Each Sunday after church services, he had made sure that she received a special hug from him to chase away the sadness in her eyes.

Today, this daughter is the mom of five children and a grandmother of ten. Once, he asked me if he should stop hugging her after church as she did not respond. I encouraged him to continue to greet her and to not give up. She needed a kind word from a godly man. Eventually, she acknowledged him. George was a father figure to my daughter, who, in time, called him "Grandpa" and Geraldine "Grandma." This daughter, now nearing her half-century birthday, remembered her "Grandpa George" and her "Grandma Geraldine" with each passing birthday until the day of their passing into heaven. Even today, she continues to honor them.

At one time in my life, while attending undergrad classes, I was recovering from being sick. These two friends volunteered to escort me to class one-hundred-and-fifty miles round trip and pick me up four hours later. While I was in class, they did a little shopping and enjoyed a nice dinner followed by a movie. They were waiting in the parking lot later after my class dismissal. They commented that they had a wonderful date night in a larger city.

These friends were about ten years older than I was. They were invited to our family gatherings even after my daughters were married. They helped us through both easy and hard times. In 2009, more than eleven years before I wrote this book, God felt their work on earth was completed. I'm sure their reward is great. We cherish the sweet memories of our times together.

My daughters and I lived in our southwestern Arizona community for almost twenty years. Our church family, friends, and acquaintances lived nearby. The years of residency and employment passed quickly. Eventually, I reaped the benefit of a mortgage-free home. A senior mentor showed me how to pay off my mortgage six years early. His advice saved me a lot of money. At the same time, I had to discipline myself to follow this advice. Godly counsel can open deaf and hearing ears.

Another con on the list was that I was now fifty-five years of age and considered a senior. What was the benefit of leaving a comfortable home and community? God knew the answer. My hindsight tells the story. God's purposes for each of his children are the best. He was not through with me yet but was just getting started.

What would I do if hired? Would I say yes? Consequently, the effort to travel four hundred miles for an interview was a favorable decision. My friend and I had a fun day. Later on, I began to imagine the outcome. What would happen to my home? Would I pick up and move that far away to metro Phoenix? My head was spinning with the thought of all that such a move involved.

I had many questions. In reality, this was an incredible happening, God was involved and at work in my life. By bedtime, I could say, "Lord Jesus, your will be done," after much prayer and reflection. I could hear the Lord say, "I have come that they may have life, and that they may have it more abundantly" (John 10:10).

Perhaps in my spirit, I knew the Lord was intentionally moving me from my small community to the big city. God had so faithfully guided me since I became single in more ways than I could even imagine. My life had taken a turn for the better, which, in my opinion, required trusting him more with each passing day. The thought of missing a God opportunity made me shudder. His steadfast love always covered me. He became a "lamp unto my feet and a light unto my path" (Psalm 119:105) through my years.

At one point, I preferred my timing, yet ultimately, I knew his timing was always the best. The repeat of my algebra class was not about my schedule. I was proud of passing it the second time around, especially seeing how the numbers came together. Through repeating this class, I learned that life includes success and failures, sometimes regardless of how much we try. Who makes it through life with only success anyway?

The day was long and productive. My black suit with the gold brass buttons fit nicely, and for a time, I felt somewhat professional. The interview went well, and time with Geraldine was always fun and special. We made it back from Phoenix safe and sound.

A sense of excitement and mixed emotions was in the air. My body now required sleep. Again before closing my eyes, my prayer went something like this. "Lord, if this Phoenix job is part of your plan for me, I will go. I will believe that you opened this door in metro Phoenix."

Morning came quickly. I was getting excited. "God, if this job is from you, I will go," I repeated. When God is in it, everything falls into place. I had experienced this many times in recent years. My home would rent. I would learn to release my house and focus on a new season in metro Phoenix. I was healthy and willing to move if this was what he wanted for my life.

I learned that when I submit to God's plans, He will work in my life. Occasionally, our ideas don't work out. The timing and the voice within our spirit play a significant factor as we follow his leading. When we heed his voice, we have the peace that passes all understanding. I wanted to rely on this inner peace as this told me that everything would be all right. This peace provided contentment, as I was learning. Listing the pros and cons was a beneficial brainstorming session.

The telephone rang within the week. The caller said, "We'd like to invite you to join our team." The caller asked me to attend my first meeting in three weeks. I asked for more time to unwind from my previous job that had ended a mere week ago and to figure out my present status. The caller said, "Just come for this meeting, and then you can return to your home to take care of matters."

Shortly after accepting this new employment, Geraldine, Gerald, and I went to the suburbs of Phoenix to find an apartment. Everything was happening so quickly. We found a perfect residence: a sanctuary with easy access to school and my job.

We also checked out the graduate program at the University of Phoenix campus. Classes would begin a few days after that first meeting I had been asked to attend. God's perfect timing was at work. Now I focused on slowing down my spinning mind. Change and adapting to a new city, new employment, new school, and new home would take a bit longer. Sometimes the body arrives before the mind.

I attended an Oral Roberts University new student weekend program before enrolling at the U of P. I was interested in obtaining a Christian counseling degree. The instructors and classes were invigorating. After consulting with my church brothers, I decided that because of my background, foundation, and the convenience of a nearby university offering a counseling graduate program, this was the right place of study. It was not essential to obtain this credential in a Christian setting. Therefore, the U of P became my school.

A realtor assisted me with renting my home down south, and at just the right time, renters moved in, all like clockwork. I did not realize at that time, that fifteen years would pass before I returned to this comfortable little southwestern home and community.

Geraldine, Gerald, and my daughter moved my household goods to Tempe. I placed the remainder of my household goods in a storage unit. In a few weeks, I took up housekeeping in an apartment about two hundred miles north of my comfy southern home. The floor of my newly found apartment served as my bed for a few days.

This new apartment became a true home. My graduate class was a short eight-minute drive while travel to my new job took a little longer, depending on traffic. I breathed a silent prayer each morning before I traveled off the exit ramp into the express lane and tightly gripped the steering wheel. I learned the art of merging into fast-moving traffic in addition to navigating the express roads. My skills improved after a few dozen attempts and a few accelerated heartbeats. The scenic tours—in other words, getting lost—lessened as well.

My mom used to say, "Nothing ventured, nothing gained." This seemed to be one my mottos.

This travel and navigating continued for about five years. What an incredible journey. God had it all worked out. My task was to be intentionally involved and to cooperate with him. My mission was to say, "Here am I, Lord, you can send me," and he did!

Who would have thought? Just like clockwork, all the events came together. I reluctantly left a dearly loved employment, and there I was, in metro Phoenix, within weeks of leaving this job. I got out of God's way, and he stepped in. He was busy working behind the scenes while waiting on me to obey him. Who would have thought?

This Phoenix journey was just the take-off of an adventurous ride. "How awesome are your deeds! Through the greatness of your power your enemies shall submit themselves to you" (Psalm 66:3).

23

Surprising Plans—Guest Speaker

*B*efore leaving my city employment, I was a guest speaker at a Parks and Recreation workshop. At this event, I announced to my colleagues that I would soon be leaving my position with the city. A woman remembered this announcement and followed up for an interview with me. Her agency was about two hundred miles north of my city.

Within a few days after my retirement, I received a call. "Do you have a job? We wanted to reach you before you begin another job. We want to invite you to Phoenix for an interview. Can you come up next week?"

Who would have thought? God took me from a trainee to a capable single woman and a polished professional in the workforce. I became a mediator and arbitrator for the Supreme Court and a hospice volunteer during this time. I was quite surprised to receive various city recognitions to include working with the Commission on Disabilities.

God was releasing his anointing, which allowed me to influence those around me. During those years, I wanted to work as though the Lord's office were near mine. Some of the older adults I worked with often said, "We can't please everyone all the time or even half of the time." God gave me a love for the older people so even the harder tasks became easier. Today, years later as an older person, I pray for strength and a desire to mow my lawn and keep up with daily tasks, and God even provides strength and the satisfaction of completing each task, which amaze me. I stand in awe of who he is and the love he has for his people. "Ask, and it will be given to you." (Matthew 7:7–8).

All along, my city job was preparing me to advance to this state position. Even so, while in the city, God used me for his plans and purposes while maturing me to take on the next assignment he had in mind. This transition finally took place fifteen years later. I had much work and learning to do as his daughter.

God, in his infinite wisdom and unbeknownst to me, had other ideas for me. Leaving this employment was a pending reality. Little did I know that this time of working with the city was a prerequisite to where the Lord was now taking me.

Ready or not, God was taking me to the next location. He answered my prayer, which was to mature in him and to take in all that he had for me. Never ever did I think that a new hurdle would include a move to metro Phoenix. I jumped in with both feet first, which opened new horizons from day one and throughout the following five years.

My faith and trust in God aided me as I moved away from my small town. He has shown himself faithful through the years, and he will surely continue to do so. Renting an apartment and eventually buying a home in the suburbs of Phoenix was the furthest thing from my mind. This new move was not even a blip on the radar until it happened.

At that time, I knew very little about transitioning into another culture or even location. Our military life had taken us into various new settings, yet my husband accompanied me. I had never attended a class or workshop on the topic of transitioning.

These types of classes would have definitely aided in military travels, adjustments, and my emotions. I did not realize that the up-and-down emotions are normal. When we enter a new situation or dwelling, we adjust more easily when we know what to expect. Feelings of displacement are real but can be addressed when we have a better idea of what to expect.

A move and acclimating to a new location also depends on a person's attitude. Transitioning takes time. Nevertheless, I was adventurous at heart, so I was excited to explore my new surroundings. However, when a loved one accompanies you, you feel more secure. Without that benefit, Jesus was clearly my all in all.

After more than fifteen years as a single, I was adjusting well. I took the opportunity to mature and become whole and healed before the move to metro Phoenix. I was surrounded by family and friends, which was a big help in this. My city employment helped introduce me to the local area and events.

God does work in mysterious ways—through timing, expansion, and opening new doors of opportunity. He knew my previous experiences would carry me through each change that was to come. One of my strengths was getting along with people. God placed within me the gift to strike up a conversation with a complete stranger.

I was recognized as the city's employee of the month, followed by employee of the year, which was a huge surprise. At the same time, I received many plaques and letters of recognition for working with various older groups. A month or so before retiring from the city, the city mayor requested that I represent him at a conference on aging in Washington, DC. Although it was a little frightening, I was honored and so excited. The unique opportunities and acknowledgments during my city employment were special winks from heaven for me. God blessed me beyond my comprehension throughout those years to build me up. The divorce and rejection and all that accompanied this transition hit me hard so that I was near rock bottom at first.

This big move to Phoenix was his way of providing another opportunity to broaden my horizons and acquire new friendships. My friendly encouraging home base was left behind, and I was heading for a new home and position at age fifty-five—a colossal undertaking.

God took care of all my needs. First of all, he gave me a gift as a tireless, enthusiastic worker. The desire to work as unto the Lord was embedded in the depths of my soul. At each new workplace, I learned so much, even until the day I left. That determined spirit never left me. Some people might think this was all a coincidence, while I call it God's gift or perhaps God's divine appointment.

And to think my daughters and I, at one time, picked up aluminum cans, ran a paper route, and sold many items from our home just to make ends meet. I was eligible for welfare, yet I chose to sell the beautiful items our family brought back from Germany instead. My mother's heart ached when we were forced to go on welfare during my childhood years, especially with those visits from the intimidating social worker.

Phoenix was like a new nation through the lens of my shortsighted eyes. However, this enormous city, country, and culture offered new horizons in a different location. I would be intimidated by some of these events and learn to walk in humility.

One of my positions with the Governor's Advisory Council on Aging (GACA) was to staff a statewide committee. Before this, I had visited local Alzheimer's residents in my hometown for several years. A pastor and I held Sunday services and visitations with the residents and with some of the nursing home people. Their name tags helped us become acquainted with them. Sundays were special visiting times. Together we sang the old-time hymns, and many residents sang along, recalling each beloved word.

Now at my new position in Phoenix, I was to write the summaries from each statewide Alzheimer committee meeting. Honestly, I didn't even know how to spell Alzheimer's. Although I was familiar with the resident's life, I knew zero about the history, trials, and studies of this condition. While at the local facility, my focus was on enjoying the people and relationships. Writing the minutes to the meeting was indeed perplexing. Thankfully, my gracious supervisor wanted me to learn this new skill, and she walked me through the learning curve of writing the minutes.

At most meetings, I felt more comfortable sitting opposite the person at the head of the table, yet my boss, a former senator, insisted I sit right next to her. It was a humbling time of great change and adjustment. Each morning before leaving my apartment, my little sanctuary, I immersed myself in prayer and communion. I asked God to help me to die to myself that I might live for him. I wanted to learn all about this new position and apply the multitude of skills. I had to focus on our heavenly Father. I did not want to let the learning curve crush my spirit.

Such a major move called for tenacity and grit. A new work culture and community would mean learning of new policies, procedures, and volumes of acronyms. I needed every second of learning I had gone through in my previous city job. God's timing in every area of my life was perfect.

Compared to this populated city, my hometown was a more like a rural area. Don't get me wrong, I loved the farm country and growing up in a rural community. I'm a farm girl at heart. I've heard it said that you can leave the farm, yet the farm cannot leave the heart of a farm girl. That's certainly applies to me!

Although acclimating to the big city was a challenge, in time, I grew to love Phoenix and my Tempe cozy second-floor sanctuary. I had many opportunities to take in various workshops given by Christian authors on books I had read. Life was busy, rewarding, and fulfilling. Life in Phoenix was most definitely a time of personal development and deepening my walk with the Lord. God's perfect timing, plan, and purpose were in effect. Little did I realize the value and importance of adapting to where I was planted. God was giving me a foretaste of what he had in mind for my future.

Phoenix was just the beginning of more adventures. As a single, I would launch into new communities, countries, and cultures. Before my move to Phoenix, my family always lived close by. If I needed a flat tire fixed or help with any problem, I could call on my family. Without a doubt, my family would have driven the nearly four hundred miles round trip if necessary, and actually, they did come to the rescue once. At the same time, God was weaning me from my family to total dependence on him.

Now unlike the previous lengthy one-hundred-fifty-mile round trip to attend undergraduate classes, graduate classes were a short eight-mile round trip twice a week. What a difference! In the beginning, my university classes overwhelmed me. The tall buildings, elevators to classrooms, thick books to read, classmates of all ages, unfamiliar faces, and class dismissal at ten o'clock at night were all a challenge. The underground parking and finding my way home safe and sound in those wee hours took courage and faith. Many students had just finished their undergrad programs. Although I had exceeded them in life experiences, their minds were bright and full of academic approaches to learning.

One night, my study group was scheduled to meet in the library on the U of A campus instead of at the U of P campus. At that time, this campus library was unfamiliar, and parking was a challenge. Finally, I found a parking spot and started walking. It was dark, and the lights were dim, at least to me. I was anxious about finding this library. A young female riding her bike on the sidewalk stopped and asked if I needed help. "Yes, can you direct me to the library?"

She started to explain the directions and then said, "I will show you." She was walking her bike, and I was walking alongside her. After a short time, there it was. Honestly, I believe she was an angel disguised as a young student.

In the gated area of my apartment complex, I took a short jaunt to my second-floor apartment. Generally, the city was quiet by this hour, yet the stairwell lighting to my apartment was dim. Once in my sanctuary, I always breathed a sigh of relief. For a very long time, a colleague from my previous work place called to check on me at about 10:15 p.m. She knew the city and the possible dangers and wanted to be sure I made it home safe and sound.

The classes and course study, although thought-provoking, were equally gratifying. I eventually relaxed and even participated in giving oral presentations and papers in front of many unfamiliar faces of all ages. I overcame the taunts and fears. Mingling with classmates brought a feeling of youth, satisfaction, and perhaps humble importance. The possession of a university ID card and a sweatshirt carried a bit of prestige for this fifty-five-year-young mama and grandma.

I needed extra energy through those years, perhaps even more than usual. Determination was implanted in my brain to achieve the career I had hoped for and envisioned fifteen years earlier as a counselee.

With hard work, a positive attitude, courage, hearty character, and with blood, sweat, and tears, I persevered. Notice I did not say perspiration dripped down my brow, but I was determined. I had paid for the two-year graduate program in advance. Who would have thought? God knew all this from the beginning. "'For I know the *plans* I have for you,' declares the Lord, '*plans* to prosper you and not to harm you, *plans* to give you hope and a future'" (Jeremiah 29:11 NIV, emphasis added). And that he did!

My strength of character spoke firmly within my spirit. "Maggie, you will have this degree and a dream come true within just a few years."

24

Pruning for Opportunities to Grow— The Telephone Call

"But the fruit of the Spirit is love, joy, peace, longsuffering, kindness, good-ness, faithfulness, gentleness, self-control." (Galatians 5:22–23).

The heartaches of the past were gone, and my life was focused on intentionally living for him. I had to follow his leading and go where he led me. I can share many lifelong positive experiences, including a productive life with major rewards. Living beyond my comfort zone produced fruit beyond my expectation, and life was wonderful with a great future ahead.

I was learning how to be single and become whole as a daughter of the King with God as my husband. I was now intentionally letting go of the past and appreciating my unique qualities. I was focusing on the positive instead of the negative. At every possible chance, I shouted out that Jesus is the answer to life.

I found new courage in Jesus, which aided in moving me out of my comfort zone. More of life was waiting for me, beyond my every expectation. And Jesus said, "He who follows Me shall not walk in darkness, but have the light of life." (John 8:12). I longed to follow the "light of the world."

It was time for a new adventure. The opportunities before us are plentiful if we are willing to be brave and obey. A single man or woman can act right away if needed; he or she does not have other responsibilities.

He was going to teach me to fly further yet again. How exciting was this? Unbeknownst to me, God planned for me to stay at my much-loved job with the city for fifteen years. I thought I would stay there until the end of my working days. But God had more for me beyond what I expected. I had to stretch not only my mind but also my location.

We can experience many new adventures if we will just step out of that comfortable rut. This was not a coincidence but a divine appointment. God was directing me into the next phase that he had for me. We might reach a certain place for a brief time, but God has more in mind. We should not just settle down and expect to stay there.

The time as a client under the care of a counselor deepened my desire to one day sit in the counselor's position. I received so much healing as a client and had a heightened passion to help others. God used this Christian counselor to get me back on my feet. Therefore, I wanted to be in that same position to encourage, support, and bring healing to the lives of others. God uses his children on earth to be his hands and feet. This concept became clearer to me with time.

The move out of a small city into the suburbs of Phoenix took all of the previous events and multiplied them. My small home town looked like a dot on a map dot in comparison to where God was taking me. Yet I was ready. I had to transition from small to large, which would take time as I was about to learn. In addition, it would take time to settle into my new employment. I was entering an unfamiliar territory and culture. Consequently, my body arrived much earlier than my mind.

The move to Phoenix, settling into a new apartment, starting a new job and entering a graduate program, all within the same week, was major. My second-floor one-bedroom flat with a small kitchen, adjacent dining area, and the end-to-end living room was a perfect set up for a single woman. The wood floor topped with a mat served as my bed for a few days until my household items arrived.

I was now living in a suburb of metro Phoenix and learning to navigate three-, four-, and five-lane highways with exits with signs and street names overhead on the by-pass. And yes, occasionally, I did miss the expressway exit. Likewise, I was intentionally learning which two-way streets and lanes turned into reverse one-way traffic in the opposite direction at certain times of the day. It took some adjusting to transition into an uninterrupted flow of traffic. Each day called for prayer and a tight grip on the steering wheel before merging into the fast lane.

My congested drive included lots of traffic, construction, and frequent highway delays. Traffic sometimes came to an abrupt stop. Other times, the by-pass was crowded with bumper-to-bumper traffic: cars, trucks, and transit buses with beeping horns on both sides. The homeless waved their signs and cups on many street corners. I prayed about who I was to give a helping hand. I had a few dollar bills to hand out, and I waited for God's nudge to see who would get those bills. The sidewalks, parking lots, and stores were crowded. Life in Phoenix was fast-paced.

My typical response was to say I took a scenic tour instead of admitting I was lost until I found the right direction. I eventually found a direct way back to my apartment after work and after class late at night. The scenic tours lessened in time. Navigating the metro area was all doable; it just required time to learn.

Back home, the streets mostly consisted of two lanes each. To think I thought these small community streets were super busy and crowded. The traffic flow in the heart of town seemed extreme at thirty-five miles per hour.

Transitioning into the unfamiliar took time and patience. But eventually, I became a near pro and came to really appreciate the big city. I liked my apartment from the moment I set foot in it. Each day was an experience, and entering into my sanctuary each night was like stepping into paradise.

Little did I realize that my five years in Phoenix was preparation for global future travels into communities, countries, and cultures.

Smaller steps are more comfortable than one big giant step from point *A* to point *Z*.

My time in metro Phoenix brought added personal development. "For this is God, our God forever and ever" (Psalm 48:14). Trees, bushes, and vines are trimmed back to boost growth and to encourage the bearing of more fruit. Yet each time that pruning comes around, we remember how God got us through the last pruning episode. God wants to continuously prune the lives of his children. "Therefore we make it our aim, whether present or absent, to be well pleasing to Him" (2 Corinthians 5:9).

Gardening, pruning trees, bushes, and vines are somewhat of a hobby and therapy activity for me. Like an artist, I examine what needs to be pruned to enhance the appearance of each portrait. I visualize growth, beauty, blossoms, and fruit and imagine what the end product is likely to produce.

Once the bottom and gangly growth and dead and broken branches are pruned, the tree thrives and becomes healthier inside and out. As Christians, we grow and, with time, become more Christlike both inside and out.

I know in my spirit that pruning takes place for our benefit, even when it hurts. "The fruit of the righteous is a tree of life" (Proverbs 11:30). "But also for this very reason, giving all diligence, add to your faith virtue, to virtue knowledge, to knowledge self-control, to self-control perseverance, to perseverance godliness, to godliness brotherly kindness, and to brotherly kindness love" (2 Peter 1:5–7).

A Christian's life includes endurance, perseverance, patience, and increasing in love and peace. Life's blunders can mean that we gain more fruit. We learn through life's journey. "Every branch in Me that does not bear fruit He takes away; and every branch that bears fruit He prunes, that it may bear more fruit" (John 15:2). "Life is hard, but there is a time and a place for everything, though no one can tell the future" (Ecclesiastes 8:6–7 CEV). The plans that Jesus has for his children require pruning with results of good fruit. "It was planted in good soil by many waters, to bring forth branches, bear fruit, and become a majestic vine" (Ezekiel 17:8).

My first graduate class kept me on my toes. The pace called for extraordinary energy and enthusiasm. I was doing reasonably well at keeping up as a new, incoming student. The problem I did encounter was that my mind was still trying to adjust to my unfamiliar territory. My body seemed to acclimate quicker and more comfortably than my brain. I kept thinking I was living in my home town instead of in my new city. The name of my home town routinely slipped out of my mouth when I should have referred to metro Phoenix instead. God-given determination made a way for me. Many times, I shouted out, "You can send me, Lord." Sometimes I wondered, if God actually did give me an opportunity to go, would I? "Whom shall I send, and who will go for us?" And I would respond, "Here am I! Send me." (See Isaiah 6:8.) I enrolled with the intent to graduate, and nothing was about to stop me, come water or high winds. I was determined to finish, even at fifty-five years of age.

My mother often mentioned my sister's name when I was home for visits. My sister lived close by and was with our mom more than I was. My sister's name automatically slipped out of Mom's lips. Since my sister was nowhere around, I just responded as if she had called my name. Now, this was fine within a family setting. It was not okay in a graduate-level classroom setting! Familiarity with the routine and surroundings came about, and in time, I began to feel at home. I was getting used to the tall buildings, underground parking, elevators to classrooms, the colossal book reads, the wide age range of classmates, their various cultures and races, the dismissal at ten o'clock at night, and the drive to my apartment in the wee hours. In time, this became routine.

My first six-week class was now behind me and Thanksgiving before me. The following morning after I completed my class and received my final grade, I was heading two hundred miles south. My suitcase was packed, and I had grabbed a bag of snacks to munch on as I drove. Soon I would be home with my family. I was so excited. This short holiday was just what a college student needed. Between transitioning into a new culture, a new job, and graduate studies, I was ready for a break.

About two months had passed since I had arrived in Phoenix. I could find my way to work, to class, and to my apartment with fewer scenic tours. I was making progress. I was acclimating to the city suburbs. It was an exciting time of stretching. Now, my family was waiting for their mom and grandma to come home. They had supported my latest quest, and I was excited to tell them of my endeavors, including settling into and becoming familiar with the city.

The feeling of accomplishment was inspiring. I had made a huge move and hiked to the other side. Maybe I didn't cross with flying colors yet flying colors weren't necessary. I was doing the best I knew how.

That last class was dismissed with a "see you in a week." I was ready for a well-deserved night's rest. Mornings came quickly. The road was waiting to see my vintage blue Honda head south. If I left early, I could beat the worst of the traffic.

Just before crawling under the bed covers, the phone rang with unexpected news that now upset my plans. My head began to throb. Defeat seized me. I needed time to absorb this news, and my trip home was now delayed. I took an extra day to do this under the security and shelter of my bed covers. Then I came to my senses. Sometimes you have to order yourself to get up and move on. I was also familiar with this. The years had passed quickly since I became single, and yet a new season was before me. The previous seasons taught me so much. During my spiritual journey through thick and thin, I learned to trust in God and who I am in him. These occasions increased my overall maturity.

I tried to figure out how I would share this news with my family. Humiliation, shame, and intimidation consumed me. The thought of failure is a powerful emotion, one that I was familiar with. The failed marriage, the failed college algebra class, and other setbacks along life's journey resonated in my mind. Life was full of success and failures. At least my life has had its share.

The enemy is out to get us. He wants us to fail and feel like failures. My mind replayed the negative thoughts of failure. *This dilemma will be my secret*, I thought. *No one will need to know about this*. In actuality, we can have ninety-nine successes and one mishap. We can receive ninety-nine compliments and one negative remark. Which do we focus on? Yes, that one mishap or negative word. I was doing just that.

In reality, I had moved out of my home from two hundred miles south to metro Phoenix. I settled into an apartment and my new employment and was finding my way to and from work and graduate classes. I could even buy ice cream before it melted, meaning that I could find my way home before it melted into a milkshake. My scenic tours had lessened. I had accomplished much since arriving in Phoenix.

The long trip home, driving through the open desert, aided in clearing my head. The scent of autumn helped remove my sad heartache and hurt feelings. Constructive thoughts were trying to filter through my despair.

What if people find out? They'll laugh or perhaps say, "I knew she didn't have it in her." The enemy was busily at work in my thought life. He wanted me to fail, give up living in Phoenix, and return home. He would have been delighted if I gave up my job and graduate program. It was time for me to pick up the pieces, put a smile back on my face, and go back to the drawing board.

As I reflected on the value of what I learned throughout the decades of my life's ups and downs, I was so thankful. I celebrated those times. We increase in knowledge and wisdom and develop a few solid character traits. The pain is uncomfortable, yet the result of the pain forms us into a more patient and productive individual.

I was familiar with both failures and successes. Both helped me in life. The surprises, the good, the could-be-better—all of these strengthened my spiritual walk. Through it all, I learned to trust in the God of the universe. I knew who I was in Jesus. At one time, I did not like myself. He now has my heart and soul, and I like what and who I have become. I like me.

As I share my stories of failure and success, they encourage others. Few people skate through life without a few bumps and bruises. Would we need God if there were no rain in our lives? That bright, beautiful rainbow follows the rainfall. We sense the freshness after a thunderstorm. Like the nitrogen that accompanies the precipitation, the flowers and grass are fresher, healthier, and grow like wildflowers. We, likewise, have a spurt of awareness and freshness when we bask in some Jesus love. After growing pains, we stand taller.

When we realize how much we have in common with others regarding our life's events, we benefit. "These things I have spoken to you, that in Me you may have peace. In the world you will have tribulation; but be of good cheer, I have overcome the world" (John 16:33).

My stories of success and failure help others when I share them. We have a tendency to believe no one else suffers like we do. We are sure that we are the only ones. Now I will freely admit that sharing my failures was a process. Until I learned the benefits of sharing, it was difficult. Once I learned to share the ups and downs or failures, success became old hat. I like openness, no hiding behind a mask. Others might not have to stay in the recovery bed as long when we share our experiences.

We can give up when life gets hard or benefit from the toughness of the journey. We then get taller, just as I did when I suffered from extremely painful leg aches and growing spurts as a child. After that painful time, Mom measured my height, and I was taller.

My mom used to say, "Everyone puts on their pants the same way, one leg at a time." What a great reminder. I heard a doctor say, "Everybody's got something." Some just hide it under that mask. I did for a time, so I am familiar with this coping mechanism. I later learned how to be transparent.

Scripture tells us that" older women should teach younger women." (See Titus 2:3.) My life was and continues to be in the Lord's hands; there is no better place to be. The older women in the church, Bible Study, and at other Christian activities taught me and nurtured me through my hardships. In the same way, I wish with all my heart to be a teacher to the younger women.

Had I known in my younger years what I know in my later years, I might have had an easier time. We older adults must teach the younger generation, women to women and men to men. Perhaps our stories will keep the younger ones from repeating the mistakes we made. Of course, in my younger years, I might not have listened. I certainly had a stubborn streak.

By now, you are wondering what my horrible, humiliating, humbling event was all about—that news that kept me in bed and under my comforting covers an extra day. The news that kept me from being with family an extra day. The caller informed me that I failed my very first graduate class at the University of Phoenix. I was embarrassed and ashamed. What a detrimental moment—my spirit was dampened, crushed beyond comprehension. Needless to say, some time went by before I could share this story.

That phone call went something like this. "This call is to inform you that you did not pass your ethics class. This class requires a B, and you received a B-. This means that you will need to repeat the class to continue the graduate program."

I asked, "Could I make up my work?"

The caller responded, "No, you will need to repeat this class if you choose to return."

This news hurt my ears and my heart. It was an industrious class, yet I was not productive enough to pass this course. I had a lot to process during my first weeks in Phoenix. Did I know little about transitioning into another culture?

I paid my full tuition except for my textbooks. I was determined. That word was imprinted on my forehead, so to speak. God made a way to pay up front. How often did that happen? Before going to Phoenix, a church administrator and I worked out the tuition numbers. I received a check from my previous employment for unused sick and vacation days. This resulted in a nice payday. Good health was in my favor, and it paid off. I had numerous sick time left to use. Between this check and my small savings, I could pay for my graduate program in Community Counseling up front. When we tallied up the numbers, we found that paying up front was the answer to saving tuition expenses. The Lord worked out everything so that I could attend graduate school.

Being a student on the main campus at that time in my life was exhilarating. Some of my fellow classmates were younger while some were middle-aged. The feeling of youth and satisfaction surrounded me. Possibly I was the oldest classmate. I had a university ID card and a sweatshirt with a university emblem on it, which offered me prestige. I had a youthful heart as an older college student.

God had faithfully demonstrated his healing power and faithfulness in previous times. I found healing even after the failed college algebra class, the preparation time when leaving my much-loved city employment, and the divorce. He uses every situation for his glory. "'For I will restore health to you and heal you of your wounds,' says the Lord" (Jeremiah 30:17). We find out that our hard times are not the end of the world.

The U of P finance person was surprised when I asked her for the total cost of the entire program. I assured her that I planned to graduate. I was now committed to studying and to a new place of employment. It was an enormous first week.

The years before living in metro Phoenix were healing and maturing years. God placed me in an atmosphere of restoration. The dreadfulness of a failed marriage was now behind me, as I was learning more about myself. My family, my church family, Geraldine, Gerald, and my place of employment facilitated my healing.

After the Thanksgiving break, I entered the classroom to retake this class. The same professor greeted me and said, "You have returned?"

I said, "Yes, I came to the university to earn my degree." The professor smiled, and that was that. Consequently, my "round two" grade improved. The day eventually came when I walked the red carpet to receive a counseling degree.

God powerfully demonstrated his faithfulness, goodness, and mercy all the days of my life (Lamentations 3:23). He used every situation for his glory. He restored the wounded heart and gives me beauty for ashes. (See Isaiah 61:3.) We find out that the hard times were to strengthen us and to place us in a better position for the future. There is life after divorce, after death, after tragedy, and after any distress that comes our way.

Each terrifying event and amazing restoration assures us that when the next unimaginable tragedy strikes, it surely will pass. God is in charge. A lovely benefit of maturing is that we appreciate life experiences more fully. The struggles and traumas become diluted and are seen as minor growing pains and valuable lifelong teachings.

I value what I have learned over eight decades. I appreciate the failures, disappointments, and the strange happenings that caused me, for a time, to hide behind my mask. I value the day I was released like a butterfly leaving its cocoon. The priceless outcome supersedes the pain.

The up-and-down emotions and how to survive or what one did to survive gave valuable insight. I so appreciated the lessons I learned. The events became a tool, a source of normalizing other people's griefs and disappointments during their painful quests.

Whether positive or negative, the experiences contributed to helping others as I sat in the counselor's seat facing a client. My sufferings and God's answers granted insight while helping others. Healing begins when situations are normalized. Others may not have to stay in the recovery bed under their security blanket as long as I did. I so value what God has taught me through the years and look forward to what he has in mind for my future.

Before graduation, the same professor whose class I failed awarded me with the "Energizer Bunny" award. No matter what I went through, with my eyes closed, I visualized my graduation ceremony. I happily walked the royal red carpet, decked in my cap and gown and a big smile to the tune of "Pomp and Circumstance." In time, that well-earned diploma was included in my portfolio. Yay! The following week, I officially sat in the counselor's seat facing the client.

God's smile, no doubt, exceeded my smile, along with the host of angels as they clapped and cheered and shouted out, "Well done, good and faithful servant" (Matthew 25:21). God wants to heal the brokenhearted and restore their souls (Psalm 147:3). "Weeping may endure for a night, but joy comes in the morning" (Psalm 30:5).

Pruning the tree—the person—brings fruitfulness that helps to normalize another tree—another person.

25

Graduate School—Practicum

*I*n graduate school, after months of study, students entered practicum training. This exercise provided a time for us to put into practice what the lectures, book work, and hours of study had taught us.

I chose to work with older adults at a senior center that was fairly nearby. I was comfortable and somewhat familiar with older adults. My previous nearly twenty years in the field of aging had offered me much insight and knowledge into their life issues. I felt at ease with this population and believed that this practicum pursuit was a great place to start in becoming a candid counselor.

Many seniors were interested and immediately signed up and, consequently, became my practicum clientele. My schedule quickly filled and overflowed, which led me to recruit a classmate to help me. Initially, I wondered if I would find sufficient volunteers who were interested in letting me practice with them as a counselor. Surprisingly, I had more sign-ups than I could effectively handle as a student with the time allotted. My classmate and I easily met our quotas.

These older adults were a diverse group. I felt privileged to spend time with this age group who had experienced nearly every one of life's various seasons. They had walked the many stepping stones of life. Their stories of different up-and-down seasons definitely enlarged my overall understanding. This rewarding and enriching time increased

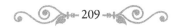

my awareness of the aging process and blessed me and boosted my confidence.

Their stories captivated me and, in some respects, were similar to the stories I had previously heard at my city job. I certainly identified with some of them, the pain that they had experienced, their ability to forgive, and their subsequent healing.

One woman, now well into her eighties, openly shared her story of sexual abuse with me. She had carried this secret throughout her entire life—not another soul had ever heard it. Sexual abuse stories were relatively new to me at that time. Through the years, however, these stories have become all too familiar. The ridged rocks of life deeply embed the heart and soul of an abused individual.

Since then, I have found that many similar stories are never shared. This is an excellent reason to find a competent counselor who can walk with a person to health and healing. Just imagine this elderly lady sharing her secret story for the first time, a story that had lodged deeply in her heart through her many decades.

No doubt, she faced endless sleepless nights thinking about this. The smooth stone of her trust was tattered, and she likely wondered who would ever believe her. She wore a mask, covering her ever-persistent gnawing story within. As she freely told her story for the very first time, her life story was not just her own. She had now unpacked the heaviness and the burden of her heart.

For learning purposes, my time together with my practicum clients was videoed with the permission of each senior. The stories of divorce, single parenting, financial loss, sexual abuse, the loss of children, and other tragic stories surfaced. My practicum was a significant learning experience for me as many older adults became vulnerable and shared their intimate life issues, their up-and-down journeys in life. I once disclosed my heart-wrenching story to a competent Christian counselor. The broken marriage trust was so devastating to me. I then worked at moving forward. Likewise, my spiritual understanding and knowledge increased. In the same way, many of these folks experienced such liberation after opening up about these heart-rending stories.

My graduate professor randomly chose a video of my one-on-one counseling sessions. Her constructive remarks heightened my therapy skills. She touched on some of the life skills that I had acquired during this intense exercise. She mentioned that I could strike a rapport with the counseling clients and maybe I would make a great social worker as well. God's gift of encouragement in me was showing itself as I worked with people. My life had included some hard knocks, and through our Lord Jesus, I overcame these and became transparent to help normalize people's problems. Our painful experiences and outcomes benefit others who are seeking answers.

While some classmates had difficulty finding a practicum site, God provided abundantly for both me and my classmate. He is an ample provider in all areas of life. Consequently, upon completion of this valuable practicum, I was further prepared to enter a full-time internship. Every client, session, varied populace, and setting helped prepare me to become a mission's counselor on assignment for the one we serve.

Life is like this. We walk through our childhood and teenage experiences and mature into adulthood as we prepare for the various seasons that follow. Our upbringing and each phase has the potential to mold us into a more Christlike person.

At age thirty-nine, the Lord provided me with a job although I had virtually no professional background. At about age forty-two, I occupied a college classroom chair. At age fifty, with much hard work, I achieved my long-awaited goal and was awarded a college diploma. Later, at age fifty-seven, I received one more much-coveted graduate-level degree.

My time, energy, and focus on God opened the gate for a future as a mission's counselor to the missionaries. My advancement included all the preparation for the next assignment. This did not happen overnight.

Whether I faced a good or a could-be-better experience, each one had the potential to equip me and prepare me for the next phase of my life. The process might include detours, significant moves one way or another, stagnant times, tough decisions, shortcuts, bumpy roads, and maybe a huge boulder to step over.

Grade school is mostly consistent for people, starting with first grade moving through the years to finally reach the twelfth grade. Sometimes a person might need to repeat grades, which can be positive even if it looks like a pause or a step backward.

Raising five daughters with eleven years in between the first and last took twenty-some years with some significant gaps. At the first nose bleed, we might have rushed to the ER. Down the line, however, with maybe the third or fourth child, we might have said something like this for a nose bleed: "Just pinch your nose and go back to playing. And please don't bleed on the rug!" Well, you get the idea.

I learned a lot about myself and others in raising my children. I believe each moment is valuable for the future. We experience sunshine and stormy, rainy, and dry days, a variety of unsettled and disruptive weather. Yet all these days shape, mold, and prepare us for the future.

God makes a way for us through every difficulty. That's exactly what he did for me. A person, a word, an encouragement, and or a Holy Spirit nudge encouraged me in my journey. Oh yes, some of these were easier and more comfortable to take, a more scenic path to follow than others.

Scripture tells us that Jesus is the Rock and all other ground is sinking sand. We have a choice. Will we build our homes and our lives on the rock or on the sinking sand? I once had a small church-shaped plaque that said, "As for me and my house, we will serve the Lord." (Joshua 24:15). In other words, never give up when life gives us sour lemons or awful trying times.

As I traveled this journey, even during the hardships, I focused on intentionally learning, encouraging, and giving hope to others. I was not always successful, but I grew along the way. Traveling through the decades of life has the potential to teach and prepare us, the students, to bring us to a place to want to help others in their journeys.

I saw the value of my different experiences to include life as a missionary. James 1:2–3 tells us to "Count it all joy when you fall into various trials, knowing that the testing of your faith produces patience." We were not counting the pain as joy, but what it produced and what we learned from it did become joy. We gained strength and endurance. These traits got us through life.

26

Internship Preparation—He Knows

"Now this is the confidence we have in Him, that if we ask anything according to His will, He hears us. And if we know that He hears us, whatever we ask, we know that we have the petitions that we have asked of Him" (1 John 5:14–15).

My internship time at a Christian agency was ideal, active, and effective, challenging me. God heard my prayer and placed me in an environment that equipped me for the future he had for me. I had a high energy level, and my supervisor brought much wisdom and knowledge to each session as she offered unique opportunities for me to gain experience as I built my confidence. She wanted to follow God's plan to train this intern and ready her for future missionary endeavors.

At this agency, I was working with families referred to the Children's Baptist Counseling Department through the State's Child Protective Services. I was one of two who raised their hands when asked about volunteer work. One day a week, I traveled into various Phoenix suburbs to provide God's healing touch to these hurting families. I often took the scenic route in my attempts to locate the homes of clients. When I put it that way—taking the scenic route—it sounded better than being lost. Needless to say, I got lost a lot.

The move from a small town to the suburbs and the big city presented a challenge for this newbie Phoenix resident. The streets were sometimes puzzling. Even so, I was determined, and I never gave up. If

I was facing north, I knew the other three directions. However, if I was uncertain of what direction I was headed, then I did not know which way to go at a certain intersection. Now my mom and my daughter know their directions by the sun. But I was wired differently.

As a play therapist, I carried a variety of counseling tools, such as a dollhouse, art supplies, play dough, board games, miniature figures, a portable sand tray, and more. These filled my car trunk and sometimes the back seat of my car, which became my office for the day. I had to determine how to best utilize play therapy, the tools, and the supplies for each family to effectively help with the difficulties. Several client visits reminded me of my childhood years. Since our family was on welfare, we had occasional visits from the state welfare lady. She arrived in fashionable clothing and drove a lavish vehicle. She wiped off our chair before sitting down. My mom kept a spotless home, and this intimidating woman wiped invisible stuff off mom's clean chair. Mom cried before and after her visit. It still amazes me how God prepared me for my future job and visits to the homes of others.

During my weekly counseling rounds, I visited a family that reminded me exactly of this state welfare lady's visits in our home. They had little furniture in their home, and what they had was piled in a corner: a divan and a soiled stool for sitting. The client occupied the couch, and the stool top was covered with food. I had a decision to make. The client pointed out the kitchen to me where I could find something to wipe off the stool. But unlike the state welfare visits to my childhood home, I had to wipe the food-covered stool clean. After that, we had a pleasant visit. I wondered if this food was intentionally left on the chair to see my reaction.

On another occasion, I left the client and immediately called my supervisor. Frantically, I said, "Lice! The family was just treated for lice. Do I need to be concerned?"

My supervisor calmly said, "Stop by the drug store and pick up lice shampoo." A personal incident with lice was a new experience. I was embarrassed when I approached a salesclerk with my dilemma. Cool and collected, she found what I needed.

En route to the shelf, she nonchalantly said, "I had a bout of lice, and this shampoo took care of the problem." God had the right person there to help with my timidity. I love the way God works and cares for his children. He is always one step ahead of us.

I did not know at that time that my suitcase would one day replace the trunk of my car and would carry the proper tools for healing around the world. God gave me on-the-job training to prepare me for my up-coming missionary travels, the next level of my walk with him. God most definitely knew which supervisor I needed to ready me for the days and years ahead in my counseling voyage.

When the time came during graduate school to locate an internship agency, I sent eight letters in search of the right position. Agencies invited me to chat and explore the possibility of working with them. I relied on my personal belief in Jesus to find the right place.

Prematurely, I accepted an agency's agreement, even completing the orientation workshop. I felt no inner peace, that peace that shows up within us when all is well with our souls. The contentment that I had relied on through the years was absent. This agency was better suited for personal growth than the other six. The eighth agency did not respond at that time.

Shortly after I accepted the position at this organization that was my second choice, the Christian agency—my first choice—called me. I was excited when the caller invited me in for a talk. The interviewer apologized for not being in touch with me earlier and said that she was on a summer break. Our conversation went well, and the stir within my heart said, "This is the place."

Now I needed to return to the agency that had originally chosen me as an intern. The nine-month internship was of great importance. I wanted to learn in the right place. Within a short time, the board at the Christian agency decided I was an excellent intern prospect. The stirring of my spirit likewise voiced, "This is the right place for your internship."

I was so surprised. God works in incredible ways. Christian Family Care Agency (CFCA) worked with children, which was one of my criteria in a job. Half of my clients would be children. This agency introduced the concept of play therapy to me. I later needed play therapy with kids as a missionary counselor for families and their children. By this time in life, my work with the city and state had taught me much about the older population concerns and general wellness. I was eager to learn the art of working with children as a therapist.

Upon graduating and eventually earning my national certified counseling and professional licensure, I then received my play therapy certification. In time, everything fell into place. The play therapy credential was valuable in the mission field because this knowledge gave me the credibility to work with parents and their children. Little did I realize that one day, this credential would take me into Pakistan, Africa, Canada, Thailand, Papua New Guinea, the Philippines, and even Israel. In addition, my assignments took me to a few stateside areas to provide counseling for children and their families.

God directs our paths and our tasks. The hymn "Onward Christian Soldiers" says it so well. We follow the cross of Jesus, and he goes before us. The Spirit within will direct our paths if we allow him to do so. Our job is to listen intently for that still, small voice.

Early into my internship, I was admittedly overwhelmed by some of the clients' issues, issues I had not yet faced. We are taught a great deal as we journey through the painful times in life, yet we face new struggles as we continue forward.

My pain led me to help others through their grief. I had walked in some of those painful shoes. My walk through this journey gave me a foundation from which to work. Not that one has to experience all the hurts and harms of life, yet walking through my many trials and recovering after divorce helped me to better understand how to relate to others and help them with their challenges.

On my way home after my first or second counseling session as an intern, I wondered about my counseling skills. I cried out to the Lord, and he heard my cry. "Lord, this is so hard. I don't think I knew what I was doing tonight."

The Spirit of the Lord touched my soul and whispered, "Maggie, counseling isn't about you. It's about me. Listen closely to my Spirit while in your sessions. My Spirit will guide you and give you the words and grace to speak. The clients that you see are sent to you by me. Listen carefully to your inner spirit, for this is me helping you. Study, pray, and pay attention to my nudging during your sessions. I will show you the way."

This word was such an eye-opener and took the pressure off me. My task was to pray, to study, and to listen to the Spirit within me. "Study yourself to be approved" by me (2 Timothy 2:15 KJV). Be prepared in all seasons of life.

I spent twenty-plus years working with older adults whom I dearly loved, yet now it was time for me to connect with our younger populace. God knew that the mission field involved all ages of clientele, including many children. Since those internship days, I refer to myself as a counselor who enjoys working with all ages.

Who would have thought? God so brilliantly brought me to this wonderful counseling internship position after the dearly loved city job. When I left that city position, I was jobless. God knew, and my task was to notice his nudges. He was guiding me for the next season of my life.

He also gave me the courage to bow out of the second-best internship position. He touched my spirit, gave me deep peace, and brought me to the perfect internship. We know that we know when it's not the commission he has in mind for us.

When we heed his way, we seem to always advance in his plan for our lives. When we follow our own inclination, we miss his best. I like being in his will. He is not a respecter of persons; he wants the best for all his children.

Yes, the best is yet to come. I wish to encourage all readers that God will walk with you through a divorce or any tragedy that you have experienced. Whether single, married, divorced, or widowed, God has a wonderful future for us if we heed his calling.

I am thankful for the past lessons, events, and opportunities. Life can be challenging, yet we can always find something for which to be grateful. With each high spot come a new lesson, a new season, and a new story. Our story is our legacy. We serve a God who offers second and additional chances. And yes, for me there was life after divorce.

27

A Long-Awaited Season—
Accepted by Wycliffe Bible Translators

"This is the confidence that we have in Him, that if we ask anything according to His will, He hears us" (1 John 5:14).

While in my back yard, tending to my shrubs and flowers, it happened unexpectedly. I was spending a quiet, peaceful time outdoors. Suddenly within my spirit, I heard the Spirit of the Lord say, "It's time to make that call to missions." Just before this visit, one year earlier, I had graduated.

I was awarded my well-earned master's degree in Community Counseling. I say "well-earned" as it took focus, commitment, discipline, and much work to earn a degree. As mentioned, I even had to repeat a class. This was the most exciting moment for those of us who proudly walked with me to this goal. My family loudly cheered on their fifty-seven-year-young mom, a moment to behold.

Before the completion of the graduate program, I was granted one thousand dollars from my place of work. This gift covered the additional money I put out toward that very first class that I had to repeat. This failure caused me much pain until I ordered myself out from beneath my comfy security blankets.

Even so, God used this failure for good. He uses our blunders, and they are never in vain. Through the years, I could share with others who missed the mark as I had in that first failed class. This happened for whatever reason, maybe to encourage another who experienced a similar problem. I believe each failure can strength us with fortitude to run the race.

"And my God shall supply all your need according to His riches in glory by Christ Jesus" (Philippians 4:19). The journey, from the inauguration of this graduate program to its completion, included willpower, discipline, determination, some blood, sweat and tears, and many joyful achievements, as well as, yes, some disappointments. Getting past a failed class helped with an issue of potential pride. My task was to stay focused from start to finish, regardless.

The suburb of Phoenix became my new place of residence for five-plus years. As a middle-aged woman, my roots were pulled up and planted two hundred miles north of my hometown. I began part-time employment with the Governor's Advisory Council on Aging (GACA). About the same time, I started my Community Counseling Graduate program at the University of Phoenix Campus. I was also dealing with some menopausal issues. This brand new season in my life was now in full swing.

My practicum began at a senior center. After graduation and after completing my internship at CFCA, I was hired part time there. I was invited to become a full-time employee, yet I was happy with my part-time position (that was often full-time) at the GACA. The flavor of both employments provided a harmonious balance.

Shortly after my arrival at GACA, I was offered a full-time job due to the illness of a staff member. This position as a program project specialist was ideal. I specialized in coordinating and implementing programs, which was my forte. This employment offered continued personal growth at a greater level than what my previous position with the city as a recreation supervisor had offered. This city position paved the way for the state position. God uses us right where we are, and while doing so, he is preparing us for the next assignment.

God uses his children mightily as he trains them now for the future. Each position comes with challenges, yet the problems broaden our outlook and increase our knowledge and skills. We are then ready for new prospects.

My morning routine while living in metro Phoenix consisted of prayer, devotions, and communion, all of which aided in giving me support and strength throughout my days in the city. I needed all that my morning devotion time gave me. Upon being refreshed, I was ready to tackle the flow of heavy expressway traffic, a day at work, an evening of client visits followed by additional study, and anything else that came up during the day.

In the refuge of my apartment, I invited the Holy Spirit to fill me up with his joy, peace, energy, confidence, and strength to accomplish the tasks of the day. The Creator of life carried me through the busy day's and evening's activity.

When the Spirit of the Lord spoke to my heart about missions while in the back yard, I knew who to call at an easily obtainable telephone number. Friends of mine had lived in Papua New Guinea for nearly eleven years. I partnered with them and knew of their various tasks. This couple's children were young before they left for missions and high school graduates and starting college upon returning from their mission assignment. I found the phone number, dialed, and spoke directly with this couple's mission organization, Wycliffe Bible Translators (WBT).

This voice within my spirit brought immediate shouts of joy and spontaneous tears. After a moment or two, the director of the mission's recruitment department and I were conversing. It was time to begin the process of becoming a mission's counselor.

Understandably, as a divorced woman, the agency needed to make sure that I had properly healed. Nearly twenty years had passed since that season in my life, and I felt healed. I mentioned to the recruiter that I knew when I needed healing. But now, without a doubt, I knew when the Lord had wholly restored me. A counselor cannot help others if they are dealing with their own unresolved issues. The Lord did an excellent job in me, and by the stripes of his Son, Jesus, I have experienced remarkable healing.

The mission's training placed significant emphasis on being healed from prior events in life before entering the mission field. Singles and couples alike face fast adjustments to the community and cultures in a foreign country. Missionaries struggle if they carry unhealed issues onto the mission field, especially since loneliness, the burden and responsibility of ministry, and spiritual warfare are constant battles.

Without proper healing, the missionary might need to return home as problems could surface while in the mission field. The missionary needed deep healing before going to an international country. The recruiter said I would be interviewed by seasoned counselors. I understood and agreed to an intense interview, which seemed positive and responsible. I had experienced God's healing for many years by that time.

Meanwhile, the process of phone interviews and an abundance of applicant paperwork started. Each step was ushering me closer to the finish line. In March 2000, I joined potential missionaries at a Mission's Quest program in California. This training consisted of an overview of missions, paperwork, study, and testing. This informative three weeks with staff and other future and some seasoned missionaries was thought-provoking. I completed all paperwork except for two documents that took additional time and thought.

The staff leader reminded me that they were waiting on those two forms. Was I all in for Jesus? I thought long and hard before signing those forms. One stated that in the event of death, the body would remain in-country unless the family paid to return it to their home country. A second form was about kidnapping and ransom. The organization would not pay anything in either of these situations. After much thought and prayer, I completed the forms.

After three weeks in Quest, I flew to Dallas in April for the personal interview. My paperwork was in process, pending an appointment before a group of mission and public counselors. The two-hour meeting with the seven counselors was intense, yet through God's grace, all went well. The interview was to assure that healing from the divorce took place before I was accepted into the counseling ministry.

I passed this test and, soon after, received an invitation to join the Counseling Department Orientation Course. By this time, I had completed my doctrinal statement and all the necessary documents. An applicant under sixty years of age was eligible for long-term missions while an applicant over this age was considered a short-term missionary. I slid into home base two days before turning sixty years of age. After all those years of preparation, I was going for all that was available, namely long-term missions.

Yes, two days before my sixtieth birthday, I was officially accepted in Wycliffe Bible Translators Missions. The application process took a year. By then, I had completed twenty-three years of employment between the city and state. I then could subsidize my mission funding with my state retirement check if needed. Also, the agency required three years of counseling experience as a pre-requisite. Between internship and my employment, I fulfilled that requirement. Just like that, everything fell into place. God's faithful timing was right on.

While living in Phoenix, I became a member of the River of Life Church, a multi-cultural, multi-racial, non-denominational setting perfect for experiencing continued spiritual growth. This church, located about ten minutes from my apartment, offered incredible fellowship. My first event there was the March for Jesus, an activity I previously participated in with my home church two hundred miles south.

Interested participants were to meet near the state capitol. I never did find my church group, so I just joined with the crowd. This amazing march ended at a nearby park where, with the array of speakers, I experienced a special God-given touch. Many people were singing, worshipping, and praising God with lifted hands and voices.

I felt unexplained heat on my hands. I opened my eyes to see if a ray of sunshine was hitting me. Although the temperature was intense, the sun, however, was not shining on me. I wondered if this was perhaps a sign of a healing ministry. I gave little thought to this incident through the years, yet as I later reflected on what happened, I believed the counseling realm was this ministry of healing. God miraculously healed me while in counseling as a client, and then, during my years as a counselor, others were healed. God was always present. I knew he used his children as his hands, feet and words. This was the case for me just as he had used the counselor that respectfully listened to my story so many years earlier.

This newly founded church was involved in street ministry, in feeding the homeless, and in throwing parties in different parks for neighborhood people. This group replaced bike tubes and tires. Old bike tubes and tires were piled like haystacks after the evening's event. Participants consumed grilled hot dogs, chips, and beverages. The hearts of many souls were touched by the Christian music, a short message, gifts to the lucky raffle winners, and an altar call at each outreach. Many people accepted Jesus into their hearts during those evenings. I loved the healing that happened in these parties at the park.

In Phoenix, our GACA event called for a parade around the Arizona Capitol. Our staff worked to encourage the older adults to join in the very first Senior 2000 Fitness program. I was privileged to coordinate and oversee this program that was beneficial to overall health.

With great ambition and a joyous heart, people of many cultures from throughout the state, including my dear friends from my home down south, followed the loud horn and the flickering yellow and red flashes of the state capitol police car as it circled the capitol. State employees came out of the buildings to cheer on hundreds of senior walkers. The air filled with jubilee on that glorious day.

Yes, I went from a small town parade in my small city to a huge parade in the capital, Phoenix—from minor to major. "Here comes the parade." From riding my decorated bike in a parade as a child to marching while I beat a drum to the parade in this huge metropolis.

I love parades. And now, who would have ever thought? God had it all planned before I knew I would move to Phoenix. Perhaps he was telling his angels during those earlier years that one day, she would march with jubilee, joined by the older population around the State Capitol. Yes, who would have ever thought?

I enrolled in the church's college-level classes and benefitted from noted speakers, such as Marilyn Hickey and others who offered workshops. I also had the privilege of volunteering at a three-day conference held by Joyce Meyers. I took advantage of as many of the plentiful conference and workshop opportunities as possible with my busy schedule. The Lord gave me opportunities that prepared me for my move to the mission field.

The busy, noisy, fast-paced city of Phoenix found a special place in my heart. My children and grandchildren came up to Phoenix during Thanksgiving and Christmas. Once the turkey and ham were in the oven, we delivered containers of food to our neighbors in need. The church began the food drive effort months before the holidays. This activity was a drive-by blessing. Today, years later, my grandchildren still speak of those times. They loved delivering food and blankets and returned the following years to help with the distribution again.

They handed out and even covered the homeless with blankets that they took to locations under the bridge and in the park. After a time, a church elder approached me about becoming a deacon, which involved in-depth training and eventual ordination. I loved the responsibilities that come along with this and stayed in this position as long as I lived in Phoenix. During my last year in the city, I joined the choir. God was continually working in my life while I attended this church.

About the second year in Phoenix, I invited my single daughter and her two sons to join me. She had been alone for a few years and needed a change. This church offered an elementary school that I felt would enrich her and her sons. I suggested that together, we purchase a home, which we did.

This home sat on a cul-de-sac road, a perfect place for two energetic boys to grow up in added safety. I experienced buyer's remorse for a time but finally got over this and made this house a home. In time, the house sold as it was time for another colossal move. My daughter remarried, and I was moving to Dallas as a missionary. This home brought healing and, eventually, a financial profit. Only God knew.

My time in Phoenix was coming to an end. I complemented my time with the GACA and earned my retirement time. My three years of counseling experience with CFCA met the minimum required time needed to join the counseling ministry with WBT. My newly acquired degree would be put to great use on the mission field.

Living in Phoenix presented an opportunity for deeper trust in the Lord. Before this, I could call my daughters for help. In Phoenix, I had to depend on the Lord for the various areas of my life. It was like a battery jumpstart, a change of a flat tire, and learning to get around. God was weaning me from dependence on the family to dependence on him.

I was one of the overseers of one of the more extensive statewide programs that brought many cultures to Phoenix. There were many enjoyable times while working and walking this state parade and in the numerous 200-miles south hometown community parades. I remembered the annual Christmas parades as the seniors walked, waved, and wished bystanders "Merry Christmas" and "Happy New Year."

It was time to sell our Phoenix home and move to Dallas. Within a week, the home belonged to another family. My real estate gal was the finest. I gave notice to the GACA and the CFCA. The years grew me up, and the opportunities with these agencies better prepared me for the upcoming season. Each step forward offered a joyous and exciting spiritual season.

Several times I was asked, "Are you sure, Maggie, that you want to leave this GACA position?" With my degree in hand and five years in this GACA position, the potential for advancement was there.

"Yes," I replied, "my calling is in the mission field." I was prepared to step into my next season in life. I waited and worked for many years to arrive to this point. The both joyful and painful journey was a long row to hoe to reach this goal. Those years called for focus and determination. By the grace of God, I made it. From elementary school years to middle-age life, yes, this was the goal. I arrived intact by the grace of God.

Now we can see why dating or becoming involved with another relationship was not in the plan for my life. He desired a tighter and always intentional relationship with God. Only through him was I able to stay focused. He made a way. And now yes, I would dearly miss my peers and Phoenix. I was very thankful for their friendship and what they taught me and what I learned during that time.

God placed me with the CFCA, the agency that taught and prepared me to be the very best mission's counselor. I will forever be grateful. God placed me in the very best setting to prepare me for the next season. "Being confident of this very thing, that He who has begun a good work in you will complete it until the day of Jesus Christ" (Philippians 1:6).

Good-byes are bittersweet. However, I had lovely memories of the years of friendships. I left better equipped.

My trusty blue Honda was now packed to the seams and took me to my home two hundred miles to the south. The time in Phoenix flew by. I left this city with much more than what I had arrived with. God provided me with the courage to complete my university studies, the three years of counseling experience, and the completion of years to retirement.

My time in southern Arizona would be short-lived. Shortly after that trip with my faithful little car, I would travel another one thousand miles east. What did God have next for me? He had led me this far and would surely continue to do so.

28

Dallas, Here I Come—Mission Assignment

"It is good to sing praises to our God...He heals the brokenhearted...Great is our Lord, and mighty in power; His understanding infinite" (Psalm 147:1, 3, 5).

The cross-country trip to Dallas from Arizona was long. The open desert range brought a sense of freedom and joy. Much work was behind me. I had jumped plenty of hurdles to arrive at this point. Some obstacles set me back, and I tripped, producing hurt, pain, and delays. Anything worth achieving takes time and work. Finishing this lap was very satisfying.

God kept me on track. This journey supplied the very best mentors, each hand-picked by God, my Comforter, security, my best friend, and the lifter of my head. I learned about our heavenly Father, who became my husband. I gained from valued teaching through the years. And finally, "I pressed toward the goal for the prize of the upward call of God in Christ Jesus" (Philippians 3:14). I reached the long-awaited goal, spurred on by the many prayers of my mother, family, and friends. People encouraged, supported, and cheered me on in this marathon.

The following Bible verse kept me going. "Commit your way to the Lord, Trust also in Him, and He shall bring it to pass" (Psalm 37:5). God walks with us as we fix and focus our eyes on him. Just a closer walk with him "My heart is steadfast, O God, my heart is steadfast" (Psalm 57:7).

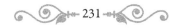

God gives bits and pieces as we journey along. Sometimes it's like walking in the dark. I knew I wanted to become a missionary, but I did not know about counseling until I went through counseling myself, almost twenty years earlier.

I stopped to see the woman who led me to the Lord before starting my road trip to Dallas. About twenty years had passed since I had stepped into her living room and repeated the sinner's prayer after her. From that moment on, I wanted to live wholeheartedly for Jesus.

My stop was a surprise visit, and might I add that she was happy to see me and hear of my travels to Dallas. She and I had celebrated my spiritual birthday throughout the years. She sent a card and note each year with encouragement and kind words. I, in turn, sent a bouquet. Without ceasing, she prayed for me through the years as God directed her.

My journey of hope and life began that day. We only want to be where he wants us to be, and God leads the way. Finally, I was now an official missionary. At one time, I considered joining the Joyce Meyer's team, but God wanted me in missions.

I once thought my life was ending, but in fact, the journey of a lifetime was just beginning. I had no idea my experience would be as astonishing and exhilarating as it turned out to be. And there is still more life ahead. I'm very much alive!

Wherever I went, I sought older women that could mentor and teach me the ways of the Lord (Titus 2:4–5). My life was strengthened in perseverance, discipline, self-control, patience, diligence, and dependability, to name a few traits. I learned to eat that elephant in the room. I learned to double my multi-tasking as I juggled different projects and tasks simultaneously.

Most importantly, I learned to step out in faith and seek God's direction. I learned much with God's help, including how to appreciate the opportunities to develop. Reflection helps put life into perspective. As I reflect on this journey, I can only say, "Yes, by the grace of God. All honor and praise I give to our heavenly Father."

This Dallas move was big for me yet not for God. "'Not by might nor by power, but by My Spirit,' says the Lord of Hosts" (Zechariah 4:6). My task was to keep pressing on with eyes focused on the one who made this possible.

I had already overcome significant challenges, and no doubt, those before me would likewise be big. Life as a single mom calls for energy. As I previously mentioned, my children participated in the usual school curriculum and extracurricular activities: from boyfriends to husbands, from bikes to cars and tire repairs to auto repairs, from fender benders to sitting before a judge. The list goes on: jobs, graduations, college, paperwork, courting, weddings, and babies. I witnessed the birth of my first eight grandchildren. These grandbabies now have children of their own.

When my children were home, they could always find me. They knew I was generally at work, in a classroom, or at church. I recall the time one of my daughters came to a Sunday event at the community center. She said, "Mom, I have something to tell you. I just ran into another vehicle. It's not too bad, just a fender bender." The other car was not damaged, just hers. She now had two fender benders on her record. Fortunately, this taught her to work even harder so she could pay off the vehicle repairs.

"For we walk by faith, not by sight" (2 Corinthians 5:7). "Now faith is the substance of things hoped for, the evidence of things not seen" (Hebrews 11:1). The early morning paper route, yard sales, and collecting aluminum cans are all vivid memories. I could spot an aluminum can from a long ways away. One daughter told people, "If you give my mom a loaf of bread, she will service your swamp cooler." I thought nothing of climbing on the roof of a home to service these units and became a twenty-year cooler veteran. That shows initiative, right?

A friend and I applied for dry down woodcutting permits for wood for the fireplace. With a chainsaw in my hands, we brought home a bundle of firewood. Like my mother, I burned wood in the fireplace, which helped to subsidize furnace costs.

I learned to paint the inside and seal the outside of our home. One summer, my vacation consisted of sealing the outside block on our house. With a paintbrush, ladder, and sun screen, I worked away. To look at my suntanned body, one might have thought I spent my vacation at the beach. Employment, college, and studies—my busy life taught me to apply myself and get up after I fell down.

I was now on my way to a new season and trusted that God would guide me in his plan. As I reminisced about where I began and where I ended up, I had more light and direction for the future. As we follow him along the path, he takes us to where he wants us to be. We know from previous circumstances that everything's going to be all right.

I felt good about reaching this long-awaited goal. A sense of freedom encircled me. Nothing worthwhile in life comes easily. God's grace enables us to work hard and gives us the ability to stay on course as we fight the good fight of faith.

I received a trophy that honored a few strong character traits and that encouraged me as I walked into the future. "There is none like You, O Lord (You are great, and Your name is great in might)" (Jeremiah 10:6).

Soon I would be in Dallas to set up housekeeping, prepare an office, and, in time, take an assignment overseas. From elementary school and a big midlife boost and acceptance into missions two days before my sixtieth birthday, life had been full of surprises. The long Arizona-to-Texas trip was a piece of cake in comparison to my life journey up to that point in life.

The traffic to Dallas was sparse. I could see for miles in every direction in the midst of open range country. The Lord and I were on the road to my first mission's assignment. Occasionally a truck shared the road with me. The booming of the radio and my voice no doubt awakened the armadillos and the prairie dogs along the way.

Although the nearly one-thousand-mile road trip was long, God's presence filled my heart to capacity and the interior of my blue Honda. God showed himself faithful and true. Whatever lay before me, I was ready to tackle it with the continued help of God. Occasional truck stops provided a beautiful stretch and needed restroom break. It was a great day for this excited single woman.

I recalled the years with the older adults and my reluctance to leave the city job. I could only image what prospects I would have missed if I had not heeded God's gentle nudge. In time, I efficiently navigated busy Phoenix. I got over the disappointment of a failed class. The trauma of finding myself single at a young age was now behind me. I was thankful for life's second and even third chances. I followed the straight and narrow path that led to fulfillment and the finish line.

I learned to let go of life's hurtful events. I learned to let go and bless my daughters as they left for college and became married adult children. I learned to let go of that tight grip on the steering wheel of my car. I learned to relax in the passenger seat and the back seat during the long trips to and from undergraduate school in Tucson. I learned to ride elevators to the top floor of a skyscraper. I learned to let go of my home and to invite renters to move in. I learned about lice treatments.

Through it all, I learned to become whole and unique and enjoy singleness. I learned of my value and discovered who I was as a single. I learned to develop myself with the help of the Lord and focus on the goal he had before me. I learned to be content in whatever state I was in. I learned to let go and let God.

A taxi cab driver once insisted on staying by my side until my car started. I am sure the angels protected me from harm at least a zillion times over. I learned that failing a class is not the end of the world. I learned to get up, brush the dust off my knees, and set foot into that same class again. I learned to eat alone in restaurants and to feel comfortable around married couples. I learned to get out of the boat and experience the water, the waves, the stormy weather, and by the grace of God, make it to the other side.

How excellent is your way, Lord Jesus, you have taught me about life. "O Lord, our Lord, how excellent is your name in all the earth" (Psalm 8:1). "These things I have spoken to you, that in Me you may have peace" (John 16:33).

I arrived at the International Summer Linguistics center on a dark evening. The young missionaries who knew I was coming were waiting for me outside the dorm. They happily helped me carry my things up to dorm room 243, my new sanctuary. One might say that my baby was born that very night, the baby that I had carried for many years. The seed planted so many years earlier finally came to fruition.

A different type of groundwork now awaited me. Missionaries go through a regime of preparation for overseas assignments. They cannot sign up today and fly out tomorrow to go on the mission field. The steps to becoming a mission's counselor were many. I completed all of them, including procuring my certifications, licensure, and a few other credentials, before my assignment to an overseas position. My graduation from an accredited university lowered the required number of client hours. I had completed many client hours in Phoenix but still needed more counseling hours. Gathering these requirements and client hours took time. My Dallas stay lasted three-plus years. I had much to learn and do.

I lived in the dormitory in a private room for about seven months, which was convenient for me. Upon my arrival at this center, I began to see clients. A counselor that specialized as a play therapist with children and their families was an excellent addition to the counseling center.

My international atlas came in handy as clients pointed out countries where they had lived and served. These clients helped to acquaint me with various countries around the world. The children efficiently pointed out their whereabouts. I was captivated and impressed as they shared stories. These children and their families blessed me with their kindness. Time with the children was gratifying and captivating. I was a student in their classroom on culture study.

Shortly after my arrival, I attended my first international mission's conference with many other counselors. Someone mentioned that I was quiet. They shared many stories, and I learned the importance of preparing for overseas counseling ministry. This group was like a power team with years of experience with missions. They were right. I felt like a total novice in comparison to these seasoned counselors. I was not ready for an overseas residency at that time.

Getting out of the boat to walk on the water and the waves can be risky. But you must leave the boat to get to the other side. Each risk draws us closer to all that God has for us.

Dallas is an ideal location for various conferences, workshops, trainings, and, of course, seeing clients. This location was a perfect place to finalize my mission's and licensure requirements. I was around seasoned, dedicated missionaries, fully committed to God's work—an impressive and awe-inspiring experience. The learning curve occasionally brought me to tears.

I eventually hoped to be invited to travel with several colleagues. My previous 1993 passport, which had taken me to Africa, Ghana, and the Ivory Coast with the Barnabas Ensemble Group, was now expired. This three-week trip to the Ivory Coast lit a fire within me. I fell in love with the people. No doubt, it prepared me for what I would soon experience once I was ready to be assigned to a third-world country. Shortly after arriving in Dallas, I applied for a new passport just in case the opportunity to travel opened up.

A medical clinic in the center among the array of other buildings and classrooms offered shots and needed immunizations for those who planned to travel out of the country. I was prepared and did all I could to be ready.

My client hours were adding up, and I was attending essential classes. My journey unfolded piece-by-piece, like a giant puzzle. I was trying to fit in all the puzzle pieces. Eventually, we will arrive if we do not give up along the way. "I will instruct you and teach you in the way you should go" (Psalm 32:8). Perhaps if we received the entire journey at one time, we would be overwhelmed. For example, we have one child, which prepares us for the next and possibly for several children.

Shortly after my arrival in Dallas, one Sunday after church, my Korean friend, who also lived in the dorm, invited me for lunch. She served Japanese noodles and an apple for dessert. I told her about my allergic reaction to apples some twenty years ago. I had not eaten as much as a bite since that time. She coaxed me like Eve did Adam. In this case, it was likely a nudge from God.

I bit off a little bite and had no reaction. Again I bit off a second bite with no response. After a few of these nibbles, I went for the whole apple. After that, I ate two and three apples per day while in Dallas. I could not get enough apples. I traded dessert for an apple. In no time, I had eaten dozens, maybe a bushel or two. Today, I'm still eating apples. God healed me and used my Japanese friend to convince me to eat his healthy fruit. This afternoon lunch was like getting out of the boat for a swim!

I had started watching Bishop T.D. Jakes on television while in Phoenix. About this time, he moved from Virginia to Dallas. I inquired as to the whereabouts of his church. I wanted to visit at least once. Well, lo and behold, the location of the Potter's House was within a very short distance from the Summer Institute of Linguistics (SIL) center. I was so excited.

Shortly after attending the first service, I completed the church's orientation course and became a member. The ten-thousand-seat capacity spread from the lower level into balconies. I never sat next to the same person during that first year. I sat in every area of the church.

One Sunday, I asked a person wearing a Guardian Angel T-shirt about this ministry. My question led me to become a member of the street ministry team where I joined their excursions into the heart of Dallas and, occasionally, Fort Worth. I loved this ministry. I had been involved in a similar ministry—a favorite—while living in Phoenix.

After several night trips into the streets, I joined the Sunday morning ministry team. The team prepared and fed the homeless a full breakfast fit for a king right there at the Potter's House. The people then advanced to the section with full bathrooms and salon chairs. They could take showers and receive clothing and shoes. Licensed beauticians provided haircuts and even perms. While the people took turns, they could receive ministry.

I was once asked to wash a person's hair. This woman had dozens of braids. Every space on her head had a twist. I asked, "How do you do this? Do I take out each braid?"

The beautician laughed. "No, just wash in between the braids." This job offered new experiences. I did it! We team members were there to bless and to provide services to those in need. Our homeless friends then attended the church service, looking as if they stepped off the "Vogue" magazine cover. They carried their own Bibles and joined the congregation. Serving with this homeless ministry was part of my special memories in Dallas.

My newly acquainted friends saved a seat for me each Sunday until I left Dallas. From that time, I sat with a friend about midway down the center aisle on the left side of the sanctuary. Eventually, I learned to know many familiar faces and friends. To meet friends, show yourself friendly—get involved.

One Sunday before joining the street ministry, I felt down and in need of a friend. I spoke these words in prayer that morning before church. I sat near a radiant older woman who soon became my friend. She was a tender-hearted, and people loved being around her. Bishop called for everyone to take the hand on the right side and their left side and stretch from one side of the aisle to the other. This older woman commented as she held my hand, "Oh, honey, your hands are so cold." She then kindly held my hands between her warm hands for a few moments. She then followed up with a gentle warm hug. This moment was the beginning of our precious friendship.

The first night I rode in the van with the Guardian Angel Team, I was the only White female, which surprised me. I thought others with my skin color would be there, yet I was okay with it and so happy to be a part of this group. One lady said to me, "Maggie, I hope you are comfortable being with us. We are so happy you have joined us. We hope you will invite some of your friends to come the next time." She soon learned that I was very content being with my special Potter House friends!

After each service, I stood in the long line to pick up a cassette tape of the service. Eventually, the recordings were out, and CDs and DVDs became popular. I listened to the messages many times. Wednesday night Bible Studies were also a favorite time. This church and the friendships were just what I needed while in Dallas.

When the time came to leave Dallas, my friends from the Potter's House treated me to a meal and night out. They gave me a photo album, and when I was in Papua New Guinea, these friends sent Christmas cards and a prayer shawl. God, you are so good at caring for your people.

Eventually, I offered a play therapy introductory workshop, and many people were interested. Play therapy and group therapy were new concepts within the missionary community. The interest made it possible for me to offer more sessions. Group play teaches compassion, helps, initiative, loyalty, diligence, responsibility, endurance, and nurturing. Working with these missionary kids was a pleasure.

After seven months of living in the dorm, I moved into an attic apartment within walking distance of my job site. I shopped at garage sales for a table, lamp, and a few things to make my little one-room apartment as cozy as possible. I took the outdoor stairs up to my living quarters for nearly three years. A few times, the snow froze on the steps, and I was stranded for a day or two. The sun shined through the window each morning and brightened this little room. It was a bit of heaven right there in the attic.

Singles have endless opportunities to become involved. When we give to others, we also receive. "It is better to give than receive." When we deliver, we receive abundantly. We don't give to receive, but it naturally comes along with giving. Fulfillment and much joy comes when we offer ourselves to others. Through the years, I have volunteered in many places. I then return to my home, filled with much joy and love. And since retirement, I have become involved in volunteering once again.

Every cell in my body experiences fulfillment and satisfaction when I can give to another in need of comfort. I am forever grateful for the people who came into my life since becoming single. Friends walked alongside me, especially during the healing phase.

God has not forgotten us. Years before, my friend openly confronted me and bravely said, "Maggie, you need to stop feeling sorry for yourself." Had she not so boldly approached me, I might have drowned in a pool of self-pity. No one told me self-pity was a sin. What a revelation!

Despite life's difficulties, with Jesus in our hearts, life becomes doable, much more relaxed, and very fulfilling. When we give of ourselves, we receive God's best. People all around us need a helping hand, perhaps just someone to listen to them.

God worked out the details so that I could travel to Pakistan and Canada while in Dallas. I treasured the time of working with the many missionary children who experienced civil unrest. Upon returning to Dallas, I was never the same. My trip to Africa in 1993 encouraged me to serve in a third-world country. I so desired to serve in a land with much hardship. The fulfillment of my wish soon followed.

"A new commandment I give to you, that you love one another; as I have loved you, that you also love one another" (John 13:34).

29

Pakistan—Assignment

My first trip to Pakistan as a Wycliffe Bible Translator (WBT) mission's counselor was a true quest. Little did I realize that many more tours would follow.

First, the trip took a long time: two-plus days through many time zones. The three of us, all counselors, started in Dallas then flew to New York, Dubai, and on to Pakistan. The trip included buses, trains, vans, and, of course, the air carrier.

I had this unique opportunity to be invited to work in Pakistan for a time. I could not turn it down, and my two traveling companions had many journeys under their proverbial belts. Since they had previously lived overseas and had taken many international trips, they seemed relaxed and confident. However, this was the first time any of us had been to Pakistan.

While traversing from one gate to another in the international terminals, I felt as if I were navigating a complicated maze. We rode buses to the various terminals that were too far to walk and then rode escalators and moving ramps as we trudged on, following the signs that led us on a hike or scavenger hunt. Miraculously, we found our way through the plethora of travelers. Overall, the trip went smoothly. We stayed in lounging areas for over-night travelers, complete with food, beverages, and souvenir shops to our liking. We three helped each other out on this challenging trip.

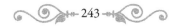

Since the three of us had gathered clothing from our Dallas colleagues that had previously lived in Pakistan, my Muslim dress was huge; three of us could have worn it at the same time. The belt around the waist and safety pins kept my garment and the bloomers in tack. Without these reinforcements, I could have easily suffered embarrassment. But overall, the garment served its purpose.

We arrived in Dubai, the last stop before entering Pakistan. We exchanged our Western blue jeans for our Pakistani dress, the *shalwar kameez*, since it was required when traveling into this country. With the long robe-like outer garment, bloomer-like pants, and a headscarf that covered everything except the eyes, we blended in with the international station traffic.

Yet we felt a bit conspicuous as our facial features did not necessarily match our garments. The last layover into Pakistan was an overnighter, and their clothing was not nearly as comfortable as our Western clothing. However, it was roomy enough, as though we were wearing pajamas, so we could stretch out for a night on the lounge chairs. Laughter and excitement bubbled up among our excited female team.

One female companion and her husband had lived in South America for many years. They had already served in various roles for twenty-five years when we met, and she and I had previously worked together for a few years. This fun, energetic woman radiated with a contagious smile wherever she went. Her husband, another jewel, and their three children were in full support of her every endeavor.

The other female companion, a single experienced traveler and missionary of many years, led us through the airport terminals. She was a tall young lady and fun, caring, and smiling. She loved people of all ages. Our young adult missionary kids (MKs) enjoyed being around this special lady. Later in her missionary career, she became a mission's counselor. Since she knew the ins and outs, she guided us through the maze with expertise. She and I worked with the MKs from the youngest to the oldest during this Pakistani venture.

The transfers in the various airports overwhelmed me. At one point, I asked my colleague if I could just tag along and if she would take care of our check-ins, etc. She agreed, and after the long flight and our arrival in Pakistan, we had made it at last. A male Pakistani greeted us at the airport entrance.

Happily, we spotted the Welcome sign with each name neatly written on it. Likewise, he appeared glad to locate us. After he managed to pack our luggage into his small van, we were headed into the heavy, risky traffic to the university. The driver dodged a variety of types of transportation. This trip was the first time I had seen several people, perhaps a family, sitting on a board placed crisscross on the back of a motorbike. Travelers freely zipped in and out of the flowing traffic—what an amazing adventure.

Even though I had a few long-distance travel adventures behind me, I felt like an inexperienced traveler on this particular trip. Other travels had included a long flight to Germany with my five daughters (six females solo), a trip for rest and relaxation to Hawaii after my husband's six-month Viet Nam assignment, and even to Africa in 1993. But none of these trips fully prepared me for this adventure.

I prayed constantly during this trip. Thankfully, God traveled along with us. His presence made the way for the three of us. No doubt, he sent his angels to guard and protect us as strangers in a foreign land. Yet God is no stranger in foreign lands since he is the Creator of heaven and Earth. He was and is familiar with Pakistan.

When Jesus went to heaven, he sent a helper. On that Pentecost day, nearly two thousand years ago, each disciple received the Holy Spirit. At one time, only Moses and the Old Testament prophets heard the Lord speak and then related those words to the people. But since that Pentecost day, the Holy Spirit resides in each person that invites him in. The Holy Spirit actively kept us safe on this trip.

We three and the driver were off, heading to our housing. This minivan driver remained silent. He did not even crack the slightest smile until we all shouted just before he slammed on the brakes to avoid hitting several people on a motorized bike. This bike had a board across the back fender the long way, hanging out on each side of the rear frame and tire. People were sitting on this board while one guy was cycling. It was a sight to behold.

Although we narrowly missed hitting the group on the bike, the driver did not seem to think it was a close call. What an amazingly busy sight with the streets so crowded with so much traffic—cyclists, cars, cow-pulled carts, and motorcycles—coasting along. Additionally, our van driver was swerving here and there, dodging animals and other moving objects. Finally, after our American shouts, he did give a big smile.

We now knew he was alive not a robot. We all laughed at that heart-stopping moment. Our laughter broke the ice. The man's expression softened, and he might've thought, *Hey, these American women are certainly full of fun.*

When we arrived at the Women's Campus, our safe place of lodging during our stay, we were assigned a room and shown where our bathrooms and shower building were located. My room reminded me of a monk's chamber with the minimal basic accommodations of a small dresser, combination table and desk, and a twin bed placed on the concrete floor. The room had a high ceiling with only one tiny window above the massive door. The small window allowed the welcome rays of sunlight to enter.

The toilets were located in another building away from our assigned rooms. We were surprised to find two types of bathrooms—a choice of a sit-down toilet or a squat-down toilet. Each type of bathroom had its own room. Our laughter filled the air. We now faced a new sight. The showers contained a large garbage can filled with water and a scoop. This scoop served as the overhead shower's running water when there was no running water, which was quite often the case.

Within a few days in the country, we took a transit bus to shop at a fabric store. I was able to purchase enough fabric for two outfits for just twenty dollars. A male seamstress, an amputee, with the assistance of his helper, measured me to exactness. The male tailor and his sewing machine were both on a rug on the floor. My garments were ready for pick up in two days. I no longer needed a belt and safety pins for my baggy pants and over-sized dress. I later became the owner of two shalwar kameez outfits.

The three of us were pleased to work with families that recently had experienced a civil unrest incident. Another team of counselors worked with the adults. The anti-government activities, such as protests and civil unrest, affected our people emotionally and physically. We enthusiastically accepted our assignments and looked forward to working with and helping our gracious colleagues that captivated our hearts in this intriguing country.

While working in Phoenix as a family therapist, I made a weekly circuit run, visiting with children and families referred by the State Family Builders program. My car trunk carried a variety of therapeutic toys for the children's play therapy sessions in their homes. These items usually included a dollhouse, furniture, creative items, miniatures for sand tray expressions, and boy- and girl-specific items.

Likewise, in Pakistan, I brought fun and challenging therapeutic tools, which were well thought-out and packed in my cargo. Much thought was given to a flexible schedule in order to meet the needs of the various ages of the children and to help aid their turbulent emotions. Thus my suitcase carried placemats to serve as sand trays, a five-pound bag of new sand, and many miniature toys. I used an assortment of art supplies to help facilitate emotional and expressive play with and without verbalizing. This included a few nurturing toys: dolls and their accessories for the girls and construction toys and more aggressive toys to help release built-up emotions for the boys.

Time spent with the children helped them to understand themselves better and to equip them for handling the stresses in their young lives. The overall outcome was very constructive. Together, the children and I had a special time of healing.

At one point, our sponsor took us for a ride through both the poverty and sight-seeing areas. This sponsor had lived there for a long time and was familiar with the region. We felt comfortable with her. Pakistani people looked on with interest and curiosity at the foreigners. Our smiles went a long way.

One night, we were taken to the Turkish and Pakistani border to watch the changing of the guards. Many Pakistani people filled the bleachers, and all of us clapped as the guards walked through the border gates, ready to entertain the spectators.

Driving through the narrow pathways to and fro was an adventure. People filled the paths, causing extensive slowing through that area. The street vendors in their shops displayed shiny, sparkly items, such as bracelets, necklaces, and watches. Hustle, bustle, and loud clamor and chaos filled the air, but we did not stop. We always carried prayer in our hearts.

On Sundays, we attended a Protestant church service. We took communion at the church altar and drank out of a standard cup. God was in this place of worship. Our university escort gladly introduced us to the culture. She drove her vehicle fast and efficient, dodging whatever might be in the way. Years later, I would notice this was similar to the way the Filipinos operate their cars.

On one occasion, we had lunch at a McDonald's. The upper seating area offered a splendid view of the busy town. Since I collect McDonald's toys, I purchased kids' meals for the surprises. I still have the Pakistani menu placemat scripted in the Islamic language.

It's difficult to explain how I felt after that first trip to Pakistan. That first trip was enormous and effective. Confidence in God and one trip to Pakistan behind me made the journey pleasurable. Interestingly enough, on my second Pakistan trip, I traveled alone, along with our Papa God.

This second trip involved a twenty-four-hour-plus layover, so I bravely took a taxi to Dubai, found a hotel, and spent the night. As I think about that trip to the city of Dubai, I can hardly believe this happened. God generously poured his anointing oil over me from top to bottom. He built a boldness and bravery within me. I can only say, by the grace of God.

I entered this refined hotel complete with the marble floors, countertops, and elegant hotel furnishings. The room I stayed in was all white as were the walls, bedding, sheets, and towels, along with a pure white bathtub, so white that my eyes squinted at the brightness. It resembled the interior of a sterilized operating room.

I only saw men and was escorted to my room by a male attendant. Feeling quite safe, I settled in and crawled into bed in need of a horizontal position. I could not think about eating. Consequently, every so often, a knock tapped on my door, waking me each time and asking if all was okay. I thought perhaps they were concerned that I didn't eat dinner. The next morning, I settled my bill and then was taken back to the airport.

Both my first and second trips offered a brand new adventure. I do not remember being afraid. Yes, I was cautious at times and I scan the crowd when out in public; perhaps I do not remember fear. On the university campus, we guests were treated with much respect; however, we were sure to stay prayed up. And when out in the public, people just stared.

Most likely, I prayed more on the second trip as my traveling partner was unseen. Traveling with a team seems safer, yet God in his faithfulness accompanied me. No doubt, the angels surrounded us the first time and certainly during my second trip as well (Psalm 91:11).

During my alone time in Pakistan, I stayed in a bed-and-breakfast run by men. They greeted me with respect. Maybe the white-hair factor offered a safety net, as did the perhaps visible angels Gabriel and Michael. My host felt I was safe, although I did experience some uncertain times. I imagine fear integrates with the idea of not feeling safe.

This time was another example of trusting the host's decision and discernment. The door to my room was very loose, and yes, I put a chair under the doorknob for additional security. Each morning, I left the premises and waited by the road for my host to pick me up.

I dressed in clothing similar to the shalwar kameez with my head covered, yet I was told that because of my white hair and age, I could expect to be treated with respect. I was about sixty-six years of age during my second visit to Pakistan. When I mentioned to my host that it would be nice to see a woman in this place of lodging, I was told that women did not work in these types of environments.

One early evening, I was invited to a single missionary's home for pizza. We sat on the floor and spent a lovely evening together. Another time, we all went to a restaurant where many other Pakistani women gathered. We women greeted each other with a smile and a nod, and we single ladies felt welcomed. One late afternoon, a single missionary and I walked the street where male vendors sold their delicious bread. These men gave us permission to take photos.

I spent time at an international school, enclosed with heavy doors and walls, surrounded with a fence so high that you could not see over it and a gate that the guard controlled. A guard was available at all times within this international school. All Pakistani homes seemed to have large solid fences and massive gates surrounding their households. When walking down the alley, you couldn't see the yards. Everything was enclosed.

Striking a great rapport with clients helps to accomplish goals. That valuable gift of encouragement given to me by God is precious in every way. Think about the gifts that God showers on you. Do you notice how these gifts help others while you get to bloom just where God plants you? I believe that these gifts are given to us so we can accomplish what God has in mind for us, for his glory.

My host and her family provided a noon meal each day. A Quick Shop located near my lodging place had various foods for snacks and the evening meal. My room came with a small refrigerator, so I had a spot to keep a snack or two. Unlike the bucket with water at the university, I always had water for a shower. This time when taking a shower, the entire bathroom was sprayed down. The drainage system worked well, so the water disappeared as soon as it hit the floor.

My host took me shopping and gave me several beautiful bangle bracelets before leaving. I had brought a few special treats for my host from home. Treats from the United States are always welcome for missionaries serving somewhere in the world.

I felt so honored and privileged to have the privilege of being asked to serve as the counselor and to provide restoration after a crisis. Those weeks offered an excellent opportunity for building character. God worked in many ways. He gets the glory for the great things he did. The culture and atmosphere were extraordinary, as was my exposure to this new country. We do serve a mighty God. "And He has made from one blood every nation of men to dwell on all the face of the earth, and has determined their preappointed times and the boundaries of their dwellings" (Acts 17:26).

I will close this chapter with this tidbit. If the woman who pierces and places a small diamond outside the nose had been available, my picture would reflect this gem. However, she was far away at the time.

30

My Mother-in-Law's Funeral—Left Out

My mother-in-law, age eighty-five, passed away in 2003, and my father-in-law, age eighty-nine, died in 2004. I made the decision to attend their funerals without a second thought. I loved my in-laws, the grandparents of my children. We faithfully corresponded with each other for nearly fifty years. Without hesitation from the beginning of my marriage to their son, I quickly referred to them as "Mom" and "Dad."

Since we first met in the mid-1950s, Fran had always been special to me. Our correspondence and visits continued even after her son and I broke up. I easily called Fran "Mom." Our hearts for each other were joined throughout the years.

I was pleased to attend this loved one's memorial service. Visiting parents was a priority for us but generally only happened once a year when the Army allowed for furlough time. We wanted our children to know their grandparents and vice versa. Our parents—my mom, and Fran and Frank—lived roughly ten miles apart. Their proximity to each other was an added convenience since our visits home involved many miles. My trips to Michigan as a single continued at least once a year and increased whenever possible in our parents' later years.

The break-up of my former spouse and I was difficult for our parents. All of our family members and friends were heartbroken and as shocked as I was. My mom dearly loved the father of her grandchildren and the husband of her second child. Since I had introduced him to her in my early high school years, she had adored this man. Mom's tears of sorrow kept her pillow moist for a very long time after the break-up of our marriage. She had loved the generational goings-on of her adult children, their husbands, and their children. She cherished the photo of her son-in-law and her together years later when he randomly stopped in to visit her. That photo was easily retrieved when she wanted to look at it.

At one point, my mother said, "I hate this divorce but will always love the father of my five granddaughters. He was so good to me." Her love for her former son-in-law continued until her death. She was a stellar example of having a loving heart. Her testimony of love and forgiveness touched many lives.

The funeral home visitation the evening before the memorial service went exceptionally well. My former husband and his wife greeted everyone as they entered the room, and I hugged them and smiled at both of them. My biological family and our friends attended that evening. Our conversation with each other and others throughout this visitation was warm and pleasant. Funerals seem to have a unique way of bringing the family together. My birth family forever treasured my former husband and his parents.

The next morning, my family and I went to the church service together. Fran's kinsfolk, who had traveled a distance to attend the funeral, greeted me with open arms. We had been friends since we first met. I so enjoyed seeing and visiting with these relatives. So many years had passed since we had been together. We talked and caught up with each other. This time together nourished our hearts with love.

My sister, her husband, my mom, brother, and I shared a pew about three seats from the back of the quaint little church. We were maybe seven or eight pews from the front of the church. We chatted about the many fun times we had with this dearly departed one. Fran's sense of humor and kindness stood out.

Grandma Fran lavished her granddaughters with letters and cards throughout the years. In turn, she received plenty of messages from our family. Letter writing was popular back in those days. A landline phone call was expensive, so letter writing was the popular way to stay in touch. The mailman dropped off and delivered letters on an almost weekly basis.

My family and I recalled Fran's sense of humor. She often cut off the heads of people in her photos. Her husband Frank shook his head as if to say, "Yup, that's Fran. What can I say?"

Fran's blue-ribbon vegetables and fruits and her homegrown hospitality were legendary. Many of my return flights to Arizona included huge red homegrown tomatoes and frozen blueberries. The berries were thawed out and ready to eat by the time I stepped off the airplane and into the hot Arizona sunshine. We loved her homegrown squash prepared like mashed potatoes. Talk about delicious! The melted butter on top that flowed into the creamy squash was like chocolate gliding over ice cream.

During our winter visits and stormy snow days, strawberries adorned breakfast table. Through the years, her granddaughters have continued to share those juicy stories. Our memories were entertaining, bringing smiles and silent laughter through this rather sad time, yet reminiscing about this lady was special for all of us.

While sitting there in that long wooden pew with my immediate family, an attractive older woman scooted in next to me. She and I greeted each other with a smile and a nod. Years had passed, so I did not recognize some of the local residents. But interestingly, she chose to sit by us when plenty of seats were available in the pew in front of us.

I had been born and raised in a slightly larger township roughly ten miles in another direction. Back then, six to ten miles was somewhat of a distance. No, it was not a horse-and-buggy ride but not a quick trip in a speeding vehicle either.

After sitting down in the pew and reflecting on these wonderful memories with my family, I opened the obituary card and began to read. In a split second, I lost my peace and went into a tizzy, at least inside.

First, I had anticipated that perhaps Dad (Frank) would invite me to sit up front in that first pew near him and the pastor. We were almost like father and daughter, so I thought that I might sit on the opposite side of his biological family.

In some ways, Frank filled in the gap of my biological father since my dad had died when I was young. In many respects, he felt like a father to me and was a kind, caring man with a great sense of humor, much like his wife. He loved his well-deserved retirement years after working in the shipyard.

Well, my expectations did not meet reality. Our open lines of communication and visits had continued throughout the years after Fran died. Out of love and respect, sadness, and optimism, I hoped to sit by him and perhaps even serve as a support. However, at times, water is thinner than blood.

As I read the obituary, for a brief moment, my heart raced, my head spun, and tears welled up. I had another opportunity to check my attitude. I failed. Have you noticed that most days provide us with the chance to check our opinions and perspectives? Now, what sparked all these emotions?

Just moments before, my family and I gladly reminisced while sitting comfortably in that padded pew about three or four seats from the back. And I fellowshipped with Fran's sister and her family before entering the church. The previous night's gathering at the funeral home also went smoothly. But my now-racing heart and spinning head were almost out of control!

Maybe my imagination and eyes are fooling me, I thought. *Let me read this obituary one more time.* Those rose-colored glasses that I was known for wearing were suddenly not so rosy. Had I lost sight of reality?

Stepparents and ex-spouses hopefully are included in the package with a second marriage when children are involved. In reality, my daughters have a stepmother. One would hope that children will have a strong relationship with their parents and with their stepparent. I did not want to be left out of this equation. But in this case, I had been left out—from the obituary.

Situations might affect our way of thinking or even our selfish thoughts and attitudes. What will we do with this decision-making process? When we ask God to mature us in various areas, he will certainly fulfill our requests and answer prayer. We often face opportunities to become more Christ-like with each passing day. While we look forward to the mountain top, deep valley disruptions might be just around the corner in our lives. These disruptions can shift us forward or backward. They can mold us into becoming more like Jesus or take us in another direction.

We might respond negatively until we realize what we are doing and shake off the incident with a mindset of "this too will pass." I faced a dilemma. I had met one more opportunity to jump another hurdle. The children that *I* gave birth to—notice the *I* word—were mentioned in this obituary; their mother was not. These were Frank and Fran's biological grandchildren and, as such, deserved to be mentioned. As their mother, God chose my body to carry and eventually birth these daughters to fulfill their destiny and for his glory. And he chose my former spouse as their dad. The Christian populace increased on Earth when our children, all five of them, were born.

I became a mom of five beautiful "fearfully and wonderfully made" (Psalm 139:14) daughters followed by handsome, fearfully and beautifully made sons-in-law, followed by numerous grandchildren and great-grandchildren. God blessed me beyond my imagination. I am so thankful to God for these children, grandchildren, and great-grandchildren.

Family dynamics have the potential to change when several sets of parents are involved. We need to accept and understand this concept. Sadly, bitterness can set in, but only if it is given permission. We would hope for a solid relationship with biological relatives and stepparents. Again, we have a decision to make and can choose whether or not we accept these realities. Even so, this acceptance might not necessarily happen overnight. It can take time to recognize the need for acceptance of these situations and allow God to take our pain and pride.

Mentors, mature friendships, and spiritual teachers can help us work through various issues. Counseling, Christian teachings, staying in the Bible, and finding a Bible-believing church all contribute to our wellness and the healing journey. People are available to help us. Healing is possible, and yes, it is a process.

The obituary listed all the children and read that this couple was the parents, which was technically a valid explanation when considering the dynamics of an extended family. But my feathers were ruffled because the biological parent of most of these children was omitted. The mama bear within me showed her belligerent side. The obituary stated a fact, yet I was not mentioned as the mother of the children.

Scripture tells us that women will have significant pain during their childbearing, yet God will spare them. If God can save a woman through childbirth, he can spare her when she is not mentioned in an obituary as the biological parent or former spouse.

In all reality, we want to positively embrace each child from a previous marriage. It can be difficult for the children when their parents separate and when the children need to integrate with another family. God, in his infinite wisdom and ways, can bring about a special sibling bond within extended families. In fact, he probably wants it that way.

The Lord might also have a big task in helping the parent who shares children and the one who has now gathered a few more in the family line. Parents can work through these obstacles, which can result in a positive outcome, but they might need time to adjust.

How many ex-spouses hurt each other by keeping the children from their spouse? The getting-back schemes only hurt the children. Jealousy steps in and takes over. A divorce is between the parents not the children. Children can be damaged, left to fend for themselves, and even swayed to take sides, especially when spouses have difficulty working through the separation issues.

When I think back to the hurts our children and other children suffered, it breaks my heart. How dare I dump further hurts on these children by keeping them from their parent who does not live at home?

I know most parents do not intend to hurt their children. Pain can drive one to make decisions or do things they would not normally do. God knows our pain and has a way of seeing us through this agony. The process of letting go and letting God take over can be challenging, yet it is possible with God's grace.

Fear sets in that we might lose our precious children or that our children will take sides. Only God can resolve this unfortunate situation if we invite him to do so. He has the answers, and we must learn to trust him and do his will instead of our will. God can help us change our ways and teach us to love, joy, peace, long-suffering, gentleness, goodness, and faith (Galatians 5:22). He can turn us around into right thinking if we intentionally make that choice.

I have seen many obituaries where the former spouse, the other parent of the deceased person's children, is mentioned. But this did not happen in my case. After traveling such a distance and working hard to honor my mother-in-law, I had to admit how much this hurt. I had to then focus on intentionally letting go of disappointment, unbelief, and hurts. What could I do with these raw emotions? The mama bear could show her discontentment in a heartbeat, and for a moment, she was certainly agitated. Now I am trying to be transparent with you all, so hang in there.

God had so graciously brought people into my single life to support and walk alongside me. My daughters are God's biggest blessings and greatest gift. He took wonderful care of us, whether we thought so or not. "Behold, children are a heritage from the Lord, the fruit of the womb is a reward. Like arrows in the hand of a warrior, so are the children of one's youth. Happy is the man who has his quiver full of them; they shall not be ashamed, but shall speak with their enemies in the gate" (Psalm 127:3–5). Integrating step-children and a stepparent into families can be challenging and rewarding. I am a grandmother of extended families. I love these grandchildren. Yet assimilating into an extended family takes more time for some than for others. Determination, perseverance, and God can bring families together.

For a few moments, as I read the obituary, I was deeply hurt. Perhaps the root of this problem stemmed from not being invited to sit next to my dearly loved father-in-law. The pain was topped off with the obituary announcement. Only God knows.

Well, the Lord did prepare me in many respects. I wanted to grow and become a worthy daughter of King Jesus. I so wanted to be in his will and do what was right. For years, I had yearned for deeper personal, emotional, and spiritual growth. Today, that yearning continues, and no doubt will continue until I make the obituary page. We are so human!

Well, this same obituary format repeated when my father-in-law passed away. Once again, as the mother of the majority of these children, my name was excluded. However, three cheers for me. I am thrilled to say that I had matured mentally, emotionally, and spiritually enough between Fran and Frank's funerals and refused to dwell on these potential negative emotions.

Yes, knowing who we are in Christ sure makes life easier. Labor scars, birthing pains, and maturing in the Lord gave me hope, courage, and that incredible peace that passes understanding. We find great comfort when we know who we are in Jesus, and we no longer need to keep up our guard.

Now here is the clincher: God showed his true wonderful colors. I loved how he did this and recognized this as a God-given gift wrapped in a beautiful bow of love. During the luncheon, after the funeral, my family sat together: my mom, siblings, and brother-in-law. As usual, we enjoyed wonderful conversation with each other and with friends. I was feeling and looking attractive. Ladies, we especially know what this is like. A good hair day and a special dress can do wonders. I was okay about not being invited to sit at the head table with our children, their dad, and their step-mom.

Envy and jealousy could have stepped in, but these attitudes were not invited to the party. In difficult times, we need to remember previous struggles and how God the Almighty Father, the Prince of Peace, carried us through. He sustained us and has proven his faithfulness in many past circumstances. Why not let him do so on this occasion as well? When my children's stepmother and their dad were alone, I walked up to them. We hugged each other. By this time, God had miraculously exchanged my hurt heart for a newly healed heart.

I was given several excellent books before my Michigan travels, and I had brought them along to pass on. One inspirational book encouraged readers to grow in the Lord. I had read this book and loved seeing more growth within myself when I finished. I had prayed about who should receive these complimentary books. I mentioned to my former husband's wife that she might like to read them. She gratefully accepted. We spoke briefly of my upcoming trip, and then she said, "We will be praying for you as you go on your mission assignment to Papua New Guinea. You are a brave woman."

Right then, the woman who sat next to me on that church pew, the third row from the back, during Fran's service approached me. What happened next was a God-given touch. I felt loved. "So sorry devil, you lose. I win! Thank you, Jesus."

This woman said, "You probably don't know me, but your mother-in-law and I have walked the country roads together during the early mornings for many years. And Maggie, she loved you so. She was always speaking of you. 'Maggie, this and Maggie, that.' I just wanted you to know that Fran loved you dearly." She then gave me a big hug and departed. Just like that, in my life one moment and gone the next, as if she were perhaps an angelic messenger bringing a word of good news, love, and healing. Now I know why she chose to sit next to me in that already crowded church pew.

I knew God sent this angel to deliver a personal, heartwarming, healing message. He knew the pain in my heart from the obituary announcement. Maybe he whispered in her ear the night before, "I have an assignment for you." She may have had a sneak preview at the obituary. She may have noticed the wetness in my eyes. Maybe she wanted to help calm the mama bear. In any case, she delivered good tidings of great joy.

Attending the funeral was significant to me. God demonstrated his blessed assurance through this woman. He knows our hearts and feels our pain. I was now prepared to get through the next funeral, Frank's, and the neglect to mention me in the obituary. Although the beautiful angel was not there, God knew I would be okay. Her kind words resonated in my heart. "Your mother-in-law loved you, Maggie."

Warmth filled my heart as I sat through my father-in-law's funeral. The obituary was just a reminder of God's love for his children and Fran's love for me. I did not need to shout out who gave birth to the children named. We choose our battles, and sooner or later, we discover that some certainly are not worth the effort. And when we do decide to fight contrary to God's will, he is always available to pick up the pieces. How sweet and reassuring is this? Yes, it all worked out. It is well with my soul.

"And He said to me, 'My grace is sufficient for you, for my strength is made perfect in weakness'" (2 Corinthians 12:9).

31

Madang Lodge—Three-Day-Stay

$\mathcal{I}$ arrived in Papua New Guinea on June 4, 2004, after being airborne for about twenty-five hours. Despite my long flight from the United States to Australia to New Zealand and, finally, Port Moresby, Papua New Guinea, into the Madang province, I was comfortably excited. I was ready to enter and explore the realm of a missionary.

The process of becoming a missionary, in reality, began during my early childhood and was now ready to birth. This dream had lain dormant as life continued after high school and marriage. After becoming single, the dream awakened and resurfaced. The journey was long and intensive, yet God sprinkled love and joy and, yes, hardship and tears through the journey. The growth, wisdom, and knowledge through the years were worth each step of the way. Of course, at times, the tears exceeded the joy. And now I had to take yet one more step, a big step, before completing this lifetime of preparation to offer counseling services to missionaries in an international office.

I now better understood the importance of entering a foreign environment with no excess emotional baggage to hinder me. The counselor, mentor, or support system could not effectively help others heal if they still struggled with their own issues. An additional consideration was the challenging of adjusting and acclimating to a third-world country.

Up to this point, my journey had an intentional focus. During the dormant season of my mission's dream, I developed in other dimensions. I learned to be productive and to multi-task by wearing many hats. Married, single, single parenting, employment, study—the list goes on and on. I believe I have earned a PhD in life.

"It is good for me that I have been afflicted, that I may learn Your statutes" (Psalm 119:71). God demonstrated his faithfulness, mercy, and grace through my entire life. As you will read, his faithfulness continues until the end of time. Although I have not yet arrived, I am further along than I was a few years ago.

After a few days of flying in a 747 jet, I had finally arrived in Madang, located on the northern coast, for my short stay. The flight into this small airport was to be my last flight for about fifty-six days. Upon completion of the Pacific Orientation Course (POC) at this training site, a smaller mission's Cessna aircraft would then take me to Ukarumpa, the location of my first mission's assignment in Papua New Guinea. My heart was giving me a cardiovascular workout as we landed at my POC boot camp site. My belly was not sure what it wanted to do.

I occupied an aisle seat as we landed in Madang, so my view of the outside world was somewhat blocked. Yet in a few moments, I witnessed an incredibly breathtaking view. Perhaps the Papua New Guinea people and I would be equally surprised to see each other. People lined up near the runway, waiting as a white-haired, fair-skinned woman, along with other Air Niugini passengers, exited the small aircraft.

Delighted, I stepped out of the aircraft and watched the native people. I had seen photos of similar scenes in movies and magazines, and yet there, before my eyes, was an actual live gallery. Pinch me. Was I dreaming?

The route to this point in life and now to begin that last ride before completing each hurdle was massive. My tear-filled eyes and wobbly knees assured me that I was alive. And yes, ready to jump through one more hoop, the last of many hoops to make it to this point. I had been through years of preparation in order to follow my childhood dream.

By now, at more than sixty years of age, a powerful range of emotions filled every cell in my body. I wanted to laugh, shout for joy, and cry all at the same time. Now that's a pretty big undertaking in itself. This was the goodness of the Lord—how could this be correctly described? Yet through this full range of roller-coaster emotions, my inner spirit experienced a miraculous sweet sense of peace and contentment. I shouted within, "I'm here, yay, three cheers. Lord, you brought me this far!"

A lifelong journey that involved keeping my eyes on the one I invited into my life many years earlier had come to pass. He promised he would never leave me (Deuteronomy 31:6 and Hebrews 13:5). We have a contract, a covenant with him. I am his, and he is mine (Song of Solomon 2:16). He has a plan and a purpose for my life as a committed Christian with a desire to follow him. This last loop was part of that, or I would have given up along the way.

Life is complicated, and only through him can we make it. He is the God of second and even third and more chances. I told him, "And today, Lord Jesus, I stand on the soil of another country, willing and trusting." That vision given to me in the elementary years of my childhood had now materialized.

Yes, the years passed. People asked why I waited so long to enter the mission field. Dreams and goals can become a reality if we don't falter or if we are willing to take advantage of additional opportunities. All these past events broadened my awareness of life.

Perhaps the following experiences all contributed to productive later years: my upbringing without a father; my widowed and single mom; our time on welfare; marriage, divorce, and singleness; and being a single parent for my family of five daughters. All of this was followed by years of study, testing in academics, successes, failures, and life's everyday happenings. This trip and forthcoming adventure, no doubt, was to be a forever memorable experience.

Missionaries are human and need time to prepare. They persevere through relentless studies and sacrifices. Their focus on the heavenly trophy keeps them on pace to reach the goal.

In addition to the many spectators waiting in front of this small terminal, native people lined the grassy area of the airfield strip. They exhibited a mixture of curiosity and congenial expressions. Their beautiful cocoa skin and short black curly hair contrasted with their white eyes and white teeth, emphasizing their welcoming smiles.

Many of the men and boys dressed in short loose pants with bare chests, and the women wore their traditional wraparound skirts called *lap laps*. Moms and young girls, many barefoot, carried babies and infants in *bilums* on their backs. Yes, I was now experiencing another culture, an ethos that I would very soon come to love so dearly.

I wondered what the onlookers thought as we travelers approached. Perhaps they, too, dreamed of traveling to another country.

I was one of the few fair-skinned people that stepped out of the aircraft that day and was met with smiles and some stares. Since they rarely saw airplanes and were not familiar with technology, they might have wondered how the aircraft managed to stay up. Both parties—the nationals and I—no doubt were filled with wonder and amazement.

Walking through the Madang Airport took only a few minutes as it was really just a hangar. My two super heavy red cargo suitcases moved up the handmade wooden ramp next to the small building. These suitcases contained an eighteen-month supply of toiletries, clothing, and an extra pair of sandals. In addition, they held some professional resources, although not as many as I would've liked to bring. Other resources had been shipped separately in a mission's crate. These suitcases and their owner made it to the final destination. We had traveled a long way.

As I stood weighed down with luggage, I watched for the western couple that was scheduled to pick me up. The trip from America to Papua New Guinea went well. Now I just had to wait for my ride. I was relieved when this pleasant and friendly couple arrived. I would spend the next six weeks with them as they would oversee the next phase of my life, namely the POC. I was so happy to have made this connection. The couple welcomed me to Papua New Guinea and introduced themselves as the temporary POC managers. They were pleased that I had arrived intact with my suitcases as occasionally travelers miss flights, and one or another is left behind. Also, airlines might misplace luggage.

Larry tossed my two red suitcases, maxed out at fifty pounds each, and heavyweight carry-on luggage unto the truck. When these brand new fully loaded suitcases slid across the oversized truck bed, they picked up a permanent stain. I decided to look the other way; after all, I had made it this far. Could I ask for more? The only way these suitcases would survive the ten-year warranty was if they stayed in the closet, hidden in their original carton for that time.

I learned that this very same oversized truck would be our taxi for the next six weeks. It would pack in a couple of dozen souls and travel up and down the Nob Nob Mountain countless times throughout our training. Understandably, Larry was in a hurry, so I just climbed in the back seat with my trusty computer hanging by its strap. Benches were placed on either side of the truck bed, and off we went.

This couple graciously invited students into their home located on the campground. Their house had all the amenities of a modern home—toilets, a bathroom, and a kitchen sink—unlike the cabins the students occupied. The couple's job was to oversee the families that would attend this required course in the rough. They were clearly in the right spot as they worked with the students.

How exciting that I made it to Papua New Guinea, all of me. My heart filled with joy. I was sure the next eighteen months would include many adventures.

The three of us proceeded to travel through the crowded, busy PNG roads and the village en route to the lodge. The drive through town seemed short. Larry freely honked the truck's horn to get people, children, dogs, pigs, and chickens to move out of the way.

The merchants were selling firewood, craft items, and garments, and fruits and root vegetables lined the streets. Bananas were piled high, unlike a small bundle at the American super market. No doubt, it took several men to carry in the heavy banana racks. The pineapples, papayas, and coconuts were organized in an orderly fashion. The sight amazed me. The collections of root vegetables resembled yams and sweet potatoes, except they were white and plump like a Michigan sugar beet.

Smoke from the cooking stoves hung in the air. The little village was alive, booming with chatter and trade. The native people either sat on the ground or squatted with their knees bent, their body weight resting on the bottom portion of their legs. No doubt, during the captivating ride through the village, my jaw fell open on several occasions.

We finally arrived at the empty, quiet lodge where I was dropped off. Larry and a porter rolled my suitcases to the front office desk and then to my room. I asked Larry if other Westerners were around. He said, "No. But you can relax. Get some rest." Unbeknownst to me, this lodge would be my resting place for a few days. Then I would be picked up and taken to the mountain-top boot-camp training ground—one more prerequisite to my assignment in this country.

The big lump in my throat grew and nearly choked me. My task was to get some rest. I considered that this couple, now acclimated to this foreign country, might have forgotten about their first week here. Yet Larry and Lucy knew I was perfectly safe at this lodge. I was the one who let doubts take over my weary mind.

I was beginning my transition into a foreign land. Today, I would not feel as vulnerable because I have acclimated to various foreign country settings since then. With years overseas and a love for the people, foreign countries feel much like home today, yet as a newbie, I did not have this feeling. Today, the "see you in three days" would not be a problem; in fact, I might even cherish this alone time.

I quickly looked over my room and checked on the available security. The noise of the nearby road, located at the end of the outdoor walk, echoed off the walls. The surrounding display of tropical plants was larger and heftier than I could ever have envisioned. They would have made a great spot for hide-and-go-seek for my grandchildren. They would have had to look hard to find their grandma in the thicket of the tropical plants. My imagination went wild with the various possibilities of what could be hiding in there.

The vegetation consisted of ferns, large orchids, poinsettias, and palm plants. Some of the animal life included red roosters, mammoth butterflies, praying mantises, and grasshoppers. God was giving me a sneak preview of this beautiful country and creation.

The window coverings were scant, barely covering the sliding patio door. If a snake or other creature wished to crawl in, the space under the patio door gave them plenty of room. The three-inch bed pad was inviting my worn body to climb in, relax, and lie down. My swollen feet from the long flight were aching to be elevated. My head was in a spin. I was ready for a good sleep in a horizontal position.

Frequent fliers know that jet lag can disrupt your biological clock. You can be sleepy in the day and wide awake through the night. But when heavy sleep fell, then noises of the evening or even the daytime startled me awake. The sudden sounds and smells of the new culture and the tropical humidity also awakened me at various times.

The geckos with their varying clicks and chit-chat kept me on edge, until I realized what was making these sounds. The residents were probably discussing and wondering among themselves who this fair-skinned woman was.

My first thought was that these respective clicks coming from the bathroom window were entering my room. I eventually mustered up enough boldness to check out the noise. The variety of birds and insects hummed through the night. The sounds of nature during the exotic tropical night were melodic yet unfamiliar and somewhat unsettling. The curtains fluttered even when closed. The sunlight shone through the closed door.

The tropical forest is unique and beautiful. The early morning sounds in Michigan were different from those in Arizona. Mourning doves cooed in Michigan, and coyotes howled in Arizona. Yet not all sounds were relaxing, and sometimes the noisy intensity of insects, birds, or coyotes overwhelmed me. But as I became accustomed to the birds' chatter and happy tunes, I learned to appreciate the enchanting melodies.

Once I was familiar with the sounds of the culture, I could more easily relax. I would have been even more comfortable had another Westerner been around. No doubt, God wanted me to take in his artistry and calm my spirit. The challenge of the unfamiliar, even knowing that God is always with us, can still be difficult.

Ghana and the Ivory Coast had similar sounds and surroundings, and I stayed there for three weeks. Yet when with a group, the newness of sights and sounds doesn't seem as scary. However, this time on my own in Papua New Guinea, was certainly an opportunity to increase my faith.

I had accepted the assignment, toiled diligently to meet all the qualifications, and trusted that everything would work out, which it did. Yet the unfamiliar surroundings can stir your imagination. In time, I became more comfortable with travel and adapting to different cultures and better acclimated to various locations with each trip.

At one point, during my first three days in Papua New Guinea, I awoke from a sound sleep with my stomach growling. The exhaustion from jet lag eased up by the third day. Soon I would travel to Nob Nob Mountain, also known as Amron Hill, or Nobanob, to the campground sight to begin my POC training.

Meanwhile, a day or two slipped by without eating, and when my hunger pains hit, it was time to investigate finding a meal. I rallied up my strength and went looking for food. I heard a noise in the kitchen area, and the thoughts of hygiene entered my mind. Previously while in Africa, I dealt with some unpleasant stomach issues. It was difficult to forget such bouts of distress.

It was now time to eat. Would I face a language barrier, I wondered? The cook met my eyes with big smile. He most likely was wondering about this White lady who had not eaten in a few days. We managed to communicate, and shortly after, the chef served me a welcoming plate adorned with chicken, eggs, toast, and fresh tropical fruit.

When I uncovered the meal in my room, ready to dive in, the whites of the egg were running into the toast. It was now decision time. I could eat the eggs as served or attempt to communicate with him and enjoy them well-done.

The cook and the translator were so gracious. I was embarrassed to even express the slightest disapproval. The deepest desire of the people was to please. The lodge staff were so humble and helpful. While in this beautiful land, I fell in love with the people. I cherish the beautiful memories of that time.

Shortly after breakfast, I wandered into the beautifully manicured gardens surrounding the lodge. The air was pleasant, and the aroma of outdoor cooking smoke aroma that often filled the atmosphere was most heartwarming. The ample-sized swimming pool water was splashed in from the waves from the large lake adjacent to the pool. Several people were swimming, and the joyful shouts from their play filled the air.

If I had seen the manicured grounds and pool area before checking into my room, I would have been able to relax more on my first day or so. The Word tells us not to be anxious, but I was anyway. My blessed sleep might have been more relaxing and calm had I obeyed the Word. Our minds can certainly play tricks on us.

The remaining day at the lodge went exceptionally well. I focused on my delightful environment and not on the what-ifs. The remaining meals in the dining area were delightful. The large windows facing the lovely tropical gardens and the waterfront gave me a spectacular view of God's beautiful creation.

The gracious hosts and the lodge stay were a bit of heaven. I imagine the chef was pleased to see this skeptical Western visitor come out from hiding to welcome the fragrance of his country. The table was always graced with tropical fruit, fresh juices, and slices of bread. The atmosphere was filled with love and wonder.

Soon Larry and Lucy arrived as promised. My big red suitcases were again picked up and with one hearty toss, thrown into the end of the truck bed. They landed in the anticipated spot—right on top of the same oil stain. Moments after a short ride through the village and busy roads, Larry was en route to the top of Nob Nob Mountain. In just a short few hours, I would become acquainted with other students who would also begin the six weeks of intensive POC training.

"Trust in the Lord, and do good; dwell in the land, and feed on His faithfulness. Delight yourself also in the Lord and He shall give you the desires of your heart" (Psalm 37:3–4).

32

Pacific Orientation Course (POC)— Boot Camp

I was excited about this Papua New Guinea mission assignment. I was now more determined than ever; boot camp was just one more hurdle to jump, and I would jump it.

The Dina, the name of the boot camp truck, was right on schedule. I was prepared to travel to the top of the mountain to start my six-week training.

The drive up the mountain to the boot camp site was steep and striking with the beauty of the tropics surrounding us as we traveled up. My heart raced and my eyes teared up as the sweat ran freely down my body. It was a typical hot, humid day in this third-world country. However, the beauty of the land overrode the discomfort of heat and sweat. I had worked years for this very day.

The full-size truck shifted down as it toiled its way to the top; the narrow dirt road was hidden in the overgrown tropical foliage. Occasionally, the greenery swiped the side of the people sitting or standing in the truck bed. While passing another vehicle on this narrow road, I held my breath and drew in my stomach as the cars edged by each other, barely a centimeter apart.

The truck traveled up and down and around one steep mountain-side curve after another. The potholes were so deep that I speculated that another large vehicle might need to pull us out if the truck ever plunged into one of these deep holes. *What if the Dina loses control,* I thought. Inevitably, it would have tumbled head over heels while picking up speed as it spiraled downward. Yet I consoled myself with the thought that maybe the thickness of the forest could stop an out-of-control vehicle. The truck driver appeared to have the situation under complete control.

The trip to the campsite in the Dina was the first of many trips to follow. The difference would be that passengers would sit on the rear wooden benches positioned on either side of the truck bed. Typically, a rider or two would stand in the middle of the truck bed, hanging onto the secured steel stationary pole.

Stepping into the truck bed called for long legs, a task in itself for this oldest trainee. After a few trips up and down that mountain, I developed a burning sensation in my behind. Sitting on those wooden benches caused a rather sizeable raw spot on my tail bone, yet I never wanted to miss a trip out. Every journey was exciting and filled with adventure.

As the Dina entered the gated rustic boot campground, I recalled my past childhood campsites. They were located in the wooded rural area of the United States, tucked away in the dense forest. This boot camp where I would live for the next six weeks, a perfect setting for training, sat on a long-standing Lutheran mission ground. This campsite was tucked away in a forest—a tropical forest in a third-world county.

Nob Nob Mountain was breathtaking, a gorgeous location for acquainting a newcomer with the country. I had a panoramic view of the ocean below and with its magnificent vibrant coral reefs springing up into the Pacific Ocean. It was like a photo of paradise.

Rich foliage surrounded most of the campsite. The banana trees and tall palms with coconuts were beautiful. Attendees were advised to stand a distance from a coconut tree, as the coconuts could easily fall on a head or body and cause considerable damage.

You could enter the compound from the front. The cabin area for lodging was a long strip of rooms with individual entrances similar to the set-up of a motel. The inside horseshoe area was inviting with greenery and a manicured grassy lawn. The greenery contained a variety of huge bugs, large colorful butterflies, and overgrown centipedes, which was quite a contrast to my back yard in Arizona. Some of the kids of trainees collected critters, so they were intrigued by the exotic, strange insects and reptiles.

My quarters, a one-room cabin, were better than roughing it in a tent, especially in this tropical terrain. This cabin had two beds. However, since I was the only single, I could take advantage of the privacy of my little bungalow after a full day of training or during a break between activities.

This basic one-room cabin with its concrete floor was located at the entrance near the gate. The board bed was topped with a slim pad for resting. The dim light near the gate served as a night light in my cabin. This room resembled the earlier church camps I had attended as a youngster, only those church camp rooms housed many bunk beds and lots of kids.

My initial thought as I entered the small cabin room was that at this late time in my life, I preferred this more upscale arrangement to the camps of my youth. In my younger years, I thought nothing of sprawling out under a tree with my sleeping bag on the ground. Now, later in life, I preferred a bed, maybe even a queen-sized bed in a nice comfortable hotel room. However, as a mom of five, my former military camp-outs and Girl Scout camping trips had prepared me for such a time as this. I was confident that this training site and room arrangement would work out just fine.

My cabin room had everything I needed: hooks to hang my clothes, a small table for accessories, and a chair to take a load off my feet. This cabin kept me dry during evening rainfalls and somewhat free from the variety of bugs. My mosquito net kept the flying insects out.

I was shocked at finding a vast million-legged granddaddy millipede on the concrete floor. I say a granddaddy as this one was titanic. I could imagine his delight had he nibbled on my Western body.

Ultimately, I focused on setting up a counseling office in six weeks, right after I finished the boot camp training. There would be no ifs, ands, or buts, as quitting for the sake of comfort was not an option. By God's grace, I would not admit defeat. I could have tossed in the towel plenty of times, taken off my tennis shoes, and said, "I'm done. I'm not built for this." But God had made a way through each hard time, and now I was 100 percent sure that with God's help, I would have an auspicious time at boot camp.

In time, I adjusted to the community toilets at the far end of the horseshoe, some distance from my bungalow. The distance, however, was a bother when I urgently needed to visit the latrine. This open-air community bathhouse sat on stilts. For the trainees to have showers with hot water, someone had to fire up the old furnace behind the bathhouse. However, the weather was plenty warm, so cold showers felt great. One bathroom facility arrow pointed to the women's bathroom, and another arrow pointed to the men's facility. The lines on either end often stretched out as the bathroom facilities stayed busy. Being an early riser was to my benefit.

Toilet stalls included a large bucket of flush water with a scoop hung on the edge as a flush device since the facility lacked flushing handles. A dip into the water bucket, and the toilet worked just fine. This creative approach worked quite well to meet our needs. We can adjust to any type of unusual expectations with the right attitude.

Another trick I learned was to wash my hair and shower using one pail of water. No doubt, I was still sudsy the first time or two. Firstly, we filled the shower stall pail with water from a nearby faucet outside the shower cubicle. Secondly, the bucket was hung on a rope extended from the ceiling with a hook attached to the sidewall. Lastly, the operator controlled the flow of water by working the round nozzle under the bucket.

It took a well-thought-out process to fully complete a shower and hair wash with only one bucket of water. After several trial and errors, I did amazingly well. The idea was to sprinkle just enough water to lather up, followed by a quick tightening of the round nozzle on the bottom of the pail. In time, I manipulated that nozzle like a pro: on-off, on-off, followed by a full-body wash in increments. We, at one point, even bathed in a creek when the rain barrel emptied due to a glitch.

I enjoyed the adventure and challenges for the most part. I believe God uses our experiences for his glory and the edification of his children. Raising a household of children certainly taught me flexibility.

Our dining area consisted of picnic tables with long benches under a wood ceiling enclosed with mesh wire. Some trainees took turns in the kitchen helping the national ladies serve and prepare food, while their hungry trainees waited for meals. Trainees then washed dishes and cleaned up the kitchen. The joint effort worked like clockwork.

Our cultural menu consisted of alligator, pork, and chicken but was mostly vegetarian. We sampled bananas of every color, shape, and size, including French-fried bananas. We also ate exotic fruits and vegetables, such as pineapples, coconuts, occasionally strawberries, taro roots, sweet potatoes, and greens similar to spinach. Each meal included homemade yogurt and granola. Sometimes we trainees had movie nights with popcorn on weekends. We drank the rainwater collected from the roof that filled the rain barrel.

Each day entailed a variety of classes, language learning, reading articles, and writing culturally related reports. We learned of the history of the country, its culture, and the necessary survival skills needed to live and work in the country's settlements. We studied the Tok Pisin trade language that kept us from getting marooned because of the language barrier. By the end of six weeks, I could converse well enough to shop at the market and operate the trade monetary system,

While visiting villages and diverse churches, we hiked the terrain and swam in the ocean. This training familiarized and prepared Bible translators and linguists for village living, while the rest of us received a better understanding of the experiences of our colleagues who would live in villages. Village living can bring stress, cultural strains, and sickness. Yet missionaries persevere through the challenges and hardships to translate the Bible.

I became acquainted with what field missionaries working in the villages experienced. The variety of classes inspired me to eagerly learn everything that the instructors taught. Translators sometimes traveled through mountains, dense bush, jungles, rivers, and streams to reach their villages. The various mission's aircraft flew close to the villages, sometimes landing on grassy areas. Although the village workers were dropped off as close as possible to their assignments, often, the missionaries had to then travel by foot, boats, and canoes however possible to reach their destination.

I received great insight as a mission's counselor. This training increased my knowledge and awareness of the country overall and what stresses my colleagues would sustain. It prepared me to better understand what a counselee coming into my office might wish to talk about, even if I had minimal understanding of their struggles. My knowledge of the challenges our missionary colleagues endured significantly grew overall.

Another goal for trainees was to be able to swim a mile. In our climbs through the mountain peaks and valleys, we navigated the tropical terrain. Usually a native accompanied us on the hikes and led the way, cutting down branches and weeds with his bush knife.

Through it all, our leg muscles and arms became buff, and our heart and lungs, stronger. The vigorous swimming and highland hikes toughened our bodies.

We sweated copiously due to the high humidity. With a God-given attitude of "I can do this," it was incredible what a person could accomplish. By the end of the six weeks, most participants could swim a mile and had hiked the mountain tops and valley lows through the tropical jungle. We had absorbed enough language to converse, could handle a lantern were able to shop in the markets, could build a cookhouse (*hous kok*), use a bush knife and could cook outdoors over a wood fire.

Before the week's stay in the village, the students were taught about the culture, anthropology, sea life, and spiritual warfare. We had dinner in a bush home and at our campsite each week, all in preparation for this week of village living. We hiked into nearby villages to see how the bush houses were fabricated and bathed in the river with limited water. Relentlessly, we worked and studied in preparation for the upcoming village week.

I appreciated the orientation. This excellent training helped to prepare me as an overall mission's counselor for debriefing missionaries who spent time in the villages and elsewhere. I admired these dedicated field workers who served as unto the Lord.

This well-ordered boot camp schedule equipped us trainees for a week of village living with national families. Each trainee received a rat box, which contained cooking equipment, a lantern, kerosene, a floor pad for our bed, and food, which we had purchased at the open market before our village adventure. Additionally, I took puzzles, a few other toys, and a Tok Pigeon songbook with words also in English, all for anticipated playtime with the children.

Soon the POC was behind me with the memories nestled in my memory bank, but now the fifth week and the last phase of village living awaited us.

I managed the full six weeks of boot camp without the use of a hairdryer, curling iron, or clothes iron. I returned to our training campground after a week of village living. I was dark brown, healthy, and happy. I would never forget this.

The boot camp staff congratulated me on making it through this vigorous training. I could keep up with the other twenty to thirty-five younger participants when it came to the mountain and valley hikes. However, my trainee colleagues outdid me in the one-mile swim.

I was once taking a truckload of cacti to the local dump. Dr. Charles Stanley, a pastor of many years, was on the radio. He said, "Every believer is called to missions as either a goer or a sender."[3] I was elated, to say the least, as I was now living my childhood dream.

With a flashlight and a favorable attitude, you and I can survive boot camp or wherever God places us. This survival skill sounds trivial, yet in general, your perspective and God matter most in life. Life does not mean a smooth ride, yet God makes life work.

How great are your works, oh Lord. "It is good to give thanks to the Lord, and to sing praises to Your name, O Most High; to declare Your lovingkindness in the morning, and Your faithfulness every night...for You, Lord, have made me glad through Your work; I will triumph in the works of Your hands" (Psalm 92:1–2, 4).

How wondrous are your ways, oh, Lord. All things are possible with you. The journey was long, yet you led the way.

[3] Charles Stanley, "The Missionary Question," In Touch Ministries, accessed September 10, 2020, https://www.oneplace.com/ministries/in-touch/read/devotionals/in-touch-with-charles-stanley/the-missionary-question-in-touch-february-26-11646262.html.

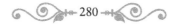

33

Village Living—A Cultural Experience

"He who calls you is faithful, who also will do it" (1 Thessalonians 5:24).

*H*e did it! The Lord our God carried me through the village living experience. Five weeks earlier, I was not ready. His grace and the process of the following weeks prepared me. I now had incredible memories, new village friends, and much gratefulness to our heavenly Father. The Papua New Guineans say, "Papa God." I like to say "Papa God," too, as this name is wonderfully personal. Oh Lord, "I will declare Your Name to My brethren; in the midst of the assembly I will sing praise to You" (Hebrews 2:12). We serve a mighty God. He loves us dearly. If he called you to do it, he is faithful to carry you through.

I can only praise and thank God for his goodness, his faithfulness, his mercy, and his grace. God is faithful. In our weaknesses, he is strong. I completed the POC, even though I was twenty to thirty-five years older than the other adults going through this boot camp training. A staff member told me that I did better than many folks half my age. God's grace carried me through. His strength was sufficient for me. "Not by my might nor by power, but by My Spirit" (Zechariah 4:6).

One young man wondered why I was there. He commented on the humility needed for the course and environment and expressed being blessed and impressed that I humbled myself to this type of training. He called me a classy lady. In reality, I felt like a pioneer woman.

I now had five weeks behind me with the major exam ahead. The final test was to join a tribal family that I had not met. I would experience living in a bush house constructed with tropical foliage. We learned that these bush houses lasted about seven years, and then they took them down and rebuilt them.

After breakfast, I hopped into the bed of the truck with my loaded rat box that resembled a footlocker and served as a suitcase. This box contained a few groceries, a pot and pan, mosquito net, kerosene lantern, and a few other incidentals. I tightly rolled my sleeping mat, and now I was ready for village living. Excitement and uncertainty flooded my mind. The boot camp director dropped me and another couple off at a designated village and said, "I'll be back in one week to pick you up. Enjoy your stay in the village."

We walked a short distance in the muddy terrain. I slipped and fell for the only time during the entire six weeks of vigorous training. My ugly, inexpensive yet superb-quality grandma-style boots paid off. Despite how unattractive they were, the leather with thick gripper hiking soles served me well. They resembled Ma Kettle's boots, but the price was right at a Dillard's warehouse, so they accompanied me. Many of the other hikers slipped while hiking through the typical forest terrain in their tennis shoes. The plentiful rainfall kept the ground wet and muddy. So in this respect, ugly boots were not so bad. These boots tell plenty of stories.

Those hiking boots deserved a place of honor for carrying me through many tough situations in the tropical jungles and a trophy for completing the incredible and productive boot camp. In hindsight, I wish I would have brought them back to the States, had them bronzed, and put them in a place of honor.

It was time to put our newly learned boot camp skills into action with the village tribe. God's love, simple gestures, smiles, and signals, along with the just-learned language, united us quickly with the village people. These few days immersed us in the middle of the national people.

I reached this season in my life by perseverance, determination, a vision, and God. His Spirit had protected me and brought me through each day and night throughout the years—my life involving much trust in the one I had invited into my heart years earlier.

The people loved us "White skins," as they called us. They reluctantly reached out first, and then I invited them to feel my hands and hair. They hesitated and then touched my hands, arms, and my white hair. Their smiles and laughter were beautiful. I fell in love with the children.

The *waspapa*, the head of the village family, took his responsibility of caring for us White folks seriously. He and his large family were pleased to see us. He gave us his bush house to live in for the week. He hung his kerosene lantern on a bamboo pool near the entrance area. The bush house door was woven from natural tropical forest materials, and the open windows had a bamboo cross-like pattern in the middle. The *lik lik* house (outdoor toilet) consisted of a hole in the ground. The lik lik house, bush house, and bathhouse were constructed with tropical forest materials by the waspapa. Meticulously, the waspapa prepared for his boot camp visitors. The wash house was ideal for a refreshing sponge bath. I gained more muscle strength from carrying water up-hill to the wash house and squatting over that toilet hole in the floor.

Our waspapa took us everywhere. Each morning at the crack of dawn, he was ready to travel: through the mountains visiting bush house churches to a school within a bush house, to a women's Bible study, to the gardens, and to see his many friends. He was so proud to support the Summer Institute of Linguistics (SIL) POC trainees. We prepared meals together and sat out on the grass on woven mats and large leaves, while we ate and told stories into the night. The stars were bright and seemed almost within reach. We laughed, prayed together, and spoke of our wonderful "Papa God." The week flew by. Waspapa was so proud to have the fair-skinned Americans living with him and his family. He cried when we said our good-byes.

The children climbed the tall coconut trees, and dropped a few coconuts down. They sliced the ends, and we chug-a-lugged the coconut juice. This drink is the best in a hot tropical setting.

Only a few of the villagers spoke English, yet we were able to communicate with gestures, smiles, and a few translators. Our newly learned language skills helped as well. I pitched in with various chores, such as carrying a five-gallon bucket from the waterfalls for drinking, going to the garden to dig out root vegetables, and taking river water to wash my clothes. The little children could easily carry a five-gallon bucket on their heads. After a few huff and puffs, I could make it up to the steep hill. The children were agile like billy goats, speedy and playful. We even popped corn over a kerosene burner stove, which was a novelty for the villagers.

This week on top of one of Papua New Guinea's tallest mountains was typically hot. The sun seemed to be within arm's reach. We were hot, sweaty, and stinky. Pail baths worked for a brief time. Occasionally a noticeable breeze blew. We ate food grown in the village garden. It was not a time to question conditions. I trusted God to care for me. I could clean up later. I remained healthy and energetic and loved the people.

The children and I played ball and put together the puzzles that I brought. We sang from a TOK Pigeon songbook and read TOK Pigeon comic books that I had brought along. In time, the children learned to put a simple twenty-four piece puzzle together. They could identify the corner and edge pieces by color and pattern and the inside pieces after some playtime.

A dozen-plus children often raced with each other. I gave them the warm up: on your mark, get set, go, and off they went. They shouted for joy when their group won. What a delightful time we had. Oh God, your children of the world, how beautiful each and every one is. "The streets of the city shall be full of boys and girls playing in its streets" (Zechariah 8:5).

One night in the village, unbeknownst to anyone, I had a very brief pity party. My lips were parched, swollen, and blistered, and my face and arms were darkened from the sun. My clothes were bleached out. I imagined I felt like a woman crossing the desert in the pioneering days on a horse-and-wagon train might feel.

I was dealing with all of that, along with thinking about the many hikes on the mountain trails in boots, wearing a skirt—of all things!—and using a walking stick for balance. Maybe it was time for a break. The paths were muddy and easy to slip on when hiking up and down mountains. The family's pigs and chickens were active under our stilted bush house and were visible between the bamboo floors. I might have been able to scratch the pig's back if the space between the bamboo poles were just a bit wider. The roosters woke us up early every morning. I would have returned in a heartbeat, but unfortunately this did not happen. Through it all, this village living will forever remain among my bucket of fond memories.

I loved the people and the village and so much appreciated their hospitality. God gently embraced me through this time of village living. We had special nighttime talks with was papa and his family and the nearby village friends. After sharing a meal together, the stories followed. The wondrous jungle beauty forever amazed me. God's sweet fragrance—the jungle, the bush, the sounds of the wildlife, and the intriguing chirps of the tropical birds—surrounded me.

I was in the interior of paradise. On top of this mountain, the vast expanse of the night sky showed its glory. God demonstrated his infinite love for the beautiful village family and their love for us. God's beauty and bountifulness captivated me. His unconditional, almighty love for his children surrounded this boot camp survivor throughout my village stay after my failed marriage. Never in a million years had I visualized spending a week in a remote village on the island of Papua New Guinea. This village experience sparked an incredible season in my life.

We exchanged gifts before parting. Papa, mama, and their many children and grandchildren received the gifts that we brought along. The children played with the puzzles and games. They, in turn, gave us beautiful handmade gifts. We Westerners have so much, and they have so little. The one most vital component between us was our love for Jesus and love for each other.

God placed me with this beautiful family who cared for me. I could not have asked for a more loving environment. How beautiful are your ways, oh Lord, our Papa God. As I previously stated, the Word tells us to "Enlarge the place of your tent, and let them stretch out the curtains of your dwellings; *do not spare*; lengthen your cords, and strengthen your stakes. For you shall expand to the right and to the left" (Isaiah 54:2–3, emphasis added). How I want to expand to the right and to the left for Jesus. He is the answer to our problems even after divorce.

A precious friend gave me a note before leaving Papua New Guinea, with the word "perseverance" written boldly on it. "Perseverance" means "a constant state of grace to a state of glory, even when it hurts." If God calls us to do it, let's do it. He makes a way. He waits for us to follow him in faith. We then experience his fragrance, his grace, his glory, and that inner peace.

As I reflect on those years of preparation, I can only conclude that we serve an awesome God. As I think about his faithfulness, I often find myself weeping. Who would have thought that because of the divorce, my life was about to begin. I am thankful and very grateful at the opportunity for new life with our heavenly Father.

The staff planned a superb picnic for the boot campers for the day after our return from the village. What a marvelous feast: Hamburgers with all the trimmings and sodas were on the menu, along with swimming. This outing was a real treat and perhaps a reward and celebration for a job well done. This ocean-side setting, with its coral reef, was ideal for snorkeling. What an amazing accomplishment. I received my certificate of achievement.

Following the barbecue, the next day, I was one of the six passengers in a missionary Cessna Skyhawk on my way to the missionary compound of Ukarumpa. In a matter of a few days, I had my very own counseling office in a third-world country. My long-awaited dream became a reality. In July 2004, I began my assignment as a mission's counselor to missionary families at the Summer Institute of Linguistics Compound in the country of Papua New Guinea.

I felt like the apostle Paul, who said, "I have fought the good fight, I have finished the race, I have kept the faith" (2 Timothy 4:7). Yes, at times throughout the journey, I wondered and wavered, but I finished the course and jumped the many hurdles that took me to Papua New Guinea.

"And they sang a new song, saying: You are worthy to take the scroll, and to open its seals; for You were slain, and have redeemed us to God by Your blood out of every tribe and tongue and people and nation, and have made us kings and priests to our God; and we shall reign on the earth" (Revelation 5:9–10).

34

Ukarumpa Arrival—Position

"I will praise you, Lord, with all my heart; I will tell of all the marvelous things you have done" (Psalm 9:1 NLT).

The day finally came, a day I envisioned since my Papua New Guinea, arrival on June 4, 2004. This was the day I had looked forward to for nearly my entire life. The mission's Cessna Aircraft picked me up in Madang and took me to Ukarumpa, the international community to the SIL Center in the Eastern highlands.

I anticipated my first Cessna aircraft ride and all that followed. Mixed emotions surfaced at first, yet the excitement outweighed the jitters. This flight reminded me of a seagull gliding in the heavens. *Hang on to your hat, Maggie*, I told myself. *You will be just fine. Just think of the range of experiences you have gone through since you arrival in this country.*

Veteran missionaries told us that seeing the ocean from a bird's eye view would add the most to our notable memories in this country. They were right. What an incredible view of the sea from above. The sparkling blue and green waters with the coral reef below and the beauty of the white caps crashing into the white sandy beach were breathtaking. In some areas, powerful waves splashed against the rock formations.

The full and occasionally very narrow view of the river streams zigzagging through the tropical vegetation was awe-inspiring. No doubt, these streams were wider than they appeared from the heights. The view downward of the puffy white clouds and sporadic rain clouds from the

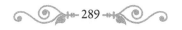

Cessna brought tears to my eyes. "Oh Lord, how incredible are your ways, your creation."

As we traveled over the village of bush houses, some had tin roofs, and others were homespun with tropical foliage. Cooking smoke rose into the sky. The country view was one of immobility and quietness. There were no neon lights, McDonald's arches, skyscrapers, cars on highways, or people. No traffic signs or red stoplights, just miles and miles of trail-like vacant dirt roads, streams, and mountain after mountain of foliage, which looked like broccoli domes from the heights. The village garden plots resembled checker boards and were spread across the flatlands with a variety of crops that burst with color. The missionaries who talked about this flight were right. Years later, this remarkable magnificent sight stays with me.

The mission compound at five thousand feet above sea level would be home for eighteen months. As we neared the airstrip, the pilot circled around and between the mountainous area in preparation for landing. The runway had foliage on the outer sides of the airstrip. People were lined up along the fenced area near the aircraft hangar. The Cessna instrument panel gauges signaled that we were about to land. The engine roared a little louder and then coasted to a stop on the concrete strip in the valley. Flying through the lavish tropical forests and over the various village houses called for excellent piloting skills.

This was a completely new adventure for me, a brand-new missionary. Years and more years had passed, waiting for that precise moment. I had eventually checked off the lengthy list of prerequisites, one by one. That list and the journey to that point stretched into ages and seasons. From an elementary student to a senior citizen eligible for a Wendy's discount card, the numerous detours greatly benefited me.

I matured in God and learned to lean on him. He became my rock and fortress, my sure foundation. I will admit that I mostly loved these years. I loved marriage and certainly have loved my children from this marriage, very much so. God blessed me beyond measure. Years later, I still have a special place in my heart for the father of my daughters. At the same time, he missed out on seeing his daughters mature into lovely women and on the many grandchildren we share. That part makes me sad. Yet life goes on, thanks to our heavenly Father.

The missionary compound greeters welcomed us with hugs, "at-a-boys" and other encouraging expressions. A group of curious natives looked on and smiled. My uncontrollable tears fell. This feat resonated within every body cell.

The community bathhouse, bucket showers, riding on the truck bed, the heat, sweat, stresses and strains and stomach ailments comes with the territory. Through it all, I was regularly happy and joyful. In reality between family and Girl Scouts, roughing it was not new to me. The over-all tearful times while in this training counted up to maybe a handful!

Within moments the luggage was in the van, and I was in the back seat proceeding to the compound. My sponsor helped me settle in. The trip to the mission center on the narrow, bumpy dirt road was captivating. The beautiful tropical forest continually intrigued me. The Papua New Guineans on the roadside were observers, sellers, and walkers. Some smiled and waved. Missionaries are transit, so seeing a new or familiar face was normal.

The guards waved us into the compound. We then headed to my sponsor's home for lunch. She invited several others that I had met in the Quest program five or six years prior. The Quest program was a three-week training program for potential missionaries hosted by Wycliffe Bible Translators held in a remote California location in the late 1990s. We learned about many aspects of missionary work, studied Scripture, listened to speakers, and much more. The leaders evaluated us to ensure that we were good candidates for missionary work.

Our luncheon reunion was warm and friendly. Several of these folks from that original training group were now married with children while others continued waiting for that right person to come along. I was about their mother's age. Perhaps they were happy to have an older person join the center's workforce. I knew the younger people about my daughter's age because we had been in training together in California, and I looked forward to talking with them further.

After lunch, my sponsor took me to my assigned home. She opened the doors, and my suitcases and I took up residence. She encouraged me to acquaint myself with my living quarters, and later, she brought me a meal. I was now alone in a translator's home on the Ukarumpa compound until October when the homeowners would return from the village.

After our dinner meal, I acquainted myself with the renter's manual, which laid on the nearby end table. This home was located near a tall steel fence that divided the compound from the village. The security guard watch station stood on stilts at the end of the oval drive and faced the side of this home. I settled in that first night. This charming small two-bedroom home with a little all-purpose room with a couch was comfy.

The contents of the renter's manual made for a nervous first night. The manual stated that the outside entrance door into the porch area had two locks, and the entry into the home had two bolts. Housing was limited, and homeowners shared their homes when in the village. The homeowner's items were stored in a locked bedroom while their household items, such as sheets, towels, pots and pans, appliances, etc., were available to the renter. The renter provided everything needed to set up housekeeping. Directions on the operation and care of these items was also included.

The handbook stated that the home had experienced several previous attempted break-ins, so it was necessary to keep the doors locked at all times, the windows closed, and the drapes pulled at night. Yes, this news made for many rough, sleepless nights. The fence located in the back of this home was too close for my comfort; however, a compound phone was next to my bed.

The guard dog security had a lot of ground to cover. They patrolled by walking, and at night, they used a truck with spotlights. They checked homes, windows, under the stilted houses, and on the border fence behind this home to search for possible hiding intruders.

The pebbles on the drive in front of the home crunched as the patrol guard walked by. One night, I woke to coughing. It sounded as if it came from my front room. I was thankful that it was only the guards walking on the dirt road. The construction of the homes was quite sparse yet perfect for the country. The wooden floors creaked when you stepped on them and occasionally shook from the earth's frequent tremors.

The very first night, the compound's siren went off, loud and scary. My colleague called to tell me what was happening. Intruders were on the compound. The siren also has a second sound if the intruders had weapons. Another siren signal goes off when all is clear. That would have been a very welcome signal; however, that did not happen immediately. Thank goodness, though, the all-clear signal sounded a short time later. I did not sleep well that night. I struggled to deal with my fears. Imaginations and feelings can be draining. God's Word says we are not to fear for he is with us. He strengthens us so that we can carry out our assignments (Psalm 91). Do we ever arrive?

My heartbeat at times exceeded what it was during boot camp mountain climbing. I could reach my cardiovascular workout rate while lying in bed. Getting out of bed to check the noise seemed risky. The nights become cold for several months of the year in Papua New Guinea, but temperatures warm up in the day time The cold wood floors comfortably creaked when someone took a step, which would alert me to anyone's presence in my residence.

Focusing on God's Word helped. When fear does show up, we have to concentrate on settling down and speaking God's Word. Be anxious for nothing (Philippians 4:6). When I am afraid, I will trust you (Psalm 56:3–4).

A friend and her husband had young visitors from the United States offer to volunteer time at the compound. We became acquainted, and these girls spent several nights with me until I felt braver and more familiar with the center's routines. We know that our uncertain times can be obstacles or a time of opportunity to trust in God. Jesus said that we would face tribulations; through trials, we acquire strength or have the ability to face the unknown. When I am having a hard time, I gain strength by the grace of God by listening to Christian music, studying, and listening to teachings. I do not allow myself to stay down for long. Like David, I encourage myself in the Lord.

We may be crushed and lose heart. Instead, God meets us right where we are. Life has a way of breaking us, but somehow, we grow and become stronger. I have seen this over and over in my faith journey. A walk of faith can indeed be stimulating, stirring, and scary as well. The seasons of life, such as my time in Papua New Guinea, can draw us closer to God. Could anyone ask for more?

The mission field adventure is like no other. I didn't always feel exuberant joy in every moment, and sometimes, I felt pain. Through it all, I did learn more about depending on God. "For when I was weak, he was strong." (See 2 Corinthians 12:9–12.) In other words, I felt physically, emotionally, and spiritually stronger. My heartbeat was in rhythm with Papa God, even when my entire body trembled from fatigue or fear.

I have great joy in knowing he walks alongside his children. My Ukarumpa counseling office became my anchor. In time, I learned to trod the beaten paths and relax in the manicured gardens filled with colorful flowers. The buckets of rain kept everything lush and green. On weekends, I walked with friends to a village church.

My colleagues and I ate an evening meal with native friends at their bush home. One night, I was invited to a girls' night out with my Papua–New Guinea friends. What an honor to be in the presence of these Proverbs 31 righteous women.

On the second day at the Ukarumpa Center, a young Asian girl knocked on my door. She was my first visitor. She gave me a recipe for homemade yogurt. The store had no yogurt, so missionaries made their own, always keeping a little aside for the next batch. I was a yogurt eater, so I was thankful for to learn this little trick.

Daylight was more exciting and filled with expectation than perhaps the nighttime. Women were not allowed to be outdoors after dark without a male escort. We took precautions for any possible intruders who may have remained within the center after the gates were locked. The days were satisfying and fulfilling with meeting new people and hearing the village stories. I especially treasured time with the national ladies as they shared their extraordinary stories of Jesus. Through it all, I could say that God was enough. Working with the clients blessed me immensely, and my schedule soon filled up.

"Let your light so shine before men, that they may see your good works and glorify your Father in heaven" (Matthew 5:16). "The Lord is my light and my salvation; whom shall I fear? The Lord is the strength of my life; of whom shall I be afraid" (Psalm 27:1). A faith walk leads to incredible blessings; this I know for sure.

I learned quickly about the store and its Monday through Friday hours from nine o'clock to five o'clock, closed on weekends. The store brands and substitutions differed, yet occasionally a few commonly known brands from home were on the shelves.

The market ran by the nationals provided fruits and vegetables. Australian apples filled the store table bin. Market days were Monday, Wednesday, and Friday from six o'clock to eight o'clock. All products were homegrown, fresh, and delicious. Before consuming any produce, I disinfected everything.

This market area was the only place we purchased anything with kina money. We charged items at the compound store, and billing took place at the end or beginning of each month. The store management delivered these goods to those of us who had no vehicles.

Many market merchants walked a long way, carrying bags filled with produce, so their mornings started early. My mission was to buy and to get the merchants to smile. I loved to smile to see if they would smile in return. That return smile was so rewarding.

The people also brought and displayed their wares on the concrete slab adjacent to the market place. Available items ranged from bouquets of flowers to handcrafted wood products to croquet items to woven tropical plant items. I loved the market. Although early, this was a great way to begin the day.

A native older man named John became a pleasant friend. He was a craftsman and also one of the ground caretakers on the compound. He once told me that he wanted to give me a gift. He wanted to carve my name on a piece of tree wood. When he delivered it, he said, "This will cost you so many kinas." He was a fun, interesting man who spoke some English. I returned to America with several of his hand-crafted pieces.

My niece sent a medium-sized box filled with a few hundred Mardi Gras traditional colored long beads to give to the national people. A person from administration thankfully accompanied me as I handed out these sparkly strands at the market. Everyone wanted a strand, even the shoppers. We recognized some people who tried to get a second strand. This event was another delightful, memorable moment.

One morning, on my early walk to work, I greeted an older woman with the usual morning greeting. She was carrying a big load on her back, and I said in Pidgeon English, "You workum plenty hard. You carry big-pela load." ("You work hard. You are carrying a big load.") She grabbed my hand and held on until we parted at the end of the road.

Before parting, she hugged me and said, "Me likum you." ("I like you.") I do not remember ever seeing her before. I think she was an angel in disguise, placed at that very spot to bless me.

I took a weekend retreat with 140 other ladies from the Ukarumpa center. We caravanned by bus and vans to the retreat area. For security reasons, some men joined us. At times, rascals placed barricades on the road and robbed passengers when the vehicles stopped. The campsite outdoor restrooms and showers were in a remote and open area. Guards patrolled these areas. Through it, all ladies were refreshed, uplifted, and ready to dive into our Monday routines. And we had no uninvited visitors during our time together.

On one of my crisis management trips, I was invited to sit in the co-pilot seat with headphones. I heard the conversation between the pilot and the radar station—how amazing! On our return, our van broke down on a mountain pass. Because I had no sunglasses, I suffered from swollen burnt eyes for several days after that. In time, the Healer had me back to normal.

On another trip, the missionary plane landed on a grassy airstrip near a village area. The village people watched from far off in the tropical tree forest. As soon as this small plane landed, the people ran out to greet us. We exchanged goods and had a time of some excellent photo shots. This surprise landing stays tucked in my memory bank.

Within several months, I was some pounds lighter. I moved into a more convenient and safer four-square apartment that was more centrally located. I now lived in one of the quarter areas, and three other female teachers had their quarter section. We shared the bathroom facilities and many interesting and fun times. Once a week, we cooked and invited the other three into our apartment.

God is honored when his children heed his call. "Here am I! Send me" (Isaiah 6:8). He openly demonstrates his awesome power. I know of times (which I admittedly regret) when I missed great blessings by stepping back instead of forward. We might not immediately recognize these benefits, yet in time, they will surface. We then see and experience his blessings and favor in our lives.

Our Papa God offers incredible opportunities, and with each, we see development and readiness for the next calling and circumstance that comes into our lives. Each time we take a risk, it becomes easier. He demonstrated his faithfulness in the previous season.

Upon my arrival, I set up my office, and shortly after that, I was given a room on the elementary school grounds. Before long, I spent a full day at this school office seeing eight to nine kids a day. The other weekdays, I saw clients at my home office and stayed busy. I loved being a mission's counselor for people with needs. In time, we offered educational workshops. We had a few marathon weekends with one workshop after another.

As a single, I offered to counsel on weekends if that was more convenient for missionaries. I so clearly remembered when I desperately needed counseling. God was faithful to provide for me and then for others when I finally met the requirements to work with others. This was not an eight-to-five job, and I was available when people requested my help.

In time, we organized a group called Woman of the Word, and the ladies came to listen to speakers and watch Christian DVDs. They loved attending these meetings. Men guarded the areas during the evening activity and escorted singles to their houses. In addition, the ladies opened a coffee house one day a week and made homemade cookies and goodies to sell. You could also purchase a beverage. Once a week, the teens prepared hamburgers, which provided another outing in this very remote setting. The store and the local national market were the only places for food, so the coffee house and the hamburger nights were big hits—another memorable time.

One week, in between clients, I walked to this place to satisfy a craving and buy a couple of homemade brownies. I ate one on the return to the office and saved the second for later after seeing a client. When I went to retrieve the second brownie, sugar ants had beaten me to this mouth-watering treat. Within an hour, the ants left no spot unseen. I was so disappointed and even considered eating the brownie with some added protein. On second thought, I surely would have overdosed on protein.

I became acquainted with the national workers in many areas of the compound. We shared the love of Jesus. I have such lovely memories of my time in this remote yet quaint area of the world.

The counseling ministry may seem far removed from the task of Bible translation; however, God provided healing to many missionaries who became wounded while doing God's work. Translators live at the front lines of spiritual warfare, in the bush environment and culture. Counselors, by the grace of God, help restore, refresh, and replenish colleagues with God's goodness. The counseling ministry encourages others so they can continue God's work.

"This Book of the Law shall not depart from your mouth, but you shall meditate in it day and night, that you may observe to do according to all that is written in it. For then you will make your way prosperous, and then you will have good success" (Joshua 1:8).

The country of Papua New Guinea, is about the size of California. Although the national language is English, the trade languages are Tok Pisin and Motu. This small country has more than eight hundred indigenous languages.

Village people need a Bible in their native tongue. They can then read and meditate on the Word and do it accordingly. I was privileged to attend several village Bible dedications, occasions adorned with God's grace. Hours, days, years, and decades go into translating a Bible into the native tongue, known as the mother tongue. The village people sing, dance, parade, and have guest speakers, and the ladies dress in beautiful white or native colorful clothing. Speakers and guests from other countries join in this glorious occasion.

The ladies carry large platters of food balanced on their heads, and then they are placed and arranged carefully on snow-white linens that cover the long tables. The men also dress in clothing typical to the culture. I often wondered where the linens and the elaborate beautiful clothing came from, as the bush houses were in remote locations. Much work went into these happy days when the village people received their own Bible.

I smiled at the children's contagious joy and play. Their smiles not only warmed my heart but the hearts of everyone around them. I will forever remember them fondly.

I shared a small room at one Bible dedication with five other women from other cultures. We ladies slept on the floor on thin mats. At another dedication, we put woven bush materials on the floor. The missionaries joined in a festive parade. The atmosphere was one of the grandest festivities. We serve an awesome God. I am deeply moved by his compassion, grace, and faithfulness.

One week, after children's Sunday school and a full meal prepared by the missionary community Sunday School teachers, the national and missionary children enjoyed licking on ice cream cones. My mission partners and I specially ordered tubs of ice cream and cones through the small compound store.

The ice cream not only landed in their tummies but covered the children's lips, nose, and chins—such a delightful treat and memory. The afternoon continued with animated VHS movies in English that accompanied my baggage. The colorful animation made up for those that didn't know English. It was an incredible day of fun and laughter.

A young boy was resting on the handle of the push lawnmower. Mowing uphill was a big job for a little guy. I approached him and suggested he pull the lawnmower up this steep hill instead of pushing it upward. Together, we worked our way to the top, huffing and puffing until we finally arrived. He extended his hand to me with a big smile.

Within a short period, missionaries throughout the country faced three crises that involved deaths. My job description included debriefing after such a huge loss. Spouses and children faced the premature deaths of loved ones, and family, friends, colleagues, and nationals needed support during their grief.

For the first of these debriefings, an administrator and I were flown to the site of the tragedy by a mission's aircraft. We depended on God's leading. Only God had answers in this situation. God came through, and by the time we left, he had calmed the waters. He uses his people on earth to be his hands, feet, and words. He leads in surprising ways during difficult times.

"It is by my Spirit," says the Lord. Sometimes, that unspeakable joy does not set in right away. We are sad to see our loved ones go, yet we are happy that we know where they are going. What would we do if we did not have a loving, caring Father who sent his Son to care for his people here on Earth and in the hereafter?

When God calls, he equips (Hebrew 13:21). "To God be the glory for the great things He does in our lives. May God open the windows of heaven and pour out His blessing on you and yours and everything you could ask or imagine for" (Ephesians 3:20–21).

35

Village Medical Run—Healing the Sick

*T*he PNG medical team made routine visits to the indigent communities to provide wellness services. The nurse's stories were so intriguing that I asked if I could ride along on the clinic's medical team run into the village. I longed for that experience and waited for that day to come around.

Once I learned Tok Pisin, it was fun to speak. The conversation was often a bit of a hit and miss, yet the national people appreciated our attempts and the trial and error. The indigenous people spoke the language of their village. Until the missionaries entered their villages, the people had no written word or even an alphabet.

Our mission compound was like a small community surrounded by village communities. The translation missionary had the task of coming up with written communication. The missionary translators lived in the village. Their first assignment was to learn the native language. Together, the village helpers and the missionaries worked on the translation of the alphabet and eventually put together words and sentences. The process required an abundance of patience and endurance.

The translator works diligently for sometimes as long as fifteen to thirty years to come up with a written language, a few Bible storybooks, and eventually, a Bible. During the process, missionaries lived in the villages for a time to learn the customs and language and to reach the village people, teaching them to read and write and sharing the good news of Jesus. They return to the compound to work and replenish their resources and supplies. I have great admiration for these missionaries.

Our boot camp hikes and, later, our group hikes often took us through isolated villages. The nationals were generally friendly and welcomed the missionaries. The children sometimes giggled a lot. I think they were intrigued by the color of our skin and hair. The children wanted to touch my white hair and fair skin. They laughed and seemed to love those moments. So did I.

One medical team took three attempts to enter a certain village. The first medical run took place in the morning after heavy rainfall the previous night. While driving up the muddy, wet, slippery dirt road toward the top of the mountain, the van slowly shifted and slid off the muddy path into the ditch. This episode abruptly ended further attempts to access this village at that time.

The second try appeared to be going well until we arrived at the village's wooden fenced-in area. The van had scarcely stopped when several villagers dashed out to confront the driver. They informed us of a dangerous situation: a tribal fight and a killing that happened the night before. His village was now on the warpath against the member of another tribe from a nearby village.

Although the villagers spoke in an unknown language, our national van driver understood their message. The expressions and the excitement in their voices convinced the driver to leave immediately. Their message was something like this. "Leave quickly, and come back another day. The villagers are in danger." The driver heard them loud and clear, so quickly, without questions, he turned the van around, and we headed back to the missions compound medical clinic.

A third medical run was scheduled a short time later. The van driver, two nurses, and I were up early with the crow of the roosters, ready to travel the mountain range one more time. This third attempt took us to another mountain top. Although it had rained the night before, this trip was a success.

The driver managed to slowly climb to the top of a relatively steep mountain, eventually ending on a mountain top overlooking a valley. The tropical forest surrounded the area. Once on a flat area, the driver circled the area while he continually honked the van horn. The sound of the horn welcomed the villagers. "Come on out, wherever you are. We have come to give medical attention to you and your children." He, no doubt, had driven this narrow path a time or two before as he seemed familiar with the area. He knew how far to go and when it was time to turn around the vehicle and stop honking.

The tropical woodland bordered the open flat area. The van driver then began on a well-driven pathway near the edge of the forest. We sat quietly at the top of the highland area. I was intrigued and asked about the honking of the horn. One of the nurses grinned. "You will see in a few minutes."

The sun was rising through the foggy patches in the valley below us. We sat in silence. The chirping birds seemed to say, "Good morning, world. It's another beautiful day." In this breathtaking setting, the valley lay low behind us, while the tropical forest on the mountain top surrounded us. We sat quietly for a few moments in expectation. Tears welled up in my eyes, and a noticeable lump formed in my throat as I beheld the creative works of Papa God.

A few trails were visible at just the right angle through the density of the forest. Once the driver parked the medical van, the two nurses, the driver, and I sat quietly waiting. But I wasn't sure for what! My curiosity was at a peak.

Suddenly, people, mostly mothers with babies in their arms, were peeping out of the thick woodland. In moments, they approached: one mom, then two and three moms, a tribe of moms holding their babies with other children of all sizes following them. A few men joined as well. What an awesome moment to watch the people exit the dense tropical forest path.

The rainfall on the top of this mountain left puddles of water, and the children delighted in splashing through them. The driver carefully dodged some of the pools, but others were centered in the pathway. One mom stopped to rinse off her little toddler in a water puddle left from the night before. *What a beautiful moment*, I thought.

"But Jesus said, 'Let the little children come to Me, and do not forbid them; for such is the kingdom of heaven'" (Matthew 19:14). The brightness and width of their smiles spoke volumes. They were happy and eager to see the medical team. They waved and shouted as their missionary friends were returning to care for them.

I was ecstatic at this beautiful sight. A few toddlers were bathed right there on the spot. Many of the younger children had bare bottoms, which simplified the bathing. I was so happy that I had joined the medical team. God cares for his people, even in the most distant lands. The forest was so striking, and my camera was clicking so as to not miss a moment of this once-in-a-lifetime experience. The medical team had again brought health, healing, and happiness.

One nurse set up a small table and a chair from the van while the driver hung a small round pan scale on the back double door of the van. The other nurse sorted through her doctor's bag. The medical team weighed babies, took temperature readings, and gave immunizations. The nurse behind the table updated the medical records, organizing and preparing for a patient review.

Moms were lined up with babies in their arms in front of the card table in an orderly fashion while the older children played happily nearby. The line of people resembled a special holiday get together. The medical team had a systematic routine and worked well with the people.

Once the parents received a shot record, the moms took the babies to the weigh-in pan that hung from the van door. Mom then sat down in the nearby chair as the medical team injected the baby's thigh with a needle as the robust cry of the child rang out.

The babies wore brand spanking new clothing, which intrigued me. The babies looked so huggable and cute in their brightly colored western outfits. The moms evidently took great care of their babies' garments. One of the nurses mentioned that her church and other nearby mission churches gave the babies these beautiful, comfortable outfits. These churches took on this ministry with great joy.

The government supplied shot records, which helped to clarify the medical history of each child. The government also provided flip flops, which helped protect the nationals against the infectious diseases found in the soil. My photos of the village medical run are priceless to me. They speak of an atmosphere of laughter, big smiles, and the fun of receiving McDonald's toys.

A few weeks before the medical run, I had traveled out of the mission compound to a nearby town with friends to visit a second-hand store. Missionaries shopped in this store with donated items from Australia and neighboring countries. Available donations resembled western thrift shops with nominal fees. I was thrilled when I spotted a few brightly colored McDonald's toys on top of a showcase. I asked if they had more and ended up with several full bags that were inside the case and in the back storage area. An adrenaline rush accompanied my purchase of these McDonald's toys.

I kept a supply of toys on hand for the just-in-case moments. These toys were precious to children with no toys. I bought all that this second-hand store had. One would think I had found a million dollars. After sanitizing and cleaning each one, the toys were ready to give away.

I handed out toys to the outstretched hands of the children and adults while the babies were given immunization shots and weighed. We had plenty of children and plenty of handouts. We first gave to shorter arms and then to longer arms, and were met with an abundance of smiles and laughter. It was a miracle. When we announced, "Children first," the adults smiled as if to say yes. The bag of toys emptied quickly. It was a joyous, precious time of fun and laughter.

The missionary compound where I lived also provided medical services for the neighboring villagers. Arrivals showed up early in the mornings, standing or sitting on the manicured grass, waiting for the doors to open. People lined up with babies in their arms, waiting patiently for their turn. The nurse lovingly handed out supplies. This expression of love for the national people is the job of a medical missionary.

The people were friendly and relational. My camera came with a display screen that I shared with the people. As they gathered around me, they were elated to see the pictures I had taken. They stared and immediately burst into joyful laughter. At that moment, I could not imagine feeling more blessed.

The country and people of Papua New Guinea, highlighted God's beauty. The welcoming smiles of the nationals, the laughter of the children, the surrounding rolling hills, and the beautiful blue sky and puffy clouds all released peacefulness. The thick vegetation, the village bush houses, the cook fires, the singing birds, the bouquets, the coconut and banana trees, and the pineapple plants all surrounded the mission center with nature's decor. Beautiful poinsettias graced the area. I fell in love with God's beautiful people, the country, and God's precious, dedicated missionaries.

The children's million-dollar smiles warmed the hearts of those passing by, who smiled in return. Those smiles would banish any grouchiness. The worship and radiance of the natives brightened the atmosphere. All of the goods and the women's eagerness to learn of our Papa God added to the delight and amazement. God provided for the missionaries through these merchants. The believers radiated him through their smiles and eyes.

Although it's been a few decades, the memory of that medical run resides in my heart even today. "Behold, I will do a new thing, now it shall spring forth; shall you not know it? I will even make a road in the wilderness and rivers in the desert" (Isaiah 43:19).

36

The Philippines—Placement

"You will keep him in perfect peace, whose mind is stayed on You, because he trusts in You" (Isaiah 26:3).

After I returned home from Papua New Guinea, I was invited to the Faith Academy International School in the Philippines as a mission's counselor for children and their families. I visited this school on my return trip to America and took up residency in Manila six months later.

I kept busy and happy during my time with family, grandchildren, and their children. Shortly after my return home, I accepted a short crisis counseling position in Pakistan. This trip tremendously enlarged my faith and my exposure to another culture.

Between travels home, visiting stateside family, and trips to Pakistan, Dallas, and the Philippines, my six-month furlough after Papua New Guinea, flew by. I accumulated an estimated fifty thousand additional travel miles during that time. This passage filled my mind in Pakistan and then in Manila: "Looking unto Jesus, the author and finisher of our faith, who for the joy that was set before Him endured the cross, despising the shame, and has sat down at the right hand of the throne of God" (Hebrews 12:2). As a man thinks so is he. (See Proverbs 23:7.) A healthy attitude plays into this. Romans 8:31 tells us, "If God is for us, who can be against us?" My leave was now behind me, and a three-and-a-half- year assignment to the Philippines lay before me.

The hectic streets and sidewalks of Manila swarmed with a busy pace. The bumper-to-bumper traffic crawled along, and I needed patience with impatient drivers. The mirror on the van that picked me up from the airport was repositioned by a vehicle that drove too close.

Neon lights flashed, and McDonald's arches dotted the city. Squatters took residency in areas near the skyscrapers. The fast-moving passenger train overhead *wooshed* as it sped along. The contrast between the Philippines and Papua New Guinea was like night and day, and I loved both countries.

My missionary aide, just like in Papua New Guinea, kept me busy for a few days. We covered a lot of territory. My medical requirements, x-rays, immunizations, and other requirements were completed in Dallas and hand-carried with me to Manila. My aide led me to the Manila quarantine office where these records were reviewed by a Filipino doctor. This doctor checked my heart, noted my age, smiled, and gave me the good-to-go signal.

We then hiked to the vehicle center to pick up a driver's license. This visit took a little longer. I had to pee in a bottle. Everyone seemed to enjoy that process except me. The procedure was complicated by a nervous kidney, dehydration, and people waiting. The stress got to me, but finally, the bottle of water I drank did the trick. Even so, the atmosphere was filled with fun and laughter.

Finally, I received my driver's license. After the preliminaries, we visited a few museums, a cathedral, and McDonald's. The weather was hot and humid; I was sweaty and dehydrated. Through it all, I fell in love with the Philippines.

Finally, after a few days' rest, it was time to leave the guest house and travel to Faith Academy, which would be my residence for the next three-plus years as a counselor at the international school. I had a few days to myself before orientation began for all the school's staff and support team.

I had a choice between two apartments in a seven-story building occupied by the mission and multi-culture families. My favorite was the studio at the end of a long hallway on the third floor. It needed work: a new toilet, a sink, and a shower. The other apartment needed work as well, yet I liked this one better. It was next to a large window that lit up the end of the hallway.

My first task was to buy a toilet and a sink. Within a week of my arrival to the Philippines, I was out buying fixtures. Fortunately, a national was available to help me shop and install these necessities. I forfeited the purchase of the shower.

God, in his infinite wisdom, was continually stretching me. Significant challenges have a way of broadening and taking us out of our boxed-in mentality whether we are ready or not. We serve a wonderful God, and the sky is the limit. No doubt, this is why God granted me a heart of adventure and the make-up of the Energizer bunny.

I had purchased a 1994 Toyota via email, owned by a Faith Academy teacher who returned to her country. After a few repairs, it was in nice running condition. My neighbor took me to the grocery store the first few times. My car sat in the parking lot for a while, as I was reluctant to attempt to navigate the heavy traffic. You had to enter the busy streets without a direct light or stop sign, which was like taking your life into your hands. Occasionally, a man just appeared and directed traffic. I was always so happy when that happened. Whichever car edges a fraction of an inch ahead gets to move out first. Driving in this environment calls for serious expertise and courage.

In time, I decided to drive to the store alone. God was watching over me as a guy was directing traffic. Pedestrians often lead traffic. I was so excited that I made it to the store. While shopping, I decided not to worry about how I would get back on this busy road. After shopping, I would do my best to return home. God provided a space between cars, so with little effort, I could scoot out. It was God as the bumper-to-bumper traffic was endless. I was elated. That was the first of many successful trips to the grocery store.

Food was plentiful. I learned to eat the foods of the culture, and occasionally, exceptional American food, such as refried beans and taco shells, made the shelf. We Westerners knew how to hoard these.

Our brain, like a sponge, can soak up negativity if we allow it to. Our focus in life, for a brief moment, can be positive or negative. While in both countries, I worked on looking at the positives. God gave me compassion for the people. I also loved their culture and was thankful for the opportunity to serve. However, there were a few negatives.

In the Philippines, I struggled with a tropical fungus on my eyes, ears, and head. It was similar to a child's cradle cap. This battle left me with a forever reminder as I face the mirror today. Adjusting to the hot and humid climate was a challenge. God's sprinkles of goodness never missed a day. His abundant faithfulness outweighed my arduous efforts. Again, these opportunities were ample openings for spiritual growth.

Each of these cultures—the United States, Papua New Guinea, and the Philippines—has their own unique flavors. It is easy to arbitrate the motives, values, and traditions of another culture based on our own culture. I know my stomping grounds, and each day in a foreign country, I learned more about an unfamiliar territory. In time, I assimilated into the new culture, and with my eyes on Jesus, I learned to look for the beauty of other cultures and their people. God daily refreshed and nourished me.

My apartment balcony view of the valley was breathtaking. My new toilet and sink worked beautifully. The flight up the stairs to the third floor gave me a great cardiovascular workout. In time, I learned to operate my two-hole washing machine, which was the greatest of victories. At the same time, I gained more patience. The apartment guards gladly carried my weekly five-gallon drinking water, a wellspring of life, to my apartment. Could anyone ask for more?

I became acquainted with my '94 Toyota. Together, we ventured out. Each day, it took me to the top of the hill to my work site. The Filipino school cook prepared special lunches each day for a nominal fee. Twice a week, she included fresh cinnamon buns. A new office air conditioner replaced the old one. The maintenance personnel found an excellent used desk and provided cubbies for my play therapy tools. These national men gladly helped with the smallest tasks. And eventually, I had an older woman mentor and friend.

The apartment steps to the third floor were eventually painted a beautiful light gray, which brightened the area. I received a cell phone. I met with the Branch Executive Board and many teachers. A young Filipino thoroughly cleaned my Toyota. The young Filipino people greeted me with "Hello, Mum." This greeting was pure music to my ears. They respected older adults with white hair, which included me.

A translator invited me to ride out to her village where I visited with the people. The counseling ministry was in full swing. My skin stayed moist and needed no creams. My boxes of counseling resources from Papua New Guinea, made it to my home in the United States after eight months.

"I have come that they might have life, and that they may have it more abundantly" (John 10:10). The voyage is not without pain and suffering. Feeling left out can so easily sneak in and zap our joy. Singles must be intentional about these intruders that will snatch all pleasure. We often deal with defeat. Jesus empowers us and can help us face any struggles we face.

Singles can always find a source of joy. A movie, a walk, prayer, praise, and worship can lift your spirits. You can also use the following outlets to reduce depression and feelings of isolation: reading the Bible, listening to teaching, volunteering, and offering to babysit so moms and dads can have a night out.

The counseling ministry existed to promote spiritual and emotional healing to colleagues and their families. When time permitted, we ministered to the native people as well. Once a week, I traveled to the other side of Manila to the main headquarters. I looked forward to this weekly visit to offer counseling services and to teach the Bible Study during the lunch hour with the Filipino ladies that worked for the Wycliffe–SIL missionaries.

Throughout the week, I stayed busy as a counselor with classes and workshops offered through the day and evening. My workshop material on DVDs was available during the day if someone wanted to watch the various programs on many important topics for personal growth. One teacher came into the counseling conference room each lunch period for nearly a year. She mentioned that she learned more during that time then what she had ever previously learned. Missionaries were hungry and thirsty for continued learning, as was I.

Each time I returned stateside, I ordered more DVD sets from the American Association for Christian Counselors. These workshops helped me maintain my continuing education status and continued to educate missionaries and me. I loved having these materials available for interested individuals and me. Evening and weekends were the perfect times to continue my studies. I was hungry and thirsty for knowledge.

Near the end of the week and on the weekends, a counselee traveled into the area for individual counseling. We spent many hours together. God knew what was ahead for this counselee who was ready to return to her homeland. Several months, maybe even a year later, we ran into each other again. She recognized me immediately, but I did not know who she was at first. When she identified herself, I remembered her very well. God had done a remarkable healing in her life and transformed her from the inside out. She loved God and her assignment. She lit up the darkest of rooms. Yes, God and his remarkable ways—who can fathom them? I never cease to be amazed. He wants to change his children's lives.

I so valued being available when a missionary flew in from other destinations for a marathon counseling weekend. We talked, shared, and sought God, and they left refreshed and a different person. Scripture says, "The unmarried woman cares about the things of the Lord, that she may be holy both in body and in spirit. But she who is married cares about the things of the world—how she may please her husband" (1 Corinthians 7:34). Volunteer opportunities for singles are plentiful. Another advantage of being single was that I could easily schedule time outside normal work hours, which might be more problematic for a married person with a family.

Wycliffe counselors collect no fees for counseling services. When I attended a workshop in Dallas, the instructor mentioned he received $150 and more per hour for his counseling services. We missions counselors looked at each other and grinned. We gained much satisfaction in assisting missionaries with life's issues of life without payment. In my opinion, serving in this capacity satisfied the soul. For me, this was the payback for the counseling services I had received at one time and for the many mentors that assisted my five daughters and me.

Until I learned the route and gained confidence, I parked my car and rode a van, taxi, or jeepney to the train station. Jeepneys were a popular mode of transportation—painted, decorated Army jeeps with open windows and two benches on each side that sat about ten people per side. The load area consists of steps to enter a long bed vehicle with a bench on either side. Other days, I sat in an overcrowded back end of the van or occupied a back seat with four or five other people, a space designed to comfortably seat three or maybe four small bodies. I could often see the road through the open rusted floor of the vehicle. There always seemed to be room for one more passenger. Sometimes you sit with one cheek on the bench. When someone moves out, you can rest your entire bottom on the bench along with maybe eighteen to twenty people crowded into the small area.

When I rode the jeepney for the first time, I asked a Filipino woman, "How does this work?" She said, "Come on, I'll show you." We crowded in, along with many other folks. I asked her how we paid for this ride. She said, "I already paid for your journey. Money is passed along until it reaches the driver's hand." She proceeded to tell me that she was a village nurse and traveled into the tribal areas on a daily basis. Through it all, I again felt so blessed. He sent this gracious woman to show me the way.

I enthusiastically climbed many steps to the top of the city to catch the train. Homeless and elderly people with cups in hand were regularly sitting on the steps to the top. I began my day with coins and bills in my pocket, ready to be placed in the open hands or cups of the homeless.

Security police checked purses and bags with a baton device at the train station entrance. Once I reached the top of the building, people jammed into the train the moment it stopped and the doors opened. They grabbed seats, and even standing room was tight. Eventually, I learned about slack time on my return travel from the SIL. I then had my choice of seats. Occasionally, en route to my drop-off point, someone offered me their spot in respect for my white hair.

I walked nearly a mile to my destination after being dropped off at the train station. Once I learned the route, my 1994 Toyota and I traveled together each Thursday. Eventually, I became familiar with the street people along my walking path. Fruit and crackers accompanied my large tote bag to pass out to these people on the way to my office. Some camped out there while others had a small drink or fruit stand. God provided safety and joy. I was in seventh heaven right there on the back roads of Manila. I stopped at a particular street-side market each week to pick up goodies. Often I carried toys in the car for the children. Our few minutes together were precious and memorable.

I became a volunteer dorm mom, which gave dorm parents a night off together. In addition, an "All for Jesus" (AFJ) program served the neighboring national community. As many as three hundred national kids showed up each Sunday morning. We enjoyed teaching, singing, dancing, and spending time with God and each other.

During school breaks and holidays, colleagues, faculty, and friends headed to the beautiful beaches and other places of interest for fun and a much-needed break. Others just relaxed at home to keep the home fires going.

Church and other activities kept me busy and so happy. I was thankful for my car and the fun in venturing out. There was always something to keep me occupied. Sometimes staying at home was restful and what I needed. I traveled by Cessna airplane into various mission areas to facilitate and participate in the child safety workshops. I got to meet missionaries in other areas and hear their many stories, which was a sweet treat.

Flying high from a bird's eye view, we have a clear picture of God's workmanship below. The beauty of the tropical forest; banana and coffee plantations; the blue and green water; and white shore sands are all so visible when seen from up high. The quaint village bush houses and garden plots are God's workmanship seen from the skies.

Filipino culture is fascinating. People greet with their eyebrows and a smile and say yes when they mean no. After being asked three times, a Filipino accepts an offer. They want to be sure the giver is sincere. The extremes in the buildings and social class in the city of Manila range from skyscrapers to squatter villages with scraps of wood and paper. I needed to understand the customs of another culture because of the possibility of offending someone.

Streets were packed with street market carts and stands selling fruits, veggies, food, kitchenware, baskets, and novelties. An armed security guard checked bags before entering buildings, the mall, and again before entering a store in a mall. The young salesclerks were respectful, attentive, pleasant, and plentiful. The people were quick to say thank you and express their appreciation for the missionary. I received plenty of both while out and about. When a Westerner was in sight, the people seemed to assume that they were missionaries.

Cars, buses, jeepneys, trikes, scooters, and motorcycles wove in and out of traffic, filling each gap. A jeepney hit my car and kept going. Because of the busyness, each vehicle has a weekly no-drive day. I once forgot about this rule and got a ticket. Yes, life on the busy streets of Manila could be chaotic. After three-and-a-half years, I became a Manila driver. My senior lady friend lived there for many years. When she was in the car with me, she constantly said, "Hurry, you can make it in that spot," or "Pass that person." Yep! She was a seasoned Manila driver and a daring one at that.

One Easter Sunday, I was invited to travel to three provinces to deliver Bibles. The indigenous people were overjoyed to have their own

Bible in their mother tongue. Missionaries lived with the people in the village, sometimes for twenty to thirty years. The people were taught to read and write. When missionaries left, the people were now self-sufficient and continued to show the generations that follow.

While there, we prayed for healings with people and took them to a hospital. For one individual, the results showed no TB yet and a slight kidney infection. People easily become dehydrated, which significantly affects their bodies. Financial support from my mission partners helped pay for x-rays, lab work, and medicine for these people.

We went into one village where a young village boy assembled a bass drum using large plastic containers. His makeshift cymbals were the size of two saucers. He rigged up a battery and jumper cable to provide juice to his speakers. His heartfelt music brought tears to my eyes. With cool sunglasses, he played like a gifted musician. His massive grin melted my heart; his radiant smile was like the morning sun.

We visited the same village on different occasions, so several of the people and I became acquainted. One grandma, very, very short in stature, offered me papaya. My missionary friend told me that this was most likely her evening meal. I did not want to take away her meal, yet my missionary friend said it would be a great insult if I refused this gift. This missionary had spent thirty years in that area of the Philippines. Everyone knew and loved her.

I was invited to teach necessary counseling skills and offer counseling services to a group of about twenty-five Asian pastors and missionaries who were preparing to go out into the mission field. Operation Blessings 700 Club sponsored this group of precious Filipinos. Many wise and grateful students desired to serve the Lord with their talents and gifts. We began each workshop with praise and worship. The Spirit of the Lord filled the room with power and might during each worship time beyond anything we had ever encountered. That week was one of much anointing for each of us.

The last night, a revival fell on us, and God healed many of those precious children from mental, emotional, and physical abuse from their childhood and time as young adults. God and I traveled a long distance by various modes of transportation to arrive at this site. I still stand in awe as I recall my experiences. Everywhere I went, a piece of my heart seemed to be left behind.

I was also invited to offer a workshop to another village tribe via translation. We traveled by air in a small missionary Cessna aircraft. We were dropped off and picked up one week later. Again, my partners helped purchase coloring books, colored pencils and sharpeners, balls, Frisbees, and puzzles for about one hundred village children. I offered PE during their recess time and visited with the people while the translator worked with the pastors. Only a few could speak English, yet we managed to communicate very well. We often prayed for the people. This tribe lived near the ocean, but no one entered the water as the undertow was so powerful and dangerous.

My mission partners and I purchased about four hundred pairs of sandal-like shoes and many large bags of rice for the children that attended the Saturday Sunday School class. The children from nearby villages faithfully came to SSS. The pastor's wife had a way with children, so between two hundred and four hundred kids sat on the floor of the church, learning Bible stories and memorizing Scripture. The children received prizes, and after class, they enjoyed a meal of rice and a piece of chicken. At the annual Christmas party, over twelve hundred children showed up. The event included food, games, prizes, and lots of entertainment. My time and memories with this church will forever remain in my heart.

Several times, I went along with a church group of volunteers to serve food in the nearby squatter villages. The children lined up with their plates in hand for a feast of rice and chicken. God blessed me beyond words during my assignment in the Philippines. We made many beautiful memories while I served in this third-world country.

I was a part of a medical team sponsored by the Wycliffe Bible Translators International, along with the Covenant Leader's Network. Many people lined up to receive treatment, and eventually, the doctors and nurses cared for all. I was much like a husband with honey-do list, busy with a variety of jobs. I had no time to become lonely or homesick as I took advantage of the many possibilities to be involved.

Life in another culture includes exciting and engaging experiences. While on a bus trip, the driver stopped for some food and a drink. I was thirsty, so I purchased a soda. The merchant opened a bottle of pop, poured it into a quart-sized baggie, and gave me a straw. The road-side stand workers kept the bottle. I later wondered if this bottle was refilled and used again. That night, my stomach became very, very sick. The moral of this short story is to be careful when a drink is poured into a quart-sized baggie. I will end this short story with an imaginary smiley face.

"But seek first the kingdom of God and His righteousness, and all these things shall be added to you" (Matthew 6:33). "For your Maker is your husband, the Lord of hosts is His name; and your Redeemer is the Holy One of Israel; He is called the God of the whole earth" (Isaiah 54:5). "For He shall give His angels charge over you, to keep you in all your ways" (Psalm 91:11).

My time in the Philippines was precious. Once there, I received many unexpected yet welcome invitations, which I gladly took. The Lord made a way and guided me. My personal belief is that everyone should go on a short- or long-term mission and spend intimate time with the God of the universe.

Scripture tells us, "Blessed is the man who trusts in the Lord, and whose hope is the Lord. For he shall be like a tree planted by the waters, which spreads out its roots by the river, and will not fear when heat comes; but its leaf will be green, and will not be anxious in the year of drought, nor will cease from yielding fruit" (Jeremiah 17:7–8).

37

Medical Stories—Provision

God provided once again, yes, one more time. Miracles never ceased. God, in an extraordinary way, took care of his children.

While living overseas, I needed an MRI procedure for a possible rotator cuff injury. Two nearby facilities offered the MRI. One hospital was a state-of-the- art facility and, yes, came with high costs.

My stateside insurance was only valid overseas in the event of a life-or-death matter. Of course, since I had to pay out of pocket, I checked each clinic, hoping for a reasonable medical fee.

The phone call to the state-of-the-art facility confirmed the high fee. Next, I contacted the older out-of-date hospital with lower fees—the only other location. In my previous employment, all my purchases required at least three price quotes. In this case, I could only ask two facilities for price quotes.

The call to the second facility amazed and blessed me beyond words. God, in his infinite ways, let me know he was taking good care of this daughter. This facility had recently purchased a brand-new state-of-the-art MRI. This machine was even more modern than the one at the more up-to-date hospital.

To top it off, the older facility was offering a substantially lower rate for the first so many MRI customers, of which I was one. God once again had it all figured out. These endearments were like receiving hugs and kisses from him, along with a wink of "I've got you covered."

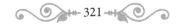

The building itself was older, yet the MRI apparatus and the person operating the machine were most definitely top-of-the-line. Consequently, the procedure did not empty my pockets. Once again, I saw this as a God-given gift. God surely does take care of his own in small and large ways.

While home on a short summer leave from the mission field, I had minor hand surgery. This stateside procedure went well, and upon my return to my overseas assignment, the removal of stitches and physical therapy was effortless as one of the missionary nurses removed the stitches. In addition, she gave me a doctor's name with a clinic nearby. Next, it was time for an orthopedic doctor visit for a referral to a physical therapy program.

The traveling orthopedic doctor, an Asian man, welcomed me into his office. He was kind and interested in my background and the reason for my time in his country. Throughout my visit in his office, he specifically asked me three times if I was a Christian.

We missionaries were encouraged to respond in differing ways in various countries. The answer to this question went something like this. "We foreigners are in your country to teach the village people to read and write. After maybe ten to fifteen years, the translator, along with the help of a village person, will produce a Bible and other books in the language of the people. We also write Bible stories, and in some cases, translate a dictionary into the mother tongue of the village occupants."

Each time the doctor asked if I was a Christian, I was faced with the choice to say yes or no. I could hear Peter as he boldly replied, "I do not know this Jesus." The crow of the rooster followed his words. A total of three times that rooster crowed loudly.

Here I was in the doctor's office. Each time he repeated the question, I told him what our people do. He was extremely grateful and indicated such by word and the expression of thankfulness followed by, "So you are a Christian then?"

I believe in obedience to authority. Who was the influence in this case? Christians, as we know, are persecuted in some countries. I proceeded to explain with the same response as before regarding the process of teaching the people to read and write, translating the Bible, and creating a dictionary. The villagers could also train their people to read and write. Then he repeated, "So you are a Christian?" I again recalled Peter's experience.

The third time, I responded yes.

He replied, "So am I," with a huge smile. He was happy and grateful for missionaries and that we would come to his country to help his people.

This doctor referred me to a nearby physical therapy clinic on the other side of his office door. He said, "Let's get you started. You can be seen today." God, the ultimate physician, blessed me beyond words during that first visit with this orthopedic doctor and each visit after that with him and the physical therapy staff.

My first therapy session immediately followed the visit with this doctor. When I went to the clinic to set up appointments, I asked what I owed for the doctor's visit. The nurse referred to my chart and said, "Um, let's see, the doctor noted a complimentary visit on your chart."

The young physical therapist assigned to me was a delight. In addition to excellent therapy, we had a fun and interesting conversation. He spoke reasonably good English and hoped to come to America one day. He was interested in obtaining a Bible that had been translated into his now-deceased grandfather's language by a missionary years earlier.

He asked, "By chance, would there be a Bible somewhere in my grandfather's mother tongue? I am interested in learning the language a bit better." What were the chances of obtaining this translation? God set us up. I was sure of this.

Yes, the mission's librarian who oversaw the many Bibles translations just happened to have one of these particular translations on her shelf. I purchased this Bible for a nominal price and carried it with me to my next session. The young therapist was so excited, so happy to receive his very own Bible in his grandfather's language. He was planning to visit his village and wanted to take this valuable book with him. He was elated, and so were his family villagers.

During our next visit, he was so energized after his journey. He brought back a woven shoulder bag uniquely handmade, which he presented with a huge smile to his missionary client—me. Isn't God amazing?

The story doesn't end there. On occasion, I brought the orthopedic doctor a bag of baked goods. The bakery conveniently located on the route to his office carried an assortment of scrumptious pastries. Some years later, I have yet to receive a bill for any of his services.

The young therapist never asked me to wash my hands before dunking one hand into the rather large paraffin wax tank. On one occasion, I casually mentioned this and suggested the possibility of many germs with all the hand dunks in this tank. He smiled, listened, and had an aha moment. On the next visit, he said, "Ms. Maggie, please wash your hands before dipping into the paraffin tank."

38

Troy—Perfect Timing

The evening before my departure, a dear missionary couple surprised me by coming to my apartment to help me finish packing. Because of their generous assistance, I was ready for that very early morning pick up. God not only provided in extraordinary ways, but he was my partner and companion throughout those mission days in the Philippines.

On December 21, 2009, my colleague drove me to the Manila International Airport. The day had arrived to begin my travel to America. My twenty-by-twenty box rested next to me in the back seat of this older, trustworthy Toyota with my leg partially sharing the resting place. A similar large box with the maximum allowable weight of fifty pounds occupied the front seat. The trunk held my large trusty red suitcases. No doubt, when my cargo and I unloaded, the car lifted considerably from the ground.

According to my colleague, a missionary kid, "A true missionary is one who can tolerate the discomfort of a fifty-pound cargo box on one leg. Inconvenience, the gift of flexibility in the moment, is a true sign of a missionary."

Yay, I passed the test. I was now a full-fledged missionary! America, here I come. After three-and-a-half years in the Philippines, I anticipated being back in the United States with my family and friends. Although I was now approaching nearly seventy years of age, I felt

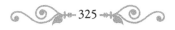

as if I were still in mid-life, full of energy and looking forward to my next assignment.

Oh yes, for certain I would miss Faith Academy, the staff, families, the Filipino people, and my work at this international school. What a blessing to have served in this country, community, and culture. I had countless amazing experiences and opportunities. And now I looked forward to a time of rest in the arms of our Papa God.

When traveling throughout the area, people only saw me, yet my unseen partner resided in my heart. His presence surrounded me at all times. I never traveled alone. God's anointing was powerful and profound, providing a sense of freedom in both my work and in other opportunities that popped up.

I freely went grocery shopping; walked the old mall; rode the jeepney, taxi, and train; drove my trusty vintage Toyota; and took whatever transportation mode the occasion required. When asked to travel to another country assignment, I was always eager and prepared to go. God provided people to assist me and to stand in the gap. When I look back, I stand in awe of God's total provision.

In addition to the one-hour car ride to the airport with a fifty-pound box partially resting on my leg, I did much more to earn this noteworthy title. Our little car was loaded down with a few other cargo boxes, including my red suitcases, computer, purse, and carry-on. Once we arrived at the airport, it took a few minutes for my leg to regain circulation. Yes, by now, I surely met the qualifications of a true missionary as I was nearing ten years of missionary service. I could not ask for more.

I left behind numerous household items for national colleagues, friends, and the staff at my apartment who so carefully and honorably cared for me and the other seventy occupants in the vintage condo. They were happy to receive clothing, a few pots and pans, and an array of other practical goods. I valued and loved these dear friends. As a token of appreciation, I left behind many toys, each individually wrapped and ready to be placed under the Christmas tree for their children.

International travelers returning to their home country from the field require an early arrival—three hours before the flight—at the international air terminal. Fortunately, young national men were readily available to accommodate passengers with their large boxes of cargo. These young men met passengers at the door, loaded their carts, lifted them onto the security belt and then back onto the carts. All this was of great help to me. Their availability lightened the mental load for other travelers as well. They knew the routine. The traveler, in turn, helped support their families with a generous gratuity. The beginning line to the ticket agent window was very, very long and did not compare to normal airport departure lines.

Once in the international departure line and through the check-in station, you enter a path that loops around and around while going through various roped-off sections. Airport personnel check and count luggage parcels, numbers, passports, and identifications several times as one works their way through this exhausting yet orderly process. You will need plenty of stamina to push and pull the loaded-down cart. You breathe a huge sigh of relief and feel a huge accomplishment once the boxes and suitcases go rolling down the conveyor.

I reached the ticket agent only to find that a middle initial was missing from my ticket yet noted on my passport. A change to my ticket to make it match the passport required an extra fee. However, after I paid the price, the ticket person behind the window said, "We are offering you a first-class seat." Wow! A first-class seat. God so graciously showered me with his goodness, surprises, hugs, and expressions of love. I was so thankful for a first-class reclining leather seat on my estimated fifteen-hour flight across the ocean.

I mentioned to the stewardess in the first-class section of the 747 aircraft that I was not sure how to act. She assured me that I would do fine. Plentiful amenities included a comfy pillow, blanket, beverages, appetizers, snacks, entrees, ice cream sundaes, fresh fruit, and cheeses, followed by after-dinner liqueurs. I did not have to regain my composure once the 747 landed. I could get up and out with no stiffness, no painful swollen ankles, and no neck and back ache—a first. I felt comfortable and rested.

My tear-filled eyes and over-joyed heart filled with praise and worship. It was as if Papa God not only was pampering me but maybe saying in his own way, "Well done, my good and faithful servant." After an intense season of focus and stamina, I was now leaving a country after three-and-a-half years. In no time, I was taking a much-needed snooze, and before I knew it, I was in Los Angeles.

"Lord, I need help to transport this cargo. I know you have a plan to get these items on the transit bus and to the departure terminal." I still become tearful as I share this story although this incident happened nearly ten years prior to writing this book. Our God. What can I say?

The hustle and bustle began once again in Los Angeles. After this whirlwind trip, I now had to ride the bus to the Southwest terminal. I would need to successfully move the entirety of my cargo—two hefty carry-on bags, red suitcases, and computer—during this transfer. With the help of a service person, we located and loaded two carts. I was glad for the rest on the journey across the ocean, since it was time to flex my muscles once again.

We walked, pulled, and pushed my load through the crowd to the bus terminal. At the bus stop, the bus driver loaded my cargo. I was now one step closer to home and breathed another sigh of relief.

I knew I fit the description of a true missionary: one who was incredibly flexible, tolerated discomfort, had mismatched clothes, and had hair that needed a comb. Perhaps time in the field fortifies and strengthens a person. We no longer worry about what others think or even what we think, for that matter.

The boxes were loaded onto the bus. I thanked the driver and a few other hearty souls. The next step was to unload these items, move to the loading area, and travel to my final destination. "Lord," I prayed, "I know you have another plan to reach my destination, so I will just sit back, catch my breath, and wait for you to work."

The adventure began when a slender, tall, handsome, young Nigerian stepped into the crowded bus looking for a seat. A seat happened to be open next to me, so I invited him to sit there. God heard my prayer and sent Troy.

Troy and I greeted each other. He then casually mentioned that his flight was early the next morning. That was my clue that this was an answered prayer. My trip was in a few hours while his flight was the next day. Troy seemed like the sort of guy that would lend a hand, even without an offer of compensation. But I then asked him if he would like to earn a little spending money. He responded willingly. God answered my prayer.

Troy unloaded my cargo while I found two carts. In moments, we trotted off to the Southwest Terminal. He signaled for me to follow him, and the adventure began. We scurried across the street, hiked the sidewalk, entered a building, navigated the crowded corridors, and entered the elevator. We traveled the maze within the airport, a trip in itself. We strolled to and fro, finally reaching the line to the check-in counter. The line was long, but we made it.

The ticket agent asked many questions; obviously she was prying. "Are you traveling together? How did you meet?" And there were more questions as well. My fair skin, unlike hers and Troy's, seemed to spark her interest. God was at work. Troy was caring and helpful in organizing each box and the bags on the top of the scale. He then loaded the cart once again and proceeded to one more area, that glorious conveyor belt.

Troy's enthusiastic attitude quickened my spirit. Now we just had one more maze before we reached the conveyor. We then would say our good-byes, and I, likewise, could say good-bye to my cargo until Phoenix. Just before offering Troy what I thought was a generous tip, the Holy Spirit nudged me. "Troy needs a little bit more. Add another bill to the total."

Troy and Ms. Maggie were both happy campers. I loved the way the Lord orchestrated this whole scenario. The Lord could not have sent a nicer person within the entire LA airport to help me out. Troy was no doubt a special angelic godsend. God blessed this daughter, and yes, God answered my prayer and Troy's as well.

We serve an awesome God. He is gracious, kind, loving, and cares deeply for his children. "Call upon Me in the day of trouble; I will deliver you, and you shall glorify Me" (Psalm 50:15).

39

Only Jesus Can Satisfy My Soul— Contentment

*I*nside the Dakar, Senegal international terminal, the light was dim. When I stepped out of this airport in 2009, the humid night air stood still and was sticky, muggy, and reeked of sweat. My instructions upon arrival were to hail a taxi to deliver me to my destination. Senegalese people lined the outer wooden fence three and four rows deep. This barrier separated the passengers from the spectators. The taxis were lined bumper to bumper behind the crowd. All of a sudden, I heard my name, "Maggie," and God made a way.

On a different trip, I was on the other side of the world, I changed flights in the Tokyo-Narita International Airport on my way to the Philippines. I had a long wait. Hundreds of people filled the well-lit passages and busy shops. All of a sudden, I heard my name, "Maggie," and God made a way.

Another time, I exited the Pakistan International Terminal. The light was bright; the air, dry. Many Pakistani spectators—ladies in their colorful shalwar kameez and men in their white, blue, or tan *sherwani*— were observing the multi-cultural array of people exiting the station. There it was, a sign that said, "Maggie," and God made a way.

While in the yard in my Tempe, Arizona home in 1999, also in my spirit, I heard my name, "Maggie . . . it's time to make that call."

Emotions filled my every cell. Laughter, tears, excitement—I knew exactly which number to call. I had become familiar with Wycliffe Bible Translators through my monthly partnership with them. The monthly envelope and resources with a toll-free number had made their way to my mailbox through the years. "Maggie, it's time," and God made a way.

Decades earlier, while attending a Christian school, the seed to become a missionary was planted deep within my heart as a seasoned disciple shared her mission field experiences. Jesus tugged at my emotions. I heard my name, "Maggie," and God made a way.

Scripture tells us that "without a vision, the people perish" (Proverbs 29:18 KJV). That vision from younger years into maturity, much like the wise men who tracked the star until it led them to their destination, kept me focused. Life's experiences, plenty of work, and eyes on the vision all kept me focused. Yes, God made a way.

In addition to locations across the country, my travels as a mission's counselor took me to Papua New Guinea, the Philippines, Pakistan, Israel, Thailand, Canada, Australia, and Africa, with several repeated trips. My resident years in Papua New Guinea, and the Philippines were extraordinary. I realized every prior experience leading up to these stays was a necessity and developed my practice of trusting in the Lord.

I valued working with clients and participating in various programs and activities as God inspired me. He sufficiently filled my cup and greatly satisfied my heart. God's gifts of much joy, strength, perseverance, and contentment made the way. Deep inside, I still carry the joy and privilege of serving meals to the squatters in the village and of preparing sandwiches and goody bags for the homeless that lived under the Manila bridges.

Colleagues and I visited the children's hospital, offering gifts and a smile. I fundraised for the Knuya Boys Home, which housed Manila street boys, and collected English and Tagalog Bibles to distribute to people without a Bible. I traveled to the northern tip of the Philippines to teach marriage and healthy sexuality through a translator. What a powerful time. A chamber pot near the bed proved to be a blessing and was better than finding the outhouse in the dimness of the night.

I treasured my times teaching with Operation Blessing in the Philippines and traveling with nurses to the middle of the tropical forest to provide medical care for the people. How I cherished the prayer walks in Papua New Guinea, even with the needed security guards surrounding us. Other times, missionaries flew in from other islands for a weekend of intensive counseling. I could share so many stories.

What a privilege to attend the Bible translation celebrations and dedications with the Kalo village people in Papua New Guinea, and the Tboli and the Kagayanen people in the Philippines. We attendees joined in the parades with other exuberant village celebrants. These celebrations were such joyful experiences. I was extraordinarily blessed to attend.

I also had the amazing privilege of distributing Bibles in smaller Filipino villages and praying for the sick who thought they had TB. When the hospital x-rays and visits proved negative, God's powerfully released his presence. The translators of their Bibles gave thirty years of their lives to complete the translation to the mother tongue. I joined this couple as they distributed this completed Scripture in the mother tongue, which was such an honor.

God kept me prepared. One early morning, while living in Papua New Guinea, an official entered my counseling office. She asked, "Maggie, can you be ready to fly in an hour? We've had another crisis. I'll fix you a hamburger to eat on the way." Only God could bring peace and restoration on three different occasions and locations after the loss of four missionaries within six weeks. We spent God-breathed time in many debrief sessions and with survivors.

Retirement! Again, in April 2013, God spoke, "Maggie." His best is always the way to go. He surely makes a way. "It is time for another season and a new chapter in your life, Maggie." Only Jesus can satisfy our souls. He has so mercifully, so graciously, done exactly that and filled me through the years.

A huge thank you goes to my partnership family and friends who joined the mission and God's calling (Matthew 28) to go into the world and preach the gospel. Your prayers, faithfulness, emotional support, encouragement, and financial gifts contributed to God's kingdom work. Thank you all for walking alongside me. Your contributions were poured into God's work throughout the world.

40

Conclusion—Never Forsaken, Forever Loved

Today, I am a better person than I was forty years ago. Not that I've arrived, but because of what God did and continues to do in my life. "Not that I have already attained, or am already perfected; but I press on, that I may lay hold of that for which Christ Jesus has also laid hold of me" (Philippians 3:12).

God gives us second and even third chances and makes use of every life experience for his glory when we commit our lives to him. He offers abundant life in many difficult situations: after a divorce, after the death of a loved one, or for a single still looking for a mate. God wants to mold and shape us, and along with growing in Jesus, his changes make you and me better people. He wants to restore broken people. I, for one, am thankful—grateful and appreciative of God's faithfulness. Singleness can lead to an extraordinary life when we allow God to guide us into his plan for you and me.

I pray that my story encourages you, dear reader, to realize that there is life and joy after divorce, becoming widowed, or while single and waiting for a husband. In some respects, after a divorce, we might think life has ended. We realize, in time, life continues and can be even better than we imagined. "Now to Him who is able to do exceedingly abundantly above all that we ask or think, according to the power that works in us" (Ephesians 3:20).

Did God use my marital crisis for his glory? I am prayerful that my life in marriage and after my marriage ended made a difference. I pray

that the talents and gifts given to me while married and through the years as a single helped people who may have crossed my path. From my childhood on, I did not realize these gifts and talents until I became single.

Yes, I recognize the gift of being a wife and mother. My mother's example helped lead the way in caring for my children. Did I do my best as wife and mother? I can say yes on both accounts. No doubt, there was room for improvement. Life included disappointment. But no matter what, the good news is God uses everything in our lives to bring us into his plan and purpose. My entire goal was to live a life holy and acceptable in God's sight. Life is a continuous season of development. Everyone struggles with issues in one way or another.

In time, I realized the leadership skills of encouragement, exhortation, energy, and getting along with people were unique God-given gifts. These gifts were amplified in my life for God's glory. You and I do not have to be super extraordinary. God gives us gifts and talents that carry us through life for our benefit and his glory. Once we realize these gifts, we just need to use them. What God gives you and me is in his best for us so that we can serve him. This gift does not mean we need to travel to Africa unless he calls us to go to Africa. It means that where God places us, we strive to honor him by doing our best.

I wanted to do my best as a wife, mother, teacher's aide, or whatever employment I had, even when serving food to someone in third-world countries or as a counselor sitting across from a client. You and I must do our very best and work as though God is right beside us.

Remember the senior lady who told me, "It's not what you know, Maggie, but your personality that keeps the senior program going and growing." Was this statement to enlighten me? God gave me a specific personality, a gift that drew older adults to the community center so that they wanted to be a part of the programs and, in some small way, a part of my life. This attraction and love for older adults was a God-given gift, a special anointing. In time, I understood this concept.

God's gifts are to enhance the lives of others. He wants his love to lighten our surroundings. Paul says, "For I wish that all men were even as I. But each one has his gift from God, one in this manner and another in that" (1 Corinthians 7:7). We recognize these gifts when we enjoy doing specific tasks: perhaps as a Girl Scout leader, coach, waitress, choir director, sales clerk, or a teacher. We treat others as we want to be treated. Perfecting our gifts and talents is a process. Likewise, our spiritual gifts mature and also differ among God's children. (See 1 Corinthians 12). We develop in him and begin to trust the promises written in the Bible. We find out the truth of God's assurances.

At one of my first large senior adult programs, I was running around like a chicken with its head cut off. My boss calmly said, "Next year's program will be a repeat and will go more smoothly." He knew practice made the program better. He was right! You and I are always improving.

Even at this later season in life, God inspires me to continually cultivate growth in him. He made a way for me as a single parent, in the classroom in my forties, and to go to Papua New Guinea and various countries in my sixties. In my seventies, I volunteered and offered Bible study lessons at the juvenile detention facility and served as a chaplain assistant at the local hospital. What will the decade of my eighties bring? God laid it on my heart, years ago, while in Israel, in that small loft, that the best is yet to come. Already, I have seen this word fulfilled in my life, but I know that the future holds even more.

When we are younger, we have more strength and stamina. When our hairs are white, our physical strength lessens. Yet we have gained a lifetime of experience, resulting in knowledge and wisdom. God is our strength when we are weak.

My feeling of failure and of being lost left me once I invited Jesus into my life. He is the answer. He is interested in taking care of his children in extraordinary ways. He made a way for this single woman, taking her from a novice to a better trained person. He took me from jobs with little responsibility and increased my sphere of influence and level of responsibility. He moved me from my small town to a large city to another state and then another country. Best of all, my five daughters are all ministers of the Word.

The Jordan River opened when the priests carrying the ark of the covenant stepped into the water, not before. The river bed split open, and Joshua and the people crossed on dry land. The act of faith and trust in God made a way through the river bed (Joshua 3:17). Moses struck the Red Sea with his staff, and the water piled high, and the Israelites passed through on dry land. Pharaoh, his finest men on six hundred chariots, and all his army were nearing. I can only imagine the fear that filled the hearts of every Israelite. They needed faith to trust that Moses's staff would open the way through the water and the children would pass through safely (Exodus 14). As a single parent, my daughters always knew where I was. They could reach me if needed when I was at work.

We need faith and trust, and as these elements develop within us, we begin our journey. God's grace enables you and me to be strong and do exploits. Raising our children as a single parent was a huge achievement. Inviting Jesus into our lives is the answer. You will be amazed at what happens when he takes over. He is the reason for my progress. You and I can stand in wonder and amazement when Jesus becomes our navigator. God uses every opportunity in life to help us achieve the goal. The development of faith and trust was a process for me. When I became single, my spirit was so broken. Today, I stand in awe as I look back and see what God has done in my life and in the lives of my children.

God leads his children into green pastures with living water, the water of life, that runs beside them. We yield to him, and the Jordan River opens, and the Red Sea divides, and the classroom offers a seat. He escorts us down the royal red carpet even as we travel to foreign countries.

David, the shepherd boy, cared for his father's flock of sheep. He learned the ins and outs of the desert in his young years. He killed a bear, a lion, and probably threw plenty of stones during his hours in the field. He developed accuracy and confidence in stone-throwing during the years of training as a shepherd. David was well-prepared when it can time to kill the nine-foot giant, Goliath. I imagine him under the stars, listening to the lions and bears crying out in the midnight hours in the wilderness. He drew close to the Good Shepherd of our souls. The Lord taught him survival, reliance, assurance, preservation, and about the safety of his presence. With boldness and confidence in God, David was ready and able to approach the gigantic man, the armored Goliath. David was maybe four- or five-feet tall. The nine-foot-high giant fell to the ground when the mighty toss of the slingshot stone hit the center of his forehead. One shot, one stone, and down went the giant. Talk about exploits!

God desires an intimate relationship with his people. We singles can rest assured that our Good Shepherd wants to restore broken lives. He wants to set us free of the burdens and hurts of a broken marriage, the passing of a spouse, or the lengthy search for a marriage partner. God knows our every thought, and he has millions of impressions of us, as many as the grains of sand (Psalm 139:18). He knows you and me better than we know ourselves. Every day, we learn more about him and ourselves. I can't imagine a single woman or a single parent facing life without the Savior leading the way. He is deeply involved in helping us finish the worthy race of life.

He carries us through every circumstance, even when we don't realize it. He increases the gifts and talents given to us from childhood forward. My widowed mom pruned her children like she trimmed and cared for her flower and vegetable garden. She cultivated, fertilized, watered, and cared for the soil, and her flowers and vegetables were premium. Likewise, she trained her children spiritually. I similarly wanted to teach my children.

Mom's strength helped me through the fatherless welfare years and having a brother with a physical disability. Each of these struggles aided in preparing me for becoming a single. You and I know that being a single mom is a difficult task, yet when we invite Jesus to help us, the job becomes doable. Hard times are to be valued, as difficult as this seems. Hard times can draw us into a deeper and more intimate relationship with Jesus.

Our children need spiritual guidance and structure while we raise them. Being raised by godly parents is a benefit, but even if parents do not teach their children, it is never too late. God brings people into our lives to mentor, counsel, and help us find the way. He faithfully grooms and shepherds us through his hands and feet here on earth.

My achievements as a single and as a single parent were about God. Keeping my focus was not always easy, especially during the earlier years, while I was learning to trust him. He leads us one step at a time. He solves life's puzzle one piece at a time. We begin to hear his still, small voice. We begin to see him at work behind the scenes of our lives, and maybe, without realizing it, we are making progress, slowly but surely. Without him, I surely would have died. This message sounds extreme, but it is the truth and my testimony. "'Not by might nor by power, but by My Spirit,' says the Lord" (Zechariah 4:6).

He becomes our pilot, navigator, anchor, and intimate partner. He lives within us, and we become his temple. When we follow him on this life's journey, he provides strength and endurance, and we rely on him.

This preparation doesn't happen overnight but takes time. We are on an adventure of maturing in Christ. "Though he fall, he shall not be utterly cast down; For the Lord upholds him with His hand" (Psalm 37:24). Just as the nitrogen in the rainfall nourishes plants and helps them grow, we grow in our relationship with him, and he gives us strength within our souls.

A spouse may abandon a marriage, but God will never forsake you and me. Now we might leave God, but rest assured, he will never leave us. He is the God of many opportunities. We learn to forgive those who hurt us, and in time, we progress hand in hand with the Savior. The sheep learn to hear and detect their Shepherd's voice, and they follow him.

The Good Shepherd picks up the lamb, holds this lamb firmly, and carries him through the desert wilderness. The wilderness teaches, prepares, strengthens, and shapes us. Our wilderness journey leads us into ministry, into serving him and then others. His light shines through us, and others want to know more about the light that brightens the room when you and I enter it.

God longs to restore and heal broken hearts. When we invite him into our lives, he gives us a brand new heart filled with love, joy, and hope for tomorrow. Yes, a brand new heart. How is this possible? Ezekiel 36:26 tells us, "I will give you a new heart and put a new spirit within you; I will take the heart of stone out of your flesh and give you a heart of flesh" (KJV).

This miracle is what God did for me. God desires to make this heart adjustment in the lives of his people. God's grace and mercy heals and restores our souls so that we can do Jesus exploits beyond our imagination. Who would have thought? He takes the ordinary and replaces it with extraordinary. Yes, who would have ever imagined it?

He took this middle-aged single woman and mom of five daughters from victim to victorious, from reduced to prosperous in him. To think I once wanted to die, and when I invited Jesus into my heart, I only wanted to live for him. Even at age eighty, I believe that "the best is yet to come." I pray my story offers encouragement to each reader.

"Not that I have already attained, or am already perfected; but I press on, that I may lay hold of that for which Christ Jesus has also laid hold of me. Brethren, I do not count myself to have apprehended; but one thing I do, forgetting those things which are behind and reaching forward to those things which are ahead, I press toward the goal for the prize of the upward call of God in Christ Jesus" (Philippians 3:12–14).

Father in heaven, our Good Shepherd, draw us to you and show us your way. Hold us tightly in your arms, close to your bosom, to your loving and caring heart. Anoint us with your healing oil. We need you. Wash away our sins and keep us pure in heart. Teach us to keep our eyes on you. Help us as single parents to raise our children in your wisdom. Thank you for being the husband to the single, widowed, and divorced. Thank you for being the Father to the fatherless children. Thank you for laying down your life on the cross of Calvary so we can live victoriously in you. Lord Jesus, you are the Savior of our minds, bodies, and souls.

Thank you that we were wonderfully made in your image. Let your light shine brightly through us so that others will come to realize that you are the way, the truth, and the life. Thank you for your sweet presence and unconditional love for your children, love beyond our comprehension. We pray all of this in the most holy name of your precious Son, Jesus. Amen.

CPSIA information can be obtained
at www.ICGtesting.com
Printed in the USA
FSHW010640310321
80003FS